Human Behavior:
The New Synthesis

Human Behavior: The New Synthesis

Mitch C. Bronston and Nils K. Oeijord

Authors Choice Press

San Jose New York Lincoln Shanghai

Human Behavior: The New Synthesis

Authors Choice Press
an imprint of iUniverse.com, Inc.

For information address:
iUniverse.com, Inc.
5220 S 16th, Ste. 200
Lincoln, NE 68512
www.iuniverse.com

ISBN: 0-595-20214-4

Printed in the United States of America

To Sydney and Hanne

Contents

Introduction

by
Mitch C. Bronston

"What really matters is what happens in us, not to us."
John C. Maxwell

"The real problem is in the hearts and minds of men."
Albert Einstein

Why do we behave the way we do? What mechanisms are at work when we smile, when we cry, when we do good things, or bad? How do we know what is good or bad? These questions, and many more, are at the core of the human condition. The full spectrum of human behavior is as complex, if not more so, than life itself, and the elegant diversification of nature.

Throughout recorded history, and certainly well before, mankind has sought to answer these, and other questions about how we respond to our environment. The ancients, it is speculated, applied the notion of *spirits* that inhabited their bodies. They must have also felt controlled by the sun, the moon, and other heavenly bodies. Natural forces were, certainly foreign to them, and their primitive notions of the world around them raised more questions than they answered. The classical civilizations developed the idea that gods and their host were in control. Every aspect of one's life was predetermined by unseen and powerful beings, who delighted in causing misery and misfortune on poor humanity. The middle ages were only slightly more sophisticated. The same idea, but with only one Supreme Being. As recently as the nineteenth century, this concept held true. Every behavior was viewed to be the result of predeterminism, and notions of good and evil were playing out their tug of war within our bodies. The cast of characters had grown to include angles and demons. Abnormal behaviors, for example, were the product of 'demonic' possession, and required a religious 'exorcism'. The person unfortunate enough to have this supernatural circus going on within his body, ended up at the mercy of some of history's cruelest individuals.

At the end of the nineteenth and beginning of the twentieth centuries, came the first true scientific approach to behavior. The advent of Sigmund Freud's psychoanalysis assumed that the mind, and not unseen spirits or demons, was the underlying precipitator of all behavior. Documentation, analysis, and pure scientific experimentation, put to rest the previous ten thousand or so years of speculation. This was, indeed, a paradigm shift. No longer was mankind the puppet of primitive forces or powerful social orders. Individuals, as well as our species as a whole, were reacting to the environment via the chemistry of the brain. This revelation in understanding has led to effective treatment for millions, and freedom from the tyranny of the unknown.

Over the last one hundred years, it has become apparent that much has evolved in the practice of psychology, and understanding of human behavior. While treatment of behavioral disorders has proven effective and far-reaching, much was, and is, left poorly understood as to the mechanisms involved in behavior as a response to the environment. Far too much emphasis has been placed on external factors via the environment itself as a precipitator of behavior. Psychology as a science itself has become inundated into every aspect of behavior in our age. It has become apparent that, even with its advanced ideas, psychology has bogged down under its own weight. It has become cumbersome and heavy. It has seemed to reach a point where a single behavior can produce many different analyses from many different psychologists. It is not unlike a room full of blind men trying to describe an elephant. Each blind individual holds a different part of the huge body. They all agree that something is in the room, and it's very large; however, only a small item can be described. One says 'tail', another says 'trunk', and still another says 'leg', and so on. By this process, the overall picture may never be fully understood. To those with sight, and from a simple distance, the vision is clear: it is an elephant. Plain and simple.

Could a new and simple approach shed some light in a blind and dark room? Could a new approach be simplicity itself? The lack of simplicity is startling in the current climate of the profession. Observe the recent focus on youth shootings in public schools. A single question of motivation to fifty different psychologists and therapists yields fifty different answers, and no one has yet answered the simple 'why' of these tragedies. Over a hundred years of advances in the field has yet to find the common denominator. The media has played a poor role as well. Continued acquiescence to 'psychology' for answers produces the same result. Perhaps it is time to step back and look at the elephant itself.

In the following chapters, we will look at a new view of behavior. A view that *includes* our species as animals, not separate from them. A view that looks at behavior in a simplified form. The tools at our command will include paleoanthropology, mathematics, ethology, neurophysiology, and forensic anthropology. We will see man from a *primal* point of view. We will see our basic instincts. We will ask 'can instincts learn?' We will travel down the road of evolution and see chemistry at work and the elegant brain that makes us who we are.

We will look at our notions of good and bad, and see how new terminology can simplify the mass of confusion that is complex behavior. Much will be discussed about 'management' of feelings, emotions, and other behavioral traits—characteristics we like to call our *personality*. We shall endeavor to describe ourselves and the wonder that we call *awareness*. Truly, man is an exquisite creature, full of mystery and beauty. *The New Synthesis* consists of 1) a new understanding of heritability, 2) a new interpretation and understanding of the broad heritability coefficient, 3) a new understanding of the human instincts, 4) a new understanding of normal and abnormal behavior, 5) a new interpretation and understanding of intellect and free will, 6) a new understanding of the behavior of genuinely identical MZA twins in different genuine free-choice environments, and 7) a new list of the human instincts.

Chapter 1 Terminology: A look ahead

by
Mitch C. Bronston

"What lies behind us and what lies before us are small matters compared to what lies within us."

Ralph Waldo Emerson

"It is striking how much of our actual behavior…can be described in reptilian terms. We speak commonly of a 'cold blooded killer'. Machiavelli's advice to his Prince was 'knowingly to adopt the beast'"

Carl Sagan

Consider the following scenario. A young man is on trial for gunning down several people during a drive-by shooting. An all too common occurrence in our present society. During the course of the trial, a parade of witnesses testifies as to the mindset of the accused. This group consists of psychiatrists, psychologists, therapists, and crisis counselors, each of which introduces evidence that describes the man's present environment. It becomes known that he came from a broken home, a drug addict mother, and an abusive alcoholic father. He was, as a boy, recruited into a street gang, and has been in and out of prison and drug rehab centers many times. He is diagnosed as bipolar manic depressive with obsessive compulsive behaviors and aggressive personality disorders. Testing shows that he has delusions of grandeur with a megalomaniac belief complex and thinks of his violent act as cleansing the earth of evil.

There is no need to discuss any possible resolution of this example; for it is fiction. Or is it? What is apparent here is that we seem to have reached a point in our culture where two things happen whenever a description of behavior is needed. An over-dependence on the environment as the cause of any kind of behavior, and a dictionary sized list of terms to define it.

First, what about the environment? How crucial is it to behavior, and is it the primary source of response? The current climate in psychology is, and has been, solidly behind the environment as the primary factor in behavior. But there is a shift occurring in scientific disciplines that would dispute that. For example, the fields of behavioral genetics and paleoanthropology point to a biological basis for behavior. To be sure, the environment is a major factor, for behavior itself does not occur without a medium in which to happen. But to say that behavior is a result of, and solely the responsibility of influencing external factors, is inaccurate. What's more, it is unwise to make diagnoses and legal decisions based on this faulty thinking. What, then, do we look at as the primary motivator in behavior, and how do we answer perplexing and complex questions about human response? The answer appears to be in biology.

Behavior is, for the most part, a product of genes and brain neuropathways. This will be discussed in greater detail in the next chapters, but for now, consider the elegant chemistry at work when living organisms move, think, behave, and act. Certainly, the environment is a factor here because it can influence *how* we *act*. An analogy would illustrate this adequately. Think of the environment as gasoline, and our body as the engine. Truly, the engine does not run without the gasoline, but all the intricate parts of the engine are the product of *physical architecture*, designed and assembled for a reactive purpose long before the gasoline is injected. Inject more gas and the engine accelerates, less, and it slows. The same is true for an organism. Behavior is a *response* to the environment. We have 'free will' (see Chapter 4), but the ultimate characteristic of that response can only act with respect to the architecture of our genes and our brain. In other words, the environment can, effectively, accelerate or slow down a potential behavior, but the engine for that behavior is already built and functional; therefore, the environment is but a catalyst.

To further illustrate this, let us look deeper into the above scenario. Just as this individual is facing his fate, another courtroom next door is in trial with yet a second gang member involved in the same incident. This individual has equal counts of the same crime; however, there is a striking difference. The accused grew up in a pleasant, suburban, middle-class neighborhood, had never used drugs, was a straight A student in school and had no prior crime history. The family was noted for community service with no background in violence, addiction, or disfunctionality of any kind. It should be noted that the accused also believed he was 'cleansing the earth of evil', and supporting testimony from another army of psychologists confirmed that this belief arose independently *before* any contact with the street gang.

If this is true, than, as stated above, the answer is biology. It is evident that, while the environment shares a role in shaping behavior, the main ingredients are already with us from birth. All that is required to precipitate any type of behavior is the chemistry of our genes and the neuropathways of our brains. Then, and only then, comes the environment in the right circumstances to initiate and manage the behaviors that we all share. It is our contention, as will be the purpose throughout this book, to submit that behavior of all living organisms, including mankind, is based in biology, and controlled by instincts. And while psychology, in its current form, does a magnificent job of helping to manage the emotions and feelings of behavior, it does not function well in describing the root biological causes of behavior. That will be, we hope, our job in this book. What, then, can we expect of the second point made above. That of the confusing, and often misleading, terminology of psychology. Can new terms, simplified, better define human, as well as animal behavior? Throughout the following chapters, we will attempt to introduce new terms. Terms that can be easily applied and descriptive of our true behaviors. Words that are understandable and simple, without deliberate 'psycho-babble'. In order to properly understand what instincts are, and how behavior happens, we need to look at the human brain and what happens inside. The following chapter will introduce us to that marvel of engineering

Chapter 2 Structure and physiology of the brain

by
Mitch C. Bronston

"Not only our pleasure, our joy and our laughter but also our sorrow, pain, grief and tears arise from the brain, and the brain alone. With it we think and understand, see and hear, and we discriminate between the ugly and the beautiful, between what is pleasant and unpleasant and between good and evil."

Hippocrates

"Lovers and madmen have such seething brains, such shaping fantasies, that apprehend more than cool reason ever comprehends. The lunatic, the lover, and the poet are of imagination all compact…"

William Shakespeare

In the course of the last 4.5 billion years of evolution by natural selection, the planet has produced a prodigious number of living species, both current and extinct. The basic composition of the DNA in all cases has changed very little over this time, but has produced a great variety of possible combinations and exquisite creatures, including man. In spite of some obvious physical differences, the molecular biology of life has evolved a common architecture in response to the environment of this planet that is common to "all" animals. Basic body, appendages of some type, and a head with two eyes, two ears, a mouth, etc. Whether a fish, a wasp, a cat, or a human, the basic form is similar. DNA has been the carrier of 'locator genes' which determine this basic shape, function, and relative placement of body parts. As we move down the evolutionary ladder to invertebrates and single celled organisms, this distinction becomes less obvious, but the rudiments of earth based architecture are apparent never-the-less.

Less apparent is the ability of DNA to carry other information, specifically genes capable of assisting the organism to adapt to the environment via behavior to insure its survival. The very nature of natural selection involves competition for control of resources and helps insure survival over less adapted organisms. But adaptation is not limited to survival alone. As physical form has evolved, so has the complex chemistry of behavioral response. This can be defined by instinct. It is apparent that DNA alone is not sufficient as the mechanism for information storage. Hence the evolution of the brain as a memory repository. This allows for greater capacity, but also greater diversity and complexity. Survival and adaptation are ever more complicated as we move up the evolutionary ladder, and the brain becomes larger and more diverse in its function. In order to understand the nature of instincts, it is necessary to first look at the structure of the human brain, and the physiology that makes it work For discussion purposes, I will limit preliminary facts to the structure and physiology of the human brain only, but it is important to note that these generalizations apply to most 'higher' animals on earth and is not limited to *Homo Sapiens* alone. It is, in fact, the very idea that human behavior is animal behavior but tempered with high innate intellect (the intellect has innate specific situational learning abilities/capacities), that allow conclusions to be made. In the following descriptions, we will use the brain model presented by Paul McLean, now accepted as a standard evolutionary model in neurophysiology. According to McLean, the modern human brain is a 'triune' structure, that is, three separate evolutionary adaptations; variations added over the last 500 million years after the Cambrian

Explosion. The human brain is composed of several parts, or levels of function, and, in its present form, is the product of over 4 billion years of evolution, specifically, about 100 million years of mammalian development, and 20 million years of primate evolution. This fact allows us to examine behaviors in other animals, and apply lessons to our own behavior. The most primitive structure of the brain is composed of the **pons**, **medulla**, and **brain stem**. These control the autonomic body functions such as breathing, heart functions and vital organ regulation. They possess very little information that can be attributed to behavior and are the earliest known brain structure present in brains. The next development in brain structure to evolve, some 350 million years ago, was the **R-complex**, or **primitive brain**. (Sometimes known as the **reptilian brain**, it is misnamed. Its source was early amphibians of the Devonian period, and only later developed in reptiles, dinosaurs, and mammals. Note: these are all separate taxonomic groups and evolved independently.) The R-complex was an extremely important development, in that it allowed organisms to acquire rudimentary intelligence and develop problem-solving capability. Along with these important features, the basics for emotion and the chemistry of instinct also surfaced. The next development in brain structure occurred quite by accident, about 65 million years ago at the end of the Cretaceous period. Dinosaurs and reptiles were the predominant life forms on the planet and mammals, while present, accounted for a small percentage of animals, mostly small rodent-like creatures. The Yucatan asteroid event destroyed most life forms on the planet, and allowed mammals to proliferate, as they were the best adapted to the new environment. The small mammalian brains developed a new and important layer of gray matter, known as the **limbic system**. It is here that most emotion is present and the area is 'pre-wired' with basic instinct information beyond what DNA can supply.

Finally, the third, and "most" important development, was proceeding during the proliferation of evolving mammals: the **neocortex**. This structure, while part of the brain as a whole, is the seat of intelligence, intellect, human initiative, and self-awareness. The primitive structures of the R-complex and the limbic system are the seat of the primal instincts, those that cause so much of our normal and abnormal behavior. Throughout the chapters of this book we will look at all of these independently. The growth of the right side of the brain before the left is purely accidental and accompanied the evolution of higher mammals, especially primates, including man. The neocortex contains two main 'mind' components, both very critical to our discussions of behavior. The first is intelligence. This term is mostly what we refer to as 'man's exclusive domain.' That, however, is erroneous. All life forms with sufficient neocortex are intelligent, just not to the same level as *Homo Sapiens*. It should be remembered that the brain itself is merely an evolutionary adaptation. It is no less important to us than the trunk is to an elephant. The **intelligence** is the sum total of our reasoning ability, experience, knowledge, and aspirations. But is not the whole picture. The second component of the neocortex is the **intellect**. How does this differ from intelligence? This part of our 'mind' is the resource manager of the information that moves about our brain, separating the primitive from the new, supervising our morals, our ethics, our emotions, and our conscience. In other words, it is the total sum of our awareness as human, and the peculiar inward view we have of ourselves. Many call it the 'soul'. Whatever it truly is, this part of our mind is the identification of our species that separates us from other living animals.

Brain physiology is a bit more complex, but must be understood in relation to structure and instinct development. One important fact must be emphasized first. Intelligence and behavior is not determined by brain size alone, as has been believed. The overwhelming majority of brain thought, intelligence, and intellect is explained by neurophysiology and not by size. Some basic facts would be helpful. The brain is not composed of truly solid matter as once thought. Instead, it is a collection of trillions of independent brain cells, or neurons. Since they do not touch each other, they cannot transmit information by conductivity alone. The mechanism for information transmission is accomplished by a plethora of chemicals called neurotransmitters. They include norepinephrine, acetylcholine, dopamine, serotonin and a variety of enkephalins such as endorphin. The relative availability and concentration of these substances determine our mood, emotional state and mental health. Other functions include regulation of sleep cycles and autonomic responses in the central nervous system. But their most important function is the building of thoughts, intellect, memory and images. This 'building' results in the formation of a string of neurons called a neurosynaptic pathway. A single pathway may be composed of a simple arrangement of a dozen or so neurons to form a memory, such as remembering your own name. Or it may consist of a billion connections to build more complex memories such as language or abstract mathematics. As one can see, the greater the complexity and size of the neurosynaptic pathway, the greater the chances that diversity and differences will occur. That is why some can play piano and others cannot, some can write complex equations, while others cannot grasp the basic fundamentals of simple arithmetic. And yet this is all normal, within the spectrum of the human condition. It is the law of statistical probabilities that allows for abnormal development of neurosynaptic pathways and its subsequent effect on what we consider abnormal human behavior. This is where our attention will be focused toward the end of this book, for it is the development of abnormal pathways that cause misinterpretation of the basic instincts and abnormal behavior as a result, It is important to note that neurosynaptic pathways do not limit themselves to the neocotex alone, but, rather, inundate the entire brain including the limbic system and the R-complex. It is this very complexity that allows our behavior to be governed by the primitive structures in the brain, and only the neocortex, with its capacity for intellect, can temper the basic instincts into behaviors that we call ethics and morals. It is also important to understand that our discussions will cover the emotions that accompany instincts, and how instincts can learn. Remember, emotions are no less important to our behavior; and, emotions are also pathways "in themselves". With this mass of neurons and neuropathways, it is easy to imagine the enormous complexity of possible behavior that can represent each human individual. Do behaviors change? And if so, is it truly a chemical change in the brain that occurs? Or are we all really the same, and just cover our true behaviors with trickery and subterfuge, as Shakespeare was fond of pointing out. The way to answer that question is to look at human evolution and human enterprise. The basic mechanism will be called a learning instinct. The following chapter will look deeply into a quantifiable approach to human behavior, how it is "inherited", manipulated by our brain chemistry, and visibly spewed out as behavioral response.

Chapter 3   The new heritability and the way instincts learn

by
Nils K. Oeijord

"The words or language, as they are written or spoken, do not seem to play any role in my mechanism of thought."

Albert Einstein

"We don't have to learn to learn because we have learning instincts."

N.K.O.

Over millions of years evolution slowly created the human brain, mind, and behavior. Therefore, to understand psychology, we must realize that psychology is a branch of biology. The key to understanding human behavior is to realize that it was designed by natural selection to solve the day-to-day problems of our hunter-gatherer ancestors. It must be remembered that our brain is comprised of neurons and their supporting structures. Neurons are cells that are connected to one another in a highly organized way. We think of these connections as neuropathways, which determine how the brain processes information.

Science has long known that the brain contains neuropathways that are specialized for different modes of perception and behavior. Just to watch a moving object you need all kinds of pathways. Some are specialized for analyzing the shape of objects, some for detecting the presence of motion and the direction of motion. Other pathways are specialized for judging distance, analyzing color, identifying the object, etc. Each individual pathway is shouting its information to higher level pathways, which check the information generated by one neuropathway against the information generated by the others. Then the processed information is handed over to even higher level pathways. Finally the processed information reaches the level of conscious awareness, and—voila!—the sight of a moving object.

Sensory receptors are connected to neurons that transmit information to your brain. Other neurons transmit information from your brain to motor neurons that are connected to your muscles. The motor neurons cause your muscles to move. This movement is behavior. However, strictly speaking, emotion, feeling, and thinking are also behavior.

The evolutionary perspective and the data collected suggest that reflexes, thinking (reasoning, decision-making, etc), learning, emotions, feelings, language, and body movements are accomplished by specialized, content-dependent neuropathways. Realizing that the function of the brain is information-processing has allowed us to resolve one version of the mind/body problem. Brain refers to the physical properties, and mind refers to the information-processing operation, of the same system. Chance mutation/natural selection is, of course, the only process that is capable of creating complex, organized behavior systems. Our random and chaotic environment (even upbringing and education are random and chaotic) cannot create natural human behavior. But there are more arguments. The argument from the low level and poverty of the input (here: input = learning possibilities) is the primary justification for saying that the basic design of behavior is innate. We can show that the basic design of behavior could not have been taught/learned. We only have to show the low level and poverty of the input. Even without input at all, normal basic behavior is often developed. Proofs: The existence of spontaneous private language in twins. The existence of normal movements, postures, gestures, and facial expressions in people that are born hearing and voice impaired.

Human behavior can be partitioned into 1) adaptations, which exist because they were selected for, 2) by-products, which exist because they are causally coupled to adaptations, and 3) noise, which was created by the random components of evolution. Our abilities to skateboard, drive cars, use computers, learn mathematics, etc, are partly direct effects and partly side-effects or by-products of our adaptations.

Obviously, only adaptations are instincts (see below) and instincts are adaptations. By-products and noise are genetic, but non-instinctual, behavior. Clearly, not all genetic behavior is functional, and not all genetic behavior is adaptive. Theories of adaptive function are important for explaining why a known instinct exists and for discovering new instincts.

It is important to realize that our neuropathways were not designed for any kind of behavior. The only kind of behavior that natural selection can design pathways for is adaptive behavior. Proof: Any pathway whose average effect was to decrease the adaptive behavior would eventually disappear from the population. Here the concept of neutral behavior is meaningless or unimportant, but, of course, by-products or side-effects exist (see above). In principle, a neuropathway could be designed to link any given stimulus in the environment to any kind of behavior. Which behavior a stimulus gives rise to must be a function of the designed neuropathways. Therefore, environments do not, in and of themselves, give rise to ordinary and appropriate behavior.

Human behavior in the present is generated by information-processing mechanisms that exist because they solved adaptive problems in the past. We must understand that human minds are calibrated to the environments in which they evolved, and that they embody information about the stable recurring properties of these ancestral environments, including situations in which adaptive errors are so costly that we have to respond appropriately the first time we encounter them.

We know that consciousness in the neocortex is just the tip of the iceberg. No information-processing machine can make all its information available to all of its parts. Therefore unconsciousness must exist. Philip

Wong and Howard Shevrin have uncovered neurobiological evidence for the human unconscious state. We cannot become consciously aware of most of our brains' ongoing activities. The only things we become aware of are a few high level "conclusions" passed on by thousands of specialized mechanisms. It's not adaptive to use the small and limited conscious mechanisms for processes other than certain parts of the learning intelligence instincts and the learning intellectual instincts (se later), and certain perceptions. An example of conscious perception: "Color" is the conscious experience that results from the processing of information by the eye and the nervous system.

A basic principle is that the same machine is rarely capable of solving two different problems equally well. Therefore our body is divided into organs. For the same reason, our brains/minds consist of a large number of neuropathways that are functionally specialized and content-dependent. We can think of each of these specialized pathways as a mini-machine that is dedicated to solving one problem. Higher level neuropathways are specialized for integrating the output of these mini-machines to produce behavior.

But, does the human mind consist of a large number of mechanisms that are functionally specialized and content-dependent, or does the mind consist of a small number of general purpose and content-independent mechanisms? This question cannot, of course, be completely answered by reasoning alone. It is an empirical question. The data collected suggests that the human mind consists of a large number of mechanisms that are functionally specialized. For example, children with Williams syndrome are profoundly retarded and have difficulty learning even very simple spatial tasks, yet they are able to make inferences about mental states. But a child with autism who has a normal intelligence and intact perceptual systems, is unable to make inferences about mental states. Clearly, **reasoning instincts** and **mind-reading instincts** exist and are highly independent. Grass looks green at both high noon and sunset, even though the spectral properties of the light it reflects have changed dramatically. Cause? The specialized, content-dependent, domain-specific, and functionally distinctive **color-constancy instinct**. No doubt about it. L. Cosmides and J. Tooby have empirically proved, in a beautiful experiment, that **cheater detection is an instinct**. They proved that cheater detection is totally domain-specific and totally functionally distinct, as if it had been designed by a computer engineer. Cheater detection is an algorithm! (Of course, by-product and noise hypotheses have been empirically eliminated.) Cosmides and Tooby have scientifically proved that human instincts exist, even in the neocortex!!

All else equal, a content-rich system will be more flexible and powerful than a content-poor one because there is little a content-poor system can infer before its operation is damaged by combinatorial explosion. To solve qualitatively different adaptive problems, our choices must be guided by qualitatively different standards. Consequently, **the mind must consist of a large number of mechanisms specialized for solving qualitatively different problems**.

From a neurological point of view, instinct always involves the neocortex, the seat of consciousness, while the reflex is confined to the lower nerve centres. We don't need to think about our reflexes. They are handled by our autonomic nervous system. But instincts (need to) think. Both reflexes and instincts help to keep us safe and healthy. All instincts are survival instincts. All reflexes are survival reflexes.

Note that both emotion and cognition consist of instincts, so there is no split between emotion and cognition. Both (specific) jealousy and (specific) logical reasoning are caused by specialized, content-dependent rules of inference, or algorithms.

Finding that a behavioural element solves a behavioural problem with reliability, efficiency, and economy is a first evidence, or so-called *prima facie* evidence, that one has identified an instinct. This kind of evidence is important for explaining why a known instinct exists, and for discovering new instincts.

Instincts are often thought of as the opposite of learning and reasoning (well-known examples are Stephen Jay Gould and Richard C. Lewontin). However, the reasoning and the learning pathways have all the characteristics of an instinct: natural, effortless, automatic, reliable, precise, fast, economical, unconscious, innate, and requires little or no instruction, even though they reside in the neocortex. So behavior is not caused by instinct or learning (alone), because learning is caused by instincts. Human behavior is more flexibly intelligent than that of other species because we have **more** instincts than they do, not fewer. The human instincts work so well that quite a lot of scientists don't realize that they exist!!! They do not realize that normal behavior needs to be explained at all!! As a result, science has generally neglected to study the most interesting machinery in the human mind!

Some researchers think that if they can show that there is information in the culture that mirrors how people behave, then *that* is the cause of their behavior. These researchers confuse cause and effect, because *that* information can, at most, only: 1) trigger actions (actions and behavior are totally different things), 2) be information for learning. But "learning" is not an explanation. "Learning" requires explanation.

The brain must have a certain kind of structure for you to learn anything at all. Even the triggering of actions needs a certain kind of brain structure to occur (or not occur) at all. Moreover, to learn specific things, there must be specific mechanisms that cause the learning to occur or not occur. These learning mechanisms must be unlearned. Therefore they must be innate. Everyday experience, common sense, studies of brain damage and behavioral disorders, etc, show that these innate learning mechanisms are specialized purpose mechanisms, not general purpose mechanisms. General purpose learning mechanisms is neither empirically nor theoretically proved to exist. Intelligence (= intelligences!) and intellect (including certain moral instincts) do not necessarily need general purpose mechanisms.

Each particular anatomical thing is fitted to a particular behavioral thing. Undoubtedly this must be believed to be so. *Gray's Anatomy*, first published in 1905, shows the anatomical modules (including the nervous system) of the human body and brain. We see no accidental by-products ("spandrels"). We see only thousands of perfect *adaptations*. Undoubtedly, the human physiology consists of adaptive chemical modules. Evolution created our almost perfectly adapted modular anatomy and physiology. If each particular anatomical and physiological modular adaptation is fitted to a particular behavior, then behavior must be believed to consist of thousands of particular modular adaptations. Everyday experience and scientific research have discovered thousands of independent or semi-independent adaptive human behaviors. Therefore, we must conclude that the human mind consists of modular adaptations (= instincts). Has the human glands for the secretion of tears? He/she knows instinctively how to cry. Has the human a mouth and a tongue? He/she knows instinctively how to chew. Has the human vocal chords? He/she knows instinctively how to make (and hear) sounds, and how to speak. (Proof: independent spontaneous language in infants). Has the human legs? The baby has a walking reflex (= the walking instinct). Modules of particular cells on the tongue register the sensations of sweet, salty, sour and bitter. These four modules are fitted to the four corresponding instincts. Has the human logical problems? He/she knows instinctively how to reason. There is no need to go on.

It's important to understand that we don't say or believe that everything that we feel, think, or do is adaptive, or that every behavioral trait of a human being is an adaptation. On the contrary, we say and know that many aspects of what we feel, think or do are evolutionary by-products, side-effects or noise. However, it's hard to find a behavioral trait without survival value. We believe, for example, that traits (instincts) like creativity, imagination, fantasy, trial-and-error learning, and even risk-taking behavior have adaptive value. Other behaviors, like choosing to remain childless is clearly non-adaptive, but is caused by our genetic ability to apply **cause-and-effect reasoning** to our life, and cause-and-effect reasoning is obvious an adaptation (an instinct). Homosexual behavior is (perhaps) not adaptive, but the love instincts and the sex instincts are adaptations. (Homosexuals have love and sex instincts.) Homosexual behavior and bisexual behavior are directly or indirectly genetic and are, of course, a part of our natural genetic variation. By the way, homosexual apes exist.

Beneath the level of individual genetic behavioral variability, all humans share certain emotions, ways of thinking, and ways of behavior by virtue of these special purpose mechanisms. Note that the individual genetic behavioral variability is nothing but the genetic variability of these mechanisms. But remember that these mechanisms can learn (more or less). This genetically based learning creates additional genetic (!) individual variability.

What effect the environment will have on behavior depends on the details of the evolved instincts. What is more important in determining an individual's behavior, his/her genes or his/her environment? This is a meaningless question because every aspect of an organism's behavior is the joint product of its genes and environment. To ask which is more important is like asking: Which is more important in causing a car to run, the engine or the gasoline? Genes and instincts allow the environment to influence the development of behavior. And genes and instincts determine how the environment influences behavior. Normal behavior reliably develops across the (ancestral) normal range of human environments because it is buffered against both environmental and genetic insults. Given a large population of people in a specific environment, to what extent can behavioral differences between these people be accounted for by differences in their genes? This is also a meaningless question because *behavior* and *action* are totally different things. The smile, as such, is genetic, but the action of a smile is environmental. Traditional psychology confuses behavior and actions. To be religious is genetic, and based on instincts, but to be Christian is not genetic. Churchgoing is a behavior based on the **instinct of ritual.**

However, traditional behavioral genetics nevertheless answers the above question by computing the (broad) *heritability coefficient.* This coefficient is a statistical measure of the genetic "contribution" to differences among individuals. It tells us what proportion of the individual differences in a population can be "ascribed to genes". For example, if we say that a specific behavior is 50 percent heritable (the coefficient = 0,50), we are saying that 50 percent of the variance in that behavior is "linked to heredity". The heritability coefficient of a behavioral trait (for example churchgoing?) can vary from one environment to the next because environments do affect development and learning. Note that the heritability coefficient tells you nothing about what caused the specific behavior of a specific individual. It's important to keep this in mind. And note that the heritability coefficient of complex adaptations is usually *low*, not high, because their genetic basis is universal and species-typical (something all of us have). This result is, of course, flawed. As I said above, the heritability coefficient does not explain what constitutes a given individual's behavioral trait. Even if the heritability (coefficient) is 50 percent (= 0,50), genes can constitute 99 percent of the trait. Moreover, the other 50 percent of the variance need not be caused by the environment, but by the measurements (for example: the researchers measure on form/off form instead of genetic differences). This is obviously the case when some researchers say that intelligence is only 60 percent heritable. Intelligence is a complex adaptation so these results are doubly flawed (see above). Moreover, intelligence is a group of learning instincts, and intelligent people tend to seek out an intelligent environment, and vice versa. More flawed! In a sense, environments are, in general, multi genetic! So heritabiliy coefficients are, in general, multi flawed.

Fortunately, the problems above were solved by Mitch C. Bronston in May 2001 by asking the question "Can we quantify how well instincts learn?" His solution is to use the (broad) heritability coefficient, but let the "environmental" part of the variance quantify how well an instinct can learn. (See more later.)

Obviously, it is meaningless to put percentages on the "contributions" made by genes (or instincts) and the environment. Take an example: a person born with "music genes" will seek out a musical environment. Practicing in that environment (a group of musical people) will switch on certain genes to create links between certain neuropathways. These links will make the person even more musical. Altered genetic activity because of environmental factors is therefore, in a sense, an indirect effect of genes. Human genes and human behavior can only be understood in the context of the surroundings. Nothing in behavioral science makes sense except in the light of evolution. A smile, in itself, is a behavior based on an instinct. The *action* of a smile is 100 percent triggered by the environment (including our brain and our body), and the smile itself is (nearly) 100 percent determined by the genes. But remember: All human instincts are, more or less, capable of (instinctual) learning. We all know that from everyday experiences. We all understand that genes do not determine actions directly. But genes determine learning instincts. And instincts determine (potential) behavior. Finally, (potential) behavior and environmental triggering determine actions. Again: Don't confuse behavior and actions as traditional psychology does. The choice of X may be culturally triggered, but the deeper reasons for choosing X do reflect an instinctual process. "Good" genes (or instincts) exploit a "good" environment much better than "bad" genes (or instincts). The difference between good (high-yielding) and bad (low-yielding) plant varieties is much bigger on good soil than on bad soil.

As a general rule, as environments become more uniform the heritability coefficient *rises* (= the "genetic" part rises). How is it possible? Because the "environmental" part is *not* environmental! It's genetic!

Environmentalists say talent doesn't exist They say the following "evidences" contradict the talent account: 1) lack of early signs, 2) evidence pointing to absence of differences in ease of learning between "talented" individuals and others, 3) exceptional levels of performance in "untalented" people, 4) "talented" individuals do not reach high levels of expertise without very substantial amounts of training. However, the logic of the **Bronston heitability coefficient** (see above) explains these anomalies. An instinct has two innate "parts" (the "basic" part and the learning part) and, naturally, the relative "size" of these parts are innate and vary from individual to individual, and from instinct to instinct. Also, of course, the speed of the biological development and maturation of these parts are innate, and vary from individual to individual, and from instinct to instinct.

In 1999 I (N.K.O.) nearly died because of blood poisoning (sepsis). During the last few minutes of consciousness before unconsciousness, I had only one instinct left: the **(sense of) sight instinct** (including the conscious part of this instinct). All thinking, all reasoning, all feelings, all emotions, all language, all hearing was gone. Total neutrality; only the sense of sight was left. I lived only at the present moment. No memories of earlier life. No thoughts about the situation. No questions. No fear. No pain. No other body senses. After my miraculous survival, I can now clearly remember these few extraordinary minutes. My wife tells me that I gradually lost all my instincts and all my consciousness in less than 20 hours. This natural experiment seems to show that each human instinct has a conscious part, and that *consciousness, rather than being holistic, consists of the conscious parts of the human instincts.* Obviously, consciousness is one kind of accessibility between 1) the senses and the brain and 2) the brain and the behavior. Consciousness contains a *part* of awareness, attention, feelings, and the "I", in addition to a (conscious) *part* of each of the rest of the human instincts, it seems. A "self" which is also real and important, are perhaps able, in limited ways, to influence its own fate. Biology cannot subtract from what it is to be human. Clearly, few, if any, animals can dispense with consciousness because of its enormous survival value. Experience tells us that conscious perceptions are strongly influenced and even determined by unconscious processes. We are conscious actors and unconscious responders. The quality of a person's thinking is partly determined by his feelings. People react differently to identical stimuli. Humans have always felt that they "know" things independently of any experience they ever had. Even when we recognize that memories must influence our minds, we feel that something else stays fixed—the thing that has those memories. When I had only one instinct left, my "I" or my "self", undoubtedly, *was* that instinct. Perhaps the "I" = the "self" = my consciousness = the conscious parts of my instincts. The last instinct left was sight. We are primates—highly visual creatures—with minds that probably evolved around this remarkable sense/instinct.

Instincts can be broken down into smaller and smaller agents of information processing. At the lowest levels, the steps have to be automatic and unanalyzed. No rational creature can consult rules all the way down. At some point a thinker must execute an existing rule in order to prevent infinite regress. The thinker can't help it. He/she must have **reasoning instincts**. When all goes well, our reasoning instincts link up into natural, appropriate, or rational behavior. Different individuals may choose differently in similar situations. Why? Well, our higher level agencies will often have *no* reasonable explanation of how the decision was made. We usually say something like "I decided to". But such expressions refer less to the processes which actually make our decisions than to the systems which intervene to *halt* those processes. Freedom of choice or freedom of will has less to do with how we think but how we *stop* thinking. We need rules for how we stop thinking. The learning instinct theory gives the answer/solution. The stop-thinking rules or mechanisms have to be directly or indirectly instinctual. The decision/choice mechanism must be instinctual. Proof/evidence: The parallel lives of MZA twins (see later). Even when we choose according to belief in values, religious belief, ideological belief, interest, taste, etc, the choice is instinctual. Proof/evidence: MZA twins research, and the other specific findings of behavioral genetics. Example: The discovery that affiliation with the Republican party is genetically determined was published in the journal *Nature*. (This discovery partly overshadowed the announcement by Government scientists that there might be a gene for homosexuality in men.)

The behavior of babies proves the existence of a large number of the human instincts. Babies have many specific emotions and feelings (even including surprise!). Emotions and feelings are instincts. No doubt about it. Babies have many specific "assumptions" (instincts) about how the world works, and what kind of things it contains. They distinguish causal events from non-causal ones. They understand intentions and goals. They read minds (infer what other people want, know, and believe). Research has shown that babies as young as five days old are sensitive to number, and that five-month-old babies can do a simple form of mental arithmetic. Acquiring concepts in children happens before they learn to speak. Three-to four-month-old babies see objects, remember them, and expect them to obey the laws of continuity, cohesion, and contact as they move, say researchers. Small babies have a grasp on gravity. They are surprised when a hand pushes a box off a table and it remains hovering in midair. A baby's preference for attractive people is established within the three to six months of life, as demonstrated in a study published in 1991. Etc. The list of unlearned behaviors (instincts) of babies is long, as predicted by the learning instinct theory.

We don't have to learn basic counting, measuring, shaping, forming, estimating, moving, calculating, proving, puzzling, and grouping. Even a blind toddler instinctively knows that the path from A straight ahead to B and then right to C is longer than the shortcut from A to C. Chimps can beat humans in computer games, and sometimes count faster than humans. Formal mathematics comes out of instinctual mathematics. This is not to say that it comes out easily. **We are all instinctual mathematicians, physicists, biologists, psychologists, and engineers.** Example: physicists don't learn to understand physics itself, but rather they discover new spontaneously "understandable" facts.

Kids respond to "new" differently. One way of discovering new instincts is to observe the child's response to the unfamiliar. This observation can even discover unlearned (genetic) differences (genetic variation) in the instincts themselves. For example: The child's response to the unfamiliar can fall anywhere along a "continuum" with extreme approach behaviors at one end and extreme avoidance behaviors at the other end.

The rest of the human instincts are genetically developed later because the adaptive problems an adolescent faces are different from those an infant faces. We all know from everyday experience that humans have instincts that are genetically adapted to their particular life stage.

If we carefully watched the development of human behavior from minute to minute we would see and understand directly that the human instincts exist and directly see and understand that the beliefs of the environmentalists are wrong. They believe in pure and genuine learning, but the arguments and facts above show that there is no such thing.

Siblings raised away from each other grow to be significantly similar to each other, with their degree of similarity being *predicted* by the number of genes they share.

The IQs of adopted children lose *all* resemblance to those of their adoptive family members and become more like the IQs of the biological parents they have *never* known.

MZ twins (monozygotic twins) are, in general, not genetically identical twins because they have different natural mutations and different genetic damages. Besides, splitting the fertilized egg often causes physical reversal or other extreme differences in physical features (including brain structures). Moreover, MZ twins, because of sharing the same placenta, actually draw apart from each other as one of them wins the competition for maternal blood supply. Nevertheless, traditional psychology says that MZ twins are identical twins. Therefore MZ twins behavioral research so far is flawed.

MZA twins are MZ twins reared apart. They were separated from birth and raised under different environments. If a pair of MZA twins are 1) genetically identical, 2) physically identical, and 3) have experienced identical conditions in the womb, and finally, 4) are raised (apart) in a free-choice society, then they will *live parallel lives*, even if they live in different environments, because of 1) they have the freedom to chose, and 2) their learning instincts are identical, and 3) their identical learning instincts actively choose what to learn. Of course, MZA twins are rare. Therefore (untalented) researchers say that the studies of MZA twins are non-representative. But the truth is that they don't like what they see. The MZA twins scare the hell out of them. **Genuinely identical MZA twins living in different free-choice environments live parallel lives.** These facts alone totally and perfectly prove our learning instincts (including character, personality, intelligence and intellect) and our new interpretation of learning, heredity and the heredity coefficient.

MZ twins (in the same pair) do not necessarily have the same genetic diseases such as schizophrenia, manic depressive psychosis (bipolar disorder), Alzheimers's disease, etc, because these diseases may be caused by random gene damage during or after the splitting of the fertilized egg. The same is true for genetic—directly or indirectly (e.g. hormonal causes in the womb)—dispositions such as for example homosexuality.

Because of the enormous importance of the life histories of MZA twins for the understanding of human behavior we now want to present a couple of quotes about life histories of MZA twins. (There exist life histories of genuine MZA twins in free-choice societies, that are much more fantastic than these, but none less fantastic.)

"Tom Bouchard's MZ 'Jim twis' were thirty-nine when reunited. Both had earlier married women named Linda, then got divorced, the married women named Betty. Both had served as sheriff's deputies in their respective Ohio towns. Without ever seeing each other, both had vacationed at the same beach resort on the Gulf Coast of Florida. Both liked working with wood and had similar basement workshops.... Each had built a circumarboreal; bench around a tree in his yard....In each case the bench was painted white. Both Jims drank Miller Lite, chain-smoked Salems, liked stock-car racing, and did not like baseball....On many different measures, Bouchard later reported their test scores were about as close as those you would expect from the same individual taking a test twice" (Daniel Seligman,1992, *A Question of Intelligence: the IQ Debate in America*). It is important to realize that it's logically impossible to explain away these parallel lives, and the parallel lives of the other genuine MZA twins in true free-choice societies, as coincidences, because the probabilities of each of these coincidences would be zero. And taken together....

"Like others who have studied twins reared apart, we have been impressed by the remarkable similarity of most MZ-apart co-twins—not just in those dimensions of aptitude, personality, or interest that we are able to measure (e.g. degree of superstitiousness), but in idiographic traits that cannot be measured in the usual sense of that term. Examples include aspects of personal style, forms of expressive behavior, pace and tempo of speech and movement, reaction to stress and excitement, postures unconsciously adopted while standing or sitting, specific fears (e.g. heights, confined spaces), focal interests (e.g. working with dogs, making guns), unusual habitual behaviors (e.g. giggling, obsessively counting things, leaving love notes about the house, and pretending to sneeze while on crowded elevators" (T. J. Bouchard (Univ. of Minnesota)).

"A pair of British MZA's who had met for the first time as adults just a month previously, both firmly refused in their separate interviews to express opinions on controversial topics; since long before they discovered each other's existence, each had resolutely avoided controversy. Another pair were both habitual gigglers, although each had been raised by adoptive parents whom they described as undemonstrative and dour, and neither had known anyone who laughed as freely as she did until finally she met her twin. Both members of another pair independently reported that they refrained from voting in political elections on the principle that they did not feel themselves well enough informed to make wise choices. A pair of male MZA's at their first adult reunion, discovered that they both used *Vademecum* toothpaste, *Canoe* shaving lotion, *Vitalis* hair tonic, and *Lucy Strike* cigarettes. After that meeting, they exchanged birthday presents that crossed in the mail and proved to be identical choices, made independently in separate cities…(N.G. Waller et al., 1992/3, Psychological Inquiry).

Identical twins, even if they live in completely different environments, tend to eat about the same amount of food. The amount of carbohydrates, fats and proteins they eat are also similar. They even eat at similar times. Genetics have a much stronger influence in pulling us to the table than do weather or social situations, says Georgia State University Psychologist John de Castro. Two identical twins separated at birth both kept themselves exceptionally clean and tidy. When asked why they did so, one replied that his adoptive mother was a model of cleanliness and tidiness, the other that he was reacting against his adoptive mother who was an "absolute slob".

Identical twins tell (from TV documentaries):

"We live parallel lives even when we are apart"

"We were reared apart, but we lived parallel lives even before we knew about each other"

"We have similar associations"

"We think similar patterns similarly"

"We have the same personality"

"We make the same errors"

"We make similar drawings, even when we are apart"

"We were always discovering things together"

"We are always doing things together"

"I can just look at him and know exactly what he is thinking"

"I can read her body language"

"Our children could not tell us apart"

"Our parents can't tell us apart".

"… can't tell us apart" Why? Because genuinely identical twins have exactly the same anatomy, physiology, behavior, voice, ways of talking, thinking style, facial expressions, gestures, postures, etc.

All known MZA cases are probably reported and described in detail in weekly magazines or TV documentaries but, unfortunately, this extremely important information is, as far as we know, largely neglected by science.

The data collected prove that genuinely identical MZA twins in different genuine free-choice environments have identical wills (definition of identical twins: see above). Note that this statement probably is the strongest support for free will that it is logically possible to find. Here the will is extremely independent of environmental factors (including other peoples' wills). Environmentalists love free will but believe that our will is determined by environmental factors!!!

We don't, in general, learn to learn. Therefore learning in itself must be genetically inherited. Obviously, what is simplistically called "learning" is a genetically inherited potential (for "learning") with certain potential, specialized, qualitative and quantitative characteristics.

No one believes that heritability means unchangeability. Behavioral geneticists, evolutionary psychologists, sociobiologists, forensic anthropologists, etc, have never believed such nonsense. Quite the contrary, these people know that humans can learn. The environmentalists' accusation of "biological determinism" is also meaningless. No one believes in "biological determinism". Behavioral science can predict human behavior only in a statistical sense because there are too many causes determining human behaviors: genetical mechanisms, physiological mechanisms, neural mechanisms (including neurotransmitters), hormonal mechanisms, pheromonal mechanisms, learning, memories, knowledge, habits, attitudes, skills, interests, character, personality, intelligence, intellect, environmental possibilities, situational triggering…*Love can be triggered by a single glance in a single moment.* The existence of instincts alone disproves "biological determinism".

Undoubtedly, one reason that some people reject the notion of "genetic behavior" is because the term is not defined before it is used. "Genetic behavior" is simply more-or-less "universal behavior". Another reason might be that some people are genetically predisposed to not to see it. Do we have other explanations of the systematic and spectacular inversions of the truth by so many intelligent and educated people?

Surprisingly, again, these intelligent and educated people don't understand the notion "a gene for behavior X". But "a gene for behavior X" is simply a gene that averaged over the other genes in the body, and averaged over the environments it appears in, probabilistically leads to behavior X. This definition is, perhaps, even consistent with the environmentalists' arguments about genetics.

We don't say or believe that "behavior is controlled by the genes". On the contrary, we say and know that behavior is controlled by thoughts, feelings, emotions, desires, beliefs, interests, happiness, sadness, sorrow, fear, anger, guilt, disgust, boredom, thirst, hunger, love of children, love of spouses, love of siblings, sex, and other learning instincts, including our inherited learning intelligence instincts and inherited learning intellect instincts.

We can control behavior. Example: We can reduce or prevent bullying behavior. However, to effectively reduce or prevent bullying behavior in a free society, we must know and understand the following nine extremely important facts about bullying behavior:

1) Bullying behavior is genetic (proved!) and shows individual genetic variation. All of us are bullies—more or less

2) Bullying behavior is triggered by certain environmental conditions. Note that the environment also includes the body and the brain of the bully. Also note that the most important aspect of the environment of any individual human being's behavioral traits (instincts) is its other behavioral traits

3) The bullying behavior mechanism has a certain learning capacity

4) After a positive learning result is achieved, the bullying behavior mechanism *in itself* still exists

5) The learning results show individual genetic variation

6) The learning result is highly specialized and situational

7) There is a certain possibility that the learning result is spontaneously unlearned

8) There exist hopeless cases such as for example psychopaths

9) Bullying behavior is highly independent of the other behaviors (instincts) of the bullying individual. This fact does not contradict point 2) above.

Each of the points above, and even each of the words used there, has "absolute" importance. Take for example the word "situational": Lenin's first act on becoming dictator was to hire the Tsar's chef, and later order a Rolls Royce from Hoopers, and Karl Marx was convinced that *Das Kapital* would finally make him rich. When Hitler attacked Norway in April 1940, virtually all of the many Norwegian pacifists threw away their broken-gun pins and without hesitation joined the Nowegian Army. In fact they were the very first personnel to reach the meeting places. Maximilien Robespierre was known for his honesty. He resigned as a judge so as not to give a death penalty. He was an advocate of democratic reforms. But after being elected a member of the Committee of Public Safety, he quickly took control of the government of France, and became the leader of the Reign of Terror. He sent his enemies, including other revolutionary leaders, and thousands of innocent people to the guillotine.

The above examples illustrate two enormously important facts about instincts:

1) Instincts are highly situational

2) Instincts are highly independent of other instincts

Bringing into awareness the reasons why we act in certain ways, gives us the power to act differently. New insights into human evolution have profound implications for how we can prevent violence and wars today.

Now it's time to sum up the following results and new insights into human behavior:

A. Human instincts are genetically inherited

B. Human instincts are potentials (potential behaviors)

C. Human instincts are situational

D. Human instincts are triggered (activated) by certain environmental situations (including the processes in the behaving individual's brain and body)

E. Human instincts are semi-independent (of the other instincts)

F. Human instincts can learn (see above)

G. The human learning is potential (see above)

H. The human learning is situational (see above)

I. Certain human learning is spontaneously unlearned

J. Human instincts, human learning, and human behaviors are buffered against both genetic and environmental insults

K. After a positive (or negative) learning result is achieved, the instinct *itself* still exists. This simple fact is surprisingly often forgotten.

Certain instincts seem to hang together, such as smiling and initiating conversation. The **instincts of friendliness and adventuresomeness** tend to co-occur reliably. Etc. Naturally, therefore, clusters of co-occurring instincts occur in certain situations. The most important aspect of the environment of any of an individual's instincts is its other instincts. Every basic instinct humans have is usually balanced by at least one other instinct. Instincts can be in conflict, both within individuals and within groups. This is **instinct competition**. It's well known that there exist **conflicting instincts** (e.g. hostility/friendship), **mutually promoting instincts** (e.g. dominance/submission), **mutually demoting instincts** (e.g. tension/relaxation), and **instinct hierarchies**. We are constantly in a state of shifting balance between the conflicting instincts. When two conflicting instincts are simultaneously strongly activated, we exhibit a number of characteristic instinctual intention movements and **instinctual ambivalent posturings**. Only when the "higher" intellectual instincts are in command can the individual deal with a situation with reason and compromise. **Emotion instincts** are grouped in pairs: joy/sadness, acceptance/disgust, anger/fear, surprise/anticipation, etc. Often there is a balance between emotional instincts and **rational instincts**. Besides, perhaps we have the ability to have feelings about our feelings. However, we cannot choose the emotions which we have. All emotions, by their very nature, lead to one or another impulse to act. The seed of all impulse is a feeling bursting to express itself in an action. We cannot decide when we have our emotional outburst. The amygdala acts as a storehouse of emotional memory, and can have us spring to action while the slower neocortex unfolds its plan for reaction. The instincts are semi-independent faculties, each reflecting the operation of distinct, but interconnected, neuropathways in the brain. Creative stupidity and able misfits (IQs 120—200) can exist because instincts are highly independent (= the mind is modular). As a matter of fact, creative stupidity and able misfits prove the existence of the human learning instincts. By the way, general intelligence tests do not measure creativity, and that is OK because the human mind is moduar. Injury, temporary ailment, lack of information, hesitation, etc, may paralyse intelligence instincts, but reflexes and basic instincts may keep us alive in the mean time. William James and Noam Chomsky pointed out that human intelligence may depend on our having more instincts, not fewer. Piaget used to say that "intelligence is what you use when you don't know what to do." Perhaps nothing enters consciousness unless it triggers an affect. With affect, any information can have meaning; whereas, without affect, the information is not noticed. "Affect without cognition is blind; cognition without affect is weak" (S. S. Tomkins). Marvin Minsky said "The question is not whether intelligent machines can have emotions, but whether machines can be intelligent without any emotions." (Experience shows that it is very often the clever people who make the worst criminals.) General intelligence tests do not measure inborn talents such as creativity, imagination, curiosity, adaptability, emotional intelligence, bodily intelligence, moral, character, personality, persistence, perseverance, interests, specific talents, co-operative attitude, sense of order, honesty, patience, enthusiasm, will power, wisdom, insight, foresight, leadership, how many things you can juggle at once, ideas, etc. And note: The intelligence-tests do not measure *intellect* (see later).

In addition to the above mechanisms, individual voluntary behavior is based on

A. The individual's perception of the situation

B. The individual's "pure" memories of events that occurred in similar situations in the past

C. The individual's immediate intentions

D. The individual's long-term goals for the future

Note, however, that perception and memory undoubtedly are instinctual. But how about interests (e.g. intentions and goals)? Well, the studies of (almost) genetically identical MZA twins in different free-choice environments prove that specific interests are genetically inherited. Therefore we are autonomous creatures. Undoubtedly, autonomy is the most important condition for the existence of free will. Clearly, if our interests were environmentally determined, free will, and even will itself, could not exist at all.

We stated above that the existence of spontaneously perfect private language in twins (independent of the language of parents or others) proves the existence of the human language instincts. Other proofs are the following facts: People with the genetic damage SLI (Specific Language Impairment) caused by a single dominant gene, score in the normal range in the nonverbal parts of IQ tests. The deaf adults occasionally discovered who lack any form of language whatsoever (no speech, no sign language, no lip reading, no writing, etc) have normal abstract-thinking instincts (including normal **mathematics instincts**). Needless to say, these people also had normal emotions, feelings, and behaviors. Even if we added inborn blindness, things would not change, specific life histories tell us. These findings seriously contradict environmentalism, and beautifully demonstrate the workings of the human learning instincts.

Man has 46 independent chromosomes and approximately 30,000 independent active genes. (The independence of genes relies on the natural process of "crossing over".) Mutations are also independent. The natural mutation frequency is roughly 1 mutation per 100,000 genes per generation, or roughly 1 mutation per fertilized egg. Why all this genetic independence? There is only one possible answer: To produce anatomical, physiological, and behavioral modularity (independence), and thereby make natural selection and evolution possible. Simplicity, beauty, elegance! In a sense, even the individual and its genes are partly independent during the processes of natural selection. Altruistic behavior might indeed evolve by means of *kin selection*. A behavior that actually kill an individual might still result in plenty of its genes being passed on to the next generation if the behavior increases the fitness of a close relative sharing many genes. In evolution genes are much more important than people. Nature kills organisms in order to let genes live into the future. Of course, the alleles are the most basic units of natural selection, but other units also exist, for example genes, instincts, anatomical organs, individuals, or even groups of individuals.

If inheritance were not discrete or modular, evolution as we know it could not have taken place. Therefore each instinct (or, at the most, small groups of instincts) must be a functionally highly discrete and genetically highly independent module. Hence if the behavioral trait X is an instinct, it should have an identifiable seat in the brain, and a set of genes that help wire it into place. Damage these genes or neuropathways, and the instinct should suffer while other instincts carry on. Spare them in an otherwise damaged brain, and you should have a retarded individual with intact behavioral trait X: an idiot savant. So idiot savants are predicted by the learning instinct theory, while environmentalism predicts that the development of an idiot savant is *absolutely* impossible. I'm sorry to say that the genetic damage to human instincts has caused the development of a substantial and steadily increasing number of idiot savants since the catastrophic pollution of the human genome began in the 1950s.

Even though we clock up more unique experiences as we age, evidence amassed over the past seventy-five years suggests that the "genetic contribution" to mental achievement and emotional characteristics **increases** with age. Example: The heritability coefficient of IQ is about 0.4 when measured in children, about 0.6 in adolescents, and about 0.8 in later maturity. The environmentalists are staring in incomprehension at these figures, but there is nothing unconceivable about them. The **Bronston heritability coefficient** (see above) directly explains these findings. The Bronston heritability coefficient tells us that the intelligence instincts' genetically determined specific learning capacities are **decreasing** with age. But, fortunately, this coefficient also tells us that the other parts of the total intelligence are **increasing**, so that the total intelligence (genetically determined!) is pretty **constant** ("= 1.0 = 100%") with age. (Individual IQ levels tend to remain unchanged from adolescence onward.) Of course, attempts to raise IQ (permanently) have failed. Both in the US and the USSR Head Start programmes that aimed to raise intelligence itself permanently totally failed. One of the most important findings of behavior genetics has been that, statistically speaking, family environment plays no consistent role in determining personality or intelligence.

Even if environmentalism was only *partly* correct, the Bronston coefficient had to *decrease* with age. Clearly, the *increasing* Bronston coefficient for human behavioral traits *proves* that human behavior is instinctive, and is not created by the chaotic and poverty-stricken environmental factors. But remember: 1) all instincts are learning instincts, and 2) all instincts are situational. Obviously, human intelligence(s) and intellect(s) depend on our having **more** instincts, not fewer.

Language instincts are an important part of the total intelligence. Most adults never master a foreign language, especially the phonology and grammar. No teaching or correction can undo the permanent error pattern. Why? Answer: The language-acquisition neuropathways are not needed once they have been used. They degenerate. Keeping the neuropathways around probably incurs costs. Therefore a critical period is centered in early childhood. These things elegantly demonstrate that the language instincts are adaptations. It's well known that there are critical periods for specific kinds of learning. The critical periods provide additional proofs of adaptive and genetic behavior.

Unused neurons may die off. This is like unused paths grow over and are not available. Neurons that are used heavily make new synaptic connections. This is like paths that are used very heavily wear away, making new connections to other paths. These changes in the brain are genetically controlled even if they may be environmentally triggered. But the instincts themselves determine if they want to react or not react.

Clearly, the increasing (with age) heritability coefficients for human behavioral traits (instincts) is *prima facie* evidence that human behavioral traits are adaptations. Hence human behavioral traits are not created by culture. But, the Bronston heritability coefficient shows that the human brain remains plastic throughout life, though not to the spectacular extent seen in childhood. All learning implies a change in the brain; a strengthening of synaptic connection. Virtually all human instincts are able to learn throughout life. However, remember that all learning, all behaviors, and even all triggering of learning and behaviors are specialized and content dependent. Remember also the genetic variation between individuals. Any parent of more than one child knows darn well how different those children are. Most parents don't believe that they can shape a child's interests, personality or intelligence. Our offspring seldom heed our warnings. Children in a family, raised in the same environment by and large, often turn out quite differently. Shared experiences involved in growing up in the same family do not make family members more similar to one another, researchers say. A domineering parent may "foster" rebellion in one child but submissiveness in another. Obviously, siblings are different from the beginning of life and develop into what they will in spite of our best effort to shape their behavior. From their parents, siblings, peers, and from the world at large, they select what they want, what they like, and what they are interested in. They ignore things that they think are boring or too difficult or too easy. As a matter of fact, the correlations between parent and child behavior could be plausibly interpreted as indicating the effects of children on their parents. Children who inherit a tendency to be sociable might elicit more interaction from their parents than introverted children. Rachel Cusk views children as the new parents. "What really matters is what happens in us, not to us" (John C. Maxwell). Parents might treat two children exactly alike but the children might interpret their parents behavior differently. If children are raised by lesbian parents, will they grow up to become homosexuals themselves? Of course, that's not the case because homosexuality is not caused by outside influences.

The correlation between adoptive parents and adopted children declines with the age of the adopted children, totally contradicting environmentalism. The correlation declines from 0.45 (= 45%) (age 7) to zero (age 17). This result is predicted by the learning instinct theory. (All explanation must be able to function as a prediction.) By the way, the IQ-correlation between "identical" twins is 0.90 (= 90%).

But how about peers? A good example of a personality that grew up without any peers is Bertrand Russell. He lost his parents very early and was educated by his grandmother. All you need is a grandmother? (Bertrand Russel's IQ was 180, Albert Einstein's IQ was 160.)

Cruelties stamp their victims' instincts with a template that regards with fear anything vaguely similar to the assault itself. But recovery from trauma happens. Unlearning and relearning are also learning. Emotional unlearning and relearning happen. The personality is malleable but elastic, and may snap back to its original shape like a rubber band. Although there was behavioral impairment in some of the Jewish survivors of the Holocaust, this tragedy gives testimony of the phenomenal adaptability and restorative power of the human mind. In general, the survivors were **not** depressed, anxious or fearful, and their personalities were unchanged. Explanation: we are all survivors of thousands of generations where cruelty was the "normal" state of affairs rather than the exceptions.

"A seventy-year-old victim of *encephalitis lethargica* has survived the pressures of an almost life-long, character-deforming disease; of a strong cerebral stimulant; and of confinement in a chronic hospital from which very few patients emerge alive. Deeply rooted in reality, she has triumphantly survived illness, intoxication, isolation and institutionalization, and has remained what she always was—a totally human, a prime, human being" O. W. Sacks, 1973, *Awakenings*. Harmondsworth: Penguin.

A *behavioral phenotype* is the type of behavior one can see clearly. *Phenotypic plasticity* is an adaptation to deal with environmental changes and stresses without changing the genes of the individual. Note that phenotypic plasticity is genetic.

The genetic phenomenon of inbreeding depression of both intelligence and physical characteristics is indicative of genetic dominance of the genes determining mental instincts. Besides, instincts are qualitative (behavioral) traits, and it's well known that qualitative physical traits are generally controlled by a few genes. There is no reason to believe that this is not the case for instincts too. On the contrary, because we know that behavioral disorders are commonly caused by a single gene. Finally, we must not forget this: the general theory of evolution tells us that the specific human instincts must correspond to a limited number of specific genes. Otherwise evolution would be impossible. Therefore it's not surprising that almost daily, it seems, another gene associated with a normal behavior (an instinct) or an abnormal behavior (a damaged instinct) is unearthed. At the same time the ineffectiveness of environmental factors are unearthed. Two examples: The effectiveness of exercise in managing depression has **not** been shown in a new meta-analysis. Data suggest that newspapers have **no** power to mould the political attitudes of their own readers.

New thinking understands that culture is to be seen as a biological adaptation. Even childhood peer groups and chimps create their own cultures. What is interesting are the huge *similarities* to be found between the people of the world: The human instincts are uniform across human cultures. The instincts (including language instincts!) are even "similar" in man and the great apes.

"Social learning"? "Cultural learning"? Mostly misunderstandings. See above. In the USSR more than 70 years (three generations) with social engineering (from birth to grave) failed horrifically. In the USA the 'prohibition era' yielded more alcoholism, drug-taking, crime, and corruption of police, than before the era. And how about the results of the many "cultural revolutions" around the world?

Ask a person to change form—think, want, and behave differently, and you probably ask the impossible, for it is the thinking, wanting, and behaving that is required to change the thinking, wanting, and behaving. Form cannot, in general, be self-changing. Besides, this project is probably, in general, statistically impossible, because it's one particular set of thinking, wanting, and behaving that tries to change another particular set of thinking, wanting, and behaving. Successful religious campaigns are **not** examples of change of behavior. X percent of the population are genetically religious. The X has **not** changed. We can of course technically change societies, but this is not the same as changing human behavior. We may change the actions but **not** the instincts themselves. However, instincts can learn. But the learning is often a scar and not a transformation. Even kindness, honesty, and other kinds of moral behavior are instinctual. Robespierre was known for his kindness, cruelty, honesty, and betrayal—**simultaneously**. Mr. X is simultaneously conservative and militant. Mr.Y is simultaneously deeply religious and a sadistic psychopath. Do you know what Karl Marx did towards his family and colleagues? "People try to change the world instead of themselves" (John Cleese).

"Unknown" factors are raising the mean IQ test scores around the world (The Flynn Effect). But it doesn't mean that people are getting any smarter. First, the expression of intelligence is not the same as intelligence. Second, the examinees are cheating: they are increasingly exposed to visual-spatial stimuli similar to the stimuli of the tests. Third, the tests are flawed. Example: Dutch men in 1952 had a mean IQ of 79 when scored against 1982 norms. Fourth, studies on nutrition have shown that vitamins or supplements have failed to reveal any impact on intelligence. Fifth, even if the test scores were correct, the cause of the raising scores might be *phenotypic plasticity* which is genetic. Sixth, the learning instinct theory perfectly explains the Flynn Effect.

David Phillips and colleagues have found that men who were smaller at birth (and later) are less likely to marry. This will cause raising mean body height. Besides, hormonal pollution and genetic damage has caused increasing body height. The son is eating junk food but he is 15 cm higher than his father. However, the son is much weaker than his father, and his back is anatomically damaged. Only different genes can cause a healthy difference in body height.

The discovery that humans have only 30,000 genes has been portrayed in some sections of the press as a victory for environmentalism. If we've got fewer genes, if there's less nature, the argument runs, then nurture must take up the slack. However, according to a report published in *Nature*, DNA's protein-building instructions may be able to combine in an unexpected way, increasing the number of possible proteins that can be generated from a given number of genes. Besides, don't forget that a single gene orchestrates the construction of a fruit fly wing. Each single gene is an enormous molecule. "In a very real sense the organism effectively transcends physical laws—even while obeying them...The necessary information [for behavioal novelty to occur is] present, but unexpressed in the constituent. The epigenic building of a structure is not a creation, it is a revelation" (J. Monod, 1972, *Chance and Necessity*). " Innate factors permit the organism to transcend experience, reaching a higher level of complexity that does not reflect the limited and degenerate environment" (Noam Chomsky, 1980, *Rules and Representations*).

People are different in fundamental ways even though they all have the same multitude of instincts. Evolution would not occur without individual genetic variation (of instincts) corresponding to individual behavioral variation. Besides, if *interactions* between genetic and environmental factors were rampant, evolution would be impossible. Therefore researchers in biogenetics find no compelling reasons to include interactions in their models. Stephen Jay Gould says "evolution cannot operate on the level of genes, because genes are invisible in nature". But genes are *indirectly* visible in nature via our *modular* instinctual behaviors. From early childhood, and highly independent of environmental conditions, people want different things. They have very different inborn motives, purposes, aims, values, needs, drives, impulses, urges, wants, etc. They instinctually believe, think, cognize, conceptualize, perceive, understand, comprehend, cogitate, etc. differently. Who is entitled to change whom?

A "long" D4DR gene implies a low responsiveness to dopamine in certain parts of the brain, whereas a "short" D4DR gene implies a high responsiveness. The novelty-seekers are much more likely to have one or more copy of the long gene. A striking example of what it means to be a novelty-seeker is the following: Among heterosexual men, those with the long genes are six times more likely to have slept with another *man* than those with the short genes. Among homosexual men, those with the long genes are five times more likely to have slept with a *woman* than those with the short genes. Matthew Stanford and Ernest Barratt have found a genetic basis for the "short fuse" (violence and aggression). Women will always love a hero, according to a study that found females value bravery above altruism when selecting men, whether it is for marriage, an affair, or a platonic relationship. Etc. Therapists reading about the new results emerging from behavioral genetics have switched from trying to treat their clients' problematic behavior to make them content with whatever their innate predispositions were. They have found that it works. Far from being a sentence, the realization of innate personality is often a release.

"Psychological conditions" are typically accompanied by an array of other medical problems. But these facts alone suggest that they are not genuine "psychological conditions". By the way, what are "psychological conditions"? Naming is not a definition. Besides, genuinely environmental explanations are outdated.

T. R. Bundy had a nurturing childhood, and he was the apple of his mom's eye. He was intelligent, had a likeable character, was a Boy Scout, and a regular churchgoer. His environmental factors was excellent, but nevertheless he confessed to murdering over 30 women and was further implicated in the murders or assaults of more than 50 victims over a 15-year period. He is not alone. This is almost a standard case. Environmental factors have, perhaps, never fully or directly explained particular cases of murder. However, around the world, behavior genetics is explaining aggression, violence and murder: An extra Y-chromosome, extreme cases of PMS, genetic damage to prefrontal cortex, genetic psychopathy, genetic mental illness, extreme cases of ADHD, genetic alcoholism, genetically determined "short fuse", and thousands of other genetic conditions are sometimes directly causing murder via an altered **aggression instinct**. Was it morally acceptable to continue to electrocute women for having genes causing extreme PMS? Thanks to behavior genetics we didn't continue to do that.

The brain of an ape or an advanced human fetus has all the same parts as an adult human. Brains produce behavior. And similar brains produce similar basic behavior. As a matter of fact, this is the only reason why they are similar. Statistically and practically apes are more moral than humans. It "could be" that our society teaches us to be cruel. However: 1) Humans create society, not vice versa, 2) In general, parents, education, religion, and the law teach us to be good, 3) Most violent films, books, etc. have happy ends (law wins), etc. Fierceness is not incompatible with compassion, fairness, valor, etc. We are simultaneous peacemakers and valiant warriors. Genetically caused independence! This is why we are flexible. This is why we have "free will". "Self-insight is harder to come by than people realize" (Nicholas Epley). We are unable to predict our behavior accurately.

Primate researchers in Asia, Europe, and the US are uncovering the instincts of the great apes. The researchers say that the lives of the great apes contain logical thinking, prediction of the outcome of a common effort, laughter, smile, crying, sorrow, fear, love, play, humor, astonishment, joy of life, empathy, awe, morality, wisdom, curiosity, exploration, inventiveness, carnivals, ceremonies, art, ambitions on behalf of their children, conversations, teaching, education, exchange of goods and services, traditions, culture, politics, aggression, violence, premeditated murders, war, cruelty, and hundreds of other "human" instincts and behavior patterns. (Stephen Jay Gould has denied consciousness to all nonhuman animals (see Steven Pinker: *How the Mind Works*, page 133)). Look at these brain weights (gm):

Blue Whale 10,000, African Elephant 7,500, Killer Whale 5,600, Bottlenose Dolphin 1,300–2,300 (average 1,700), Human 900–2,000 (average 1,400), Gorilla 500–1,000, Chimpanzee 350–600. Several species have larger brains than humans, compared to the body size. Besides, there is nothing special with the anatomy of the human brain. The great apes even have a language module. Environmentalism and its twin idea *speciesism* are horribly wrong—both scientifically and morally. All living species must be highly intelligent in a broad sense in order to survive. Intelligence is always specialized intelligence (adaptations) for a specialized way of life. Put a group of ten young, healthy and intelligent Norwegians into the Rain Forest. They are probably going to die because of lack of specialized intelligence, not because of lack of survival possibilities.

It's easy to see (if we look carefully) the consistent appearance of the genuine behavioral trait X (the individual's variant of the instinct X) throughout a family's pedigree. Example: It's easy to see the consistent appearance of genuine religious beliefs and genuine no religious beliefs, throughout a family's pedigree. Different variants of the same instinct X (different behavioral traits X) are caused by different alleles (se above). It's a mystery how the environmentalists are able to believe that different alleles have no effects on behavior. A specific behavioral trait in a specific individual is, of course, determined by a specific combination of alleles cooperating with other alleles in the genome. Therefore we may, in general, look many generations back in order to find an individual with exactly the same variant of the trait, and if the particular combination is rare, we may never find it. In families were a lot of living or written information exist for many individuals in many generations back, it is extremely fascinating to learn how genuine variants of specialized behavior of all kinds appear and disappear throughout the generations. No environmental causal chains exist between the owners of these behaviors. And these behaviors are extremely specialized and distinct. Therefore learning is totally ruled out. Here is a new area of research.

The life histories of extraordinary people, of all kinds and all ages, from all sorts of environments, are important evidences *for* the human instincts and important evidences *against* environmentalism. These cases are so extreme and the arguments from the low level and poverty of the input are so strong, that learning is absolutely ruled out. The life histories of people with physical brain damage, genetic brain damage, trauma, etc, are also extremely important research areas for the science of human instincts. Finally, the new cognitive science of early development ("what infants know") gives us exceedingly interesting, sensible and accurate information about the human instincts, intelligences and intellects. If we use a broad and general definition of instinct: "specific genetically inherited neuropathways that can specifically create behavior and learn" then all ordinary and appropriate behavior, including intelligences and intellects, are instincts.

All instincts are learning instincts (se above). Your instincts learn at their best when the **pleasure instinct** or the **caring instinct** is activated. If there are too much for the instincts to handle, the **anxiety instinct** is triggered. People's **concentration instincts** work best when the demands on them are a bit greater than usual, and they are able to give a bit more than usual. An enormous number of case histories tell us that "lower" instincts need not be satisfied before "higher" instincts can be satisfied or triggered. (Therefore "Maslow's Hierarchy of Needs" is, in general, incorrect.) The same case histories often tell us about the existence of talents. But the environmentalists reject the existence of talents. However, now, it's logically impossible to do that, because the overwhelmingly confirmed theory of learning instincts proves that the potential qualitative and quantitative capacities for all kinds of learning must be inborn. The following case history proves that genius and talent exist and that "mathematics" instincts exist. If ever there were a human individual with inborn mathematical ability it would be Srinirasa Ramanujan, a poor, unedjucated Indian, born in 1887, who was one of the greatest and most unusual mathematical geniuses who ever lived. He was very poor. Ramanujan, his brother, and his parents lived in a one-room home. He had no mathematical education. As a matter of fact, it can be argued that, for Ramanujan, a formal education was beside the point. He poured out math results, using excess wrapping paper to scribble down his enormously complicated formulas. This genetically determined genius didn't, in general, need to write down the complex proofs! He was so obsessed with his mathematics, in fact, that he did not want to stop to eat. Ramanujan's mother had to feed him at mealtimes so that he would be free to continue writing while he ate. The other mathematical geniuses of the world were shocked when they studied his results. Ramanujan's work in the area of number theory is exactly what physicists need when they work on the 26-dimensional mathematical models of string theory more than 100 years later! Do we need more evidence? Well, here it is: Karl Friedrich Gauss was a mathematician at the age of two. In the history of mathematics, there may never have been a child as precocious as Gauss—by his own account he worked out the rudiments of arithmetic before he could talk.

If the mathematical abilities of geniuses are inborn, and they certainly are, then the mathematical abilities of "ordinary" people must also be inborn. And if mathematical abilities are inborn, and they are, why shouldn't other kinds of less complex mental abilities be inborn? Do we need more evidence? Well, Wolfgang Amadeus Mozart was a composer at the age of three (while I, Nils K. Oeijord, is totally unmusical at the age of 54). And Benjamin Wood was a member of Mensa at the age of two. For all kinds of human abilities there exist a lot of case histories that prove beyond the doubt of reasonable people that all kinds of human abilities are inborn (= consist of learning instincts). Note that the kind of learning that the environmentalists believe in, is totally ruled out by the learning instinct theory. But remember that the Bronston heritability coefficient measures how well an instinct can learn. This kind of learning, however, is an inborn ability, but, of course, it's a potential ability. Remember also that **the effects of mobility and learning augment rather than eradicate the effects of instinctual differences on behavior.**

Remember the specialized, content-dependent mechanisms of the mind. These mechanisms are instincts. Only instincts can learn. General intelligence doesn't exist, but some people may be generally intelligent (methods of measurement: IQ-tests, etc.). "Intelligence" consists of a group of intelligence instincts. Intelligence without emotions is weak or perhaps impossible. Emotions without intelligence are blind. Therefore, **in a sense, all instincts are intelligence instincts.** We cannot axiomatize human behavior. So forget about general learning such as general classical conditioning, general operant conditioning, and general reinforcement. Experience and research show that IQ cannot be changed much by experience or education. This fact alone suggests that the IQ as such (including the learning part) is genetically determined. Furthermore, these findings are predicted by the learning instinct theory and the new interpretation of the heritability coefficient (se above). Statistically, it seems, man does not respond to better education by being a basically and permanently better person, perhaps because the will itself remains unchanged. Using the mind to fight mind, is difficult.

The functions subsumed in the term intelligence are compatible with the learning instinct theory. These functions are: stimulus apprehension, perception, attention, discrimination, stimulus generalization, learning (seeing regularities in the world), learning-set acquisition, remembering, thinking (e.g. seeing relationships), problem solving, etc.

However, it's not enough to be "intelligent". We also need intellect. Intellect consist of moral, wisdom, emotional intelligence, introspection, empathy, sympathy, friendliness, non-violence, nuanced social behavior, fairness, objectivity, insight, foresight, patience, curiosity, creativity, enthusiasm, sense of freedom, character, personality, courage, honesty, purpose, goals, planning, decision making, etc, in addition to balanced intelligence instincts. The intellect helps us to deal nimbly with competing demands and conflicting strategies. Intellect is balance. Intellect is behavioral management. Intellect is a lot of survival instincts. In a sense, the intellect has to be—by definition—"more" innate than "lower" instincts because it must be more buffered against both the inner and the outer environments than the lower instincts are. (*Personality* = a person's unique combination of consistent behavioral traits. A *behavioral trait* = a specific variant of an instinct. A *character* is required to evoke an emotional response and to be believable, compelling, persuasive, and sincere.)

Specific instinctual behavior appears and disappears according to particular circumstances. The circumstances in which an instinct is active, and the significance attached to it, vary enormously. Note that *innateness* refers to the measurable probability that an instinct will be activated in a specified set of environments, not to the certainty that the instinct will be activated in all environments.

Instincts "defeat" instincts and create survival abilities such as adaptability flexibility, malleability, variation, alternatives, new strategies, new habits, novelty, creativity, intuition, trial (and error), opportunism, exploration, new knowledge, quirkiness, sloppiness, unpredictability, broad potential, redundancy, stability, etc.

Purpose and purposeful striving toward ends and goals may be an essential part of instinctive behavior. When examined closely, the list of instincts in this book can give examples of instincts that can combine to create genuine instinctive *teleonomic* behavior.

It's almost impossible to stop the human instincts. Looking at nothing turns out to be quite hard to do. Our eyes and brain will not stop seeing, even when they have to invent the world from nothing. Instincts are also activated while we sleep: Dreams. Blind children and sighted children gesture at the same rates and use the same gestures while speaking. Blind children gesture even when they are aware the listener is blind. **Groups of deaf children spontaneously develop a perfect sign language. Deafness cannot stop the language instincts!** The explanatory power of the learning instinct theory is enormous. The theory easily explains historical processes. An example: People with abnormal instincts (e.g. psychopaths) become dictators (what else?) because they instinctively want to become dictators. The results: Human instincts such as thinking, judgement, and creativity are systematically repressed and stunted. People become anxious (**anxiety instinct** activated) and do not trust each other (**distrust instinct** activated), and there is a possibility of sudden conflict and violence (**aggression instinct** activated). In the end the **physical violence instinct** is simultaneously activated in a large number of people. The resulting situation has many names. This is not merely a simplistic description. 40 percent of the Germans voted for Adolph Hitler because they didn't know what a psychopath is. (Psychopathy is genetic.)

The Penguin Dictionary of Psychology revised by Harvey Wallerstein lists only *eight* human instincts in traditional psychology: life instinct, death instinct, sexual instinct, social instinct, herd instinct, religious instinct, repulsion instinct, and collecting instinct. Do we think the human mind is that simple? Many traditional psychologists have suggested to banish the term "instinct" from the psychologist's dictionaries. Other psychologists only say "Handle with care." Edward O. Wilson says: "Because of its vagueness the term "instinct" is seldom used in technical literature anymore, …" Vagueness? No! The concept of instinct is totally clear even for the people in the streets and it ought to be clear for scientists as well. If you understand that **laughter, sorrow, happiness, anger, etc. are instincts**, then you know perfectly well what an instinct is. An innate behavioral characteristic of humankind (an instinct) is an adaptation to certain circumstances. This adaptation may often be "unfortunate", such as anger, "short fuse", etc. Even R. Leaky didn't understand the human instincts: "I do not believe that violence is an innate characteristic of humankind, merely an unfortunate adaptation of certain circumstances", he declared. As a matter of fact, instincts **are** adaptations activated in **certain** circumstances, and the results are often unfortunate.

The textbooks of psychology *avoid* the use of the word instinct by using a large number of *synonymous* words and expressions: drives, basic drives, urges, instinctive urges, instinctive behavior, natural tendencies, motives, natural motives, predispositions, innate predispositions, human potentials, natural responses, the deeply ingrained parts of the human psyche, the quintessential aspects of human psyche, the most elementary rules of human behavior, the biological roots of behavior, genetic behavioral traits, man's unique behavioral traits, general behavioral traits of the human species, humankind's propensities, innate propensities, behavioral traits of mankind, the universals of human behavior, universal human mental attributes, the predispositions human beings display, the elements of human nature, human nature, biological mandates, specialized mental mechanisms, mental mechanisms, the commonality of human nature, our evolved mental mechanisms, the fundamentals of our nature, genetically influenced behavioral characteristics, genetically influenced behavioral predispositions, the basic structure of human behavior, human faculties, the fundamental aspects of human behavior, natural [behavioral] needs, [behavioral] needs, etc, etc.

Phobias, philias, manias, perversities, and mental disorders are *abnormal* instincts. Abnormal instincts are, in general, products of normal genetic variations, natural mutations, or gene damages. An understanding of normal and abnormal human instincts makes it easy to understand personality disorder. For example, a psychopath is an individual with an abnormal **feeling-of-guilt instinct**, an abnormal **affection-and-sense-of-mercy instinct**, an abnormal **affective-fixation instinct**, and an abnormal **feeling-of-anxiety instinct**. Of course, therapy, use of drugs, operation, or prison do not cure psychopathy. Phobias, philias, manias, perversities, and mental disorders teach us how normal instincts work (= how the mind works). Unfortunately pollution damages instincts via gene damage. **The genetic damage to the human instincts is catastrophic.**

If we want to understand and explain human behavior in detail, we need a list of all basic elements (instincts) of human behavior. If we don't have, or don't use, such a list, a detailed explanation and even a detailed description is, in general, impossible. Examples: Desmond Morris says religion is *appeasing*. Richard Dawkins says religion is *viruses on the mind*, Stephen Jay Gould sometimes says religion is *moral*, and sometimes says religion is *comfort*, Karl Marx said religion is an *addiction*, psychology books don't say anything at all, and so on. Steven Pinker says: "We can't have ethics unless we hold someone responsible for their behavior; we can't hold them responsible for their behavior unless we believe that the behavior is not directly caused." But **moral instincts** (ethics) are logically and genetically independent of the **punishment instinct**. On other planets there may exist humanlike creatures lacking one of these categories of instincts, or both. Our language consists of elements (inborn universal grammar, inborn universal word-producing mechanism, etc), our body language consists of elements (inborn specialized movements, positions, etc), and our behavior consists of elements (inborn instincts). You cannot talk correctly about quantum mechanics if you don't know the correct words (concepts) of quantum mechanics. You cannot talk correctly about human behavior if you don't know the correct words (instincts) of human behavior. The enormous intellect Noam Chomsky, and the equally enormous intellect Steven Pinker, have beautifully explained the language instincts. Chomsky's "the argument from the poverty of the input" is exceedingly important for the understanding of the language instincts. But we have to continue. Language is behavior. And the "argument from the poverty of the input" is equally important for the other human instincts. As a matter of fact, it's *more* important. The "language of the non-language-part of behavior" has a larger and more complex "universal grammar" and a larger "universal word-producing mechanism" than the "language of the language-part of behavior". The list of instincts in the Appendix of this book contains many of the most important elements of human behavior. Each element on the list is spontaneously and clearly understood, and automatically used, by all normal minds (and most abnormal minds) without any special instruction. Each element is totally universal. All fiction writers use these elements automatically, and their readers "absorb" them automatically. They are the human instincts.

Chapter 4   *The five primal instincts and abnormal behavior*

by
Mitch C. Bronston

"I have never, in all my various travels, seen but two sorts of people, I mean men and women, who always have been, and ever will be, the same. The same vices and the same follies have been the fruit of all ages, though sometimes under different names."

Lady Mary Wortley Montagu

"There are many humorous things in the world: among them the white man's notion that he is less savage than the other savages."

Mark Twain

Up to this point we have looked very deeply at the neocortex, that part of the human brain that is responsible for our intelligence, our intellect, and many of our 'pure' situational learning instincts. We have seen how instincts learn and how they change to accommodate new experiences in the environment, and what that does to our behavior. We might ask, at this point, what, then, is the difference between the "other" functions of the neocortex, the intelligence, and the intellect? While both are considered 'conscious' mechanisms, they perform separate tasks. The intelligence is the sum of our knowledge, experiences, fantasies, creative spirit, and reasoning instincts. Current terminology does not distinguish between that and intellect. For our purposes in discussing human instincts and behavior, we have applied a new definition to intellect because it appears to perform a different function, and is related to how instincts learn. For now we can call it the manager or the central processing unit of the neocortex. Very much like a computer, it applies its sorting ability to a "nebulous" collection of thought processes we humans like to call ethics and morals. In other words, the difference between right and wrong behavior. Dictated by our societies and civilization, parameters are applied to define how we should behave. Intelligence (= intelligence instincts) alone is not a sufficient mechanism to control behavior. "Pure" instincts, certainly, are not either since they tend to precipitate "innate" behaviors. What, then, helps this mass of information and collection of "platooned" instincts actually learn (adapt)? This would be the intellect and its ability to supervise the communication between primitive instincts and intelligence instincts. (However empathy, sympathy and other 'good' instincts are also at work.) We will devote an entire chapter to the intellect, but we need to look at another type of instinct that is much older and ancient than the learning instincts of the neocortex. These are the primal instincts; innate mechanisms that reside deep in the animal brain, and appear to account for most of our normal and abnormal behavior. It should be remembered that in McLean's description of the brain, there reside two layers of ancient tissue, the limbic system and the R-complex. These are most certainly the seat of much of our unconscious thought and memories, and we will contend that what we classify as abnormal behavior often originates in this part of the brain. We may refer to it as the animal brain, and, indeed, the instinctive behaviors it produces are nothing short of true animal behavior.

It has been discussed that psychology is effective in dealing with emotions and feelings, but little is understood about our animal beginnings. It is primarily designed that way because, as a species, we have perceived ourselves as separate from the animals and therapists have basically ignored our humble beginnings. Our religious and social institutions also contribute to this misinformation by design. That leaves the basic cause of our abnormal behavior untouched and untreated, rendering us impotent in helping to allow old instincts to relearn a new function in a changing environment. How important are the emotions in this process? They are critical to our understanding of primal behavior, for we will contend that where emotion is present, a primal instinct is the root cause, and must be addressed. The limbic system and the R-complex have given us the animal instincts of survival. This spans a period of time that is nearly 700 million years of evolution. From about the Cambrian period onward, great diversity in many species has occurred, and the combined knowledge of individual survival has been passed down to us, *Homo Sapiens*. We can say that the neurophysiology of our animal brain is the chemical equivalent of every species that has ever existed since that growth spurt called that Cambrian Explosion occurred. The rudiments of the R-complex, and later, the limbic system, have survived mass extinctions, subspeciation, and bursts of punctuated equilibria throughout our evolutionary history. It is amazing how durable this tissue and its instincts appear to be. It is also amazing how different species, separated by long periods and epochs, can exhibit the same behavior. How do we know this? Studies of current animal species and data from the fossil records confirms that, in spite of changes in physical architecture, behavior has remained fairly constant over this time frame. In other words, living things have behaved pretty much the same way since life first evolved. It is man, with his great intellect and ability to change his behavior, who now can actually manage behavior and change the environment. What type of instincts do we find in the animal brain? And what type of behavior can we expect from such a primal source? This chapter will provide an overview of the primal instincts and a look at abnormal behavior. Succeeding chapters will look at individual behaviors and how they affect our daily lives. We have reclassified current terminology into an understandable format that helps describe our most fundamental nature, and look at how we might behave when primal instincts dictate our response.

As already stated, we are, all of us, animals first and moral, intelligent beings second. Our humanity is the 'evolution' of civilization based mostly on intellect. Our 'ordinary' instincts are a product of 'prewired' brain physiology. They are certainly more evolved in *Homo Sapiens* than other animals, but present, non-the-less, in the great diversity of life. There are two basic instincts from which we derive our survival concepts. These instincts are "present" in information supplied by DNA and controlled by the nucleotide sequences of our genes. They are most certainly primordial, and predate even Cambrian life forms. They are, simply, self- preservation and reproductive. All living creatures as old as life itself have these two instincts. They help keep us alive, make us aware of predators or danger, and help us pass our species adaptations to the next generation. The next three instincts are more esoteric, because they require a brain to be present. They can be referred to as abstract instincts because of their requirement for complex neurosynaptic pathways found only in organisms with brains. The first is the instinct for territorialism, simply defined as the behavioral mechanism for the need to have territory to live. The second is the instinct for social hierarchy, defined as the behavioral mechanism for the need to interact with members of our own or other species in a way that exemplifies position and dominance. The third is the instinct for ritualism, illustrated by repetitive behavior in response to our environment. As simple as these sound, they are, in fact, the complex result of evolution of individual survival techniques. The correct 'prewiring' of our brains is the normal pattern of information given to us at birth and comes from primordial genes in our DNA and specific neurosynaptic pathways in the three levels of the brain. The normal spectrum of behavior throughout our species is filled with many examples. Here are but a few: Our self-preservation is in play when we dodge an object or run from fire. Our reproductive instinct is most evident in our loving behavior toward a mate or offspring. Territorialism is the mechanism involved when we feel pride in our country or our rabid loyalty to a favorite sports team. Certainly our ownership of property (home, possessions and money) is territorialism. Ritualism is dominant in our expression of religious belief, daily activities, and courtship. Hierarchy dominates our social interaction with others and our perceptions of the world around us, particularly our self-esteem. These are the normal expressions of the five instincts. It is easy to see that no one instinct governs any one behavior, rather, a combination of one or more instincts can be applied in almost every known behavior. It is interesting to watch higher mammals, excluding man, because the intellect is less developed and the primal instincts are dominant in controlling their behavior. As stated, primal instincts are not limited to mammals, just "better" developed. Fish swim in schools, bees and other insects divide the work load, all examples of hierarchy and territorialism. Higher mammals mark their living and hunting area for the same reason that humans have bank accounts or addresses on their homes. The list of normal behavior is endless, but it is important to note that just about all human activity can be explained by these five instincts. This is particularly evident when the 'prewiring' is abnormal and instinct becomes more than normal expression. This happens more frequently than we would like, but it is a fact of life and part of the diversity of our species. That is were we will turn our discussion. There are many causes of abnormal 'prewiring' Genetic mutation, causing DNA to alter its instructions, injuries to the brain and its ability to accurately perceive its environment, and incorrect balances of brain neurotransmitters are some examples. Conclusively, any alteration in the way the individual perceives his or her environment can result in abnormal behavior. Remember that 'civilization' is defining our parameters of what is normal and that is governed by intellect, not basic instincts. So what are examples of abnormal responses to the five instincts. A seemingly normal man rapes and kills a woman in a park. Rape is about power and sex. As one can see, in this case, this man's perception of reproductive and hierarchy instincts are miswired and he behaves in the only normal way he can. To take what he wants by force. In his mind, he sees himself as better than the woman, who is only beneath him in the social order, and in confusing this instinct, along with reproductive and certainly territorial desires, he rapes! A fourteen year old boy, ignored and tormented by classmates, opens fire with an assault rifle, killing several students and a teacher. The public and news media search endlessly for the 'why it could happen' answer. Understanding the basic instincts makes it easy. This young man may have suffered from periods of unbalanced neurotransmitters in the brain, common to just about everyone at some point, but accompanied by cruel torment from his peers, his perception was one of danger to his existence and misreading the social hierarchy. His response is to correct the situation and restore the hierarchy as he sees it by eliminating those responsible for his loss of self-esteem. This is biochemistry, not psychology, which the public misses entirely in their search for answers.

A 'despotic leader' invades a neighboring country. The world's response is to mobilize its forces and make war on this nation and its 'demented' leader. The objective is to 'restore' the normal balance of power at the cost of over 100,000 dead. The explanation: territorialism and hierarchy at its worst. The perceptions of the despotic leader and the perceptions of the responding nations are altered by instincts nearly 4 billion years old. Instinct overcomes intellect with great regularity among all species, but is particularly destructive in man with his enormous quantity of both. Perception of normal instinct can be altered even in normal individuals by the introduction of chemical substances that change neurotransmitter activity levels. This is one of the most common afflictions of our age. The use of psychotropic drugs can suppress the intellect and enhance the instincts in many. This is not true in all cases, but a significant percent of the population of the planet has the propensity to react adversely to alcohol and other mood altering drugs. Murder, rape, burglary, destructive rage, and assault, are very common among perfectly well behaved people who chemically alter their neuropathways and let the five primal instincts determine their actions. Again this is biochemistry, not social conditioning and our society needs to understand this to find a solution to the problem. One final example illustrates that abnormal perception of the primal instincts can affect large numbers of people at the same time. A religious cult, convincing a group of people that a spaceship is awaiting them behind a comet to take them to heaven, commits mass suicide and, again, we ask why. How could this happen? The answer is in the misinterpretation of data supplied by the instincts for ritualism and hierarchy. Most all religious practice is designed to satisfy these two basic instincts, but in this case, the people involved may have been 'prewired' from birth, and, most likely, had been that way most of their life. This tragedy was enhanced by an appalling lack of hierarchical understanding of the way the universe is put together, and a twisted understanding of religious motivation. Religious fanaticism finds its basic roots in the need to satisfy these instincts. Intellect seems to have failed, as it usually does in all cases such as this. Religious fanaticism is global in scope and does not limit itself to cults. Observe the Middle East, Bosnia, the Indian subcontinent, or the southern USA, and you will find the common denominator is ritualism and hierarchy, and the characteristic lack of application of intellect. The vast majority of our species deal with these instincts relatively peacefully, but there are always examples of those 'prewired' to abnormal behavior. The next time a bomb goes off in front of an abortion clinic, the 'prewired' brain map of the individuals responsible will need no additional explanation.

In all of the previous examples, one common theme surfaces over and over again. The five basic instincts are present in all humans, as in other species, but it is how we react to their influence that determines our behavior. There appear to be only two possible environmental influences that motivate our behavior. Satisfaction of our instincts, or a challenge to them. These external motivations also seem to be associated with deep emotion and feelings. Observing animal behavior without the tempering effect of powerful intellect, illustrates this equitably. Domesticated animals, for example, display their instincts openly, and the associated emotions surface simultaneously. A hungry house cat will notify its human companion immediately, exhibiting the instinct of self-preservation (need for food) as a challenge to itself. Eating, subsequently, will satisfy that instinct, and the accompanying purr will display the associated emotion. A school of fish squeezed into a small tank and separated into two equal coed groups by a glass partition will exhibit agitation at the challenge to its instincts for reproduction and loss of territorial integrity, and will stop mating, some dying with in days. A second control group in a wider area without challenging constraints, will show no stress and behave normally. When the glass partition in the first group is removed and the area is expanded, the school reforms and prodigious mating ensues until neither group can be distinguished in scope or behavior. It is clear that challenge to the basic instincts can be offset by satisfaction. In *Homo Sapiens*, our instincts are under constant bombardment from the environment, and challenge is ever present. Satisfaction usually rewards us with feelings of comfort or happiness. The challenge of loneliness is offset by the inclusion of a companion, satisfying our hierarchical instinct and reproductive instinct if the companion is a potential mate. We are challenged by confusing sensory input moment by moment, resulting in ritualistic practice to help us cope with more familiar patterns. Sometimes the 'prewiring' is distorted in the brain, and ritualism becomes obsession. Such is the case in obsessive compulsive disorders and religious fanaticism. Our overwhelming need to recognize and satisfy the challenges to our instincts can be both beneficial or dangerous. Both challenge and satisfaction are the product of exquisite chemistry in the brain and DNA, and have a plethora of negative and positive emotions that accompany them, also governed by elegant chemistry in the brain. It is the unknown factors of intellect that allow us to choose how we will behave. How do challenge and satisfaction work within individual behaviors? And are primal instincts capable of learning? In the next chapters we will examine each behavior separately and look at the intellect as the controlling mechanism.

Chapter 5   The primal instincts of hierarchy, territorialism, and ritualism

by
Mitch C. Bronston

"I am absolutely convinced that no wealth in the world can help humanity forward…money only appeals to selfishness and irresistibly invites abuse."

Albert Einstein

"It is clear that many instinctive desires…are in their nature of short duration; and after being satisfied, are not readily or vividly recalled."

Charles Darwin

Of all of the primal instincts, the behavior associated with hierarchy is, by far, the most consuming. Living organisms that possess a significant neural network in the brain develop powerful social behaviors, and interact in ways that allow them to dominate the resources of the environment. Because of the evolutionary oddity that allowed *Homo Sapiens* brains to diversify over other organisms, the primal instincts as a whole are more pronounced and varied in humans, and the instinct of hierarchy in particular. Remembering the definition of hierarchy: competing for resources through position and dominance; it is essential for human beings to excel over others in "every" interaction. This behavior is evident from the simplest situations to the most bizarre. The consequences may be benign, or they may be devastating. Whatever the case, hierarchical behavior seems to dominate all other instincts in most individuals. Remember too that powerful emotions are involved in the orbiting cycle of challenge and satisfaction. That is to say, our hierarchical neural pathways are constantly being challenged, leading to the behavioral reaction, followed by satisfaction, and back again. The emotional tides ebb and flow accordingly and the individual experiences the full gamut from, say, sadness to happiness. This cycle may repeat as many as a thousand times a day to some degree depending on the perceived needs of the individual. Note that perceived is important because the need is not always essential for survival. The perception in all of us is that we must dominate, in some way, those around us, or natural selection "will eliminate us." In other words, it is *not* in our nature to be kind and pleasant to others in every situation. This sounds horrible until one understands that the primitive brain evolved in nature for the purpose of survival, and civilized behavior is mostly the product of intellect. All of the rules, regulations, policies, procedures, laws and social applications we practice as humans, are the invention of the neocortex alone, and not the meanderings of the R-complex and the limbic system. While it is true that house pets and other higher mammals can use their neocortex, it is not as well developed as humans, hence, they can be trained, but cannot take this behavior to the next level and adapt it permanently. Once they are removed from the interaction with humans, they will revert to pure instinctive behavior, and the civilized training they received will be ignored.

We all have the capacity to revert to primitive instinctive behavior. What holds that in check is the intellect. That is where our conscious efforts toward civilization reside; neural pathways inundating the neocortex. The layer of the brain that exploded with growth and diversity some 850,000 years ago. Prior to that, *Homo Sapiens* was barely able to compete with other primate species. It has been suggested that our most recent cousins, *Australopithecines*, *Homo Erectus*, and *Homo Habilis*, could not adapt to the changing environment, and became extinct, while *Homo Sapiens* adapted, moving onward because of the growing size and complexity of the brain. It is important to note that there is no evidence of so-called civilization until about 100,000 years ago. Social structure appeared only periodically, but most bands of humans lived primarily on their primal instincts, following herds of animals they could hunt, and adapting as they moved. There is little doubt that hierarchy played a major role in survival. Those without this well developed instinct, perished, and natural selection has endowed us with an ample genetic gift from that time. It is easy to conclude, therefore, that this dominant instinct is the surviving trait of those early and vulnerable humans as they scratched and clawed their way out of the caves into the skyscrapers of the present. It is indeed fortunate that we all have this well evolved series of neural pathways. It gives us desire, competitive spirit, leadership qualities, and many other admirable traits that allow us to better our position in the environment. But in the great diversity of humankind there is an equal tendency to dominate at the expense of others. Remember, we are only a short step away from our primitive ancestors, and we all have the capacity to do harm if our perceptions of survival are challenged. In other words, we can all kill on a whim, injure another randomly, and, at any moment, any one of us can satisfy some challenge to our hierarchy by eliminating the competition. We are held in place, for the most part, by 12,000 years of laws and human excellence in building a greater society, through our neocortex and its capacity for altruistic understanding. (Note that humans also have pure altruistic instincts.) That is how we define civilization, and separate ourselves from the animals. But as diverse as mankind is, abnormal behavior is constantly present in every society on the planet. Abnormal behavior is defined as behavior outside of the parameters of a civilized society. It can range from mild hierarchical domination of a single individual, to mass genocide of an entire population. The purpose of this discussion is not to root out the next Adolph Hitler. This exercise is to help us understand the daily "trauma" of individual hierarchical challenge and the associated response mechanism. That is where this discussion will center.

In all fairness to the contemporary use of psychology, a few thoughts are necessary. Modern psychology is, as many know, based, to some extent, on a specific structure of the mind, namely ego, super ego, and id. The key here is mind. Instinct refers to brain structure and is based on neurophysiology and the "triune" brain as described by Paul MacLean; the R-complex, the limbic system and the neocortex as produced by evolution. Psychology tends to wander in many directions to describe human behavior, and becomes complicated and heavy. It doesn't need to be. Primal instincts vs intellect is fairly simple and describes human behavior as animal behavior modified by our innate intellect. The intellect, is defined here as that which "consciously" recognizes and modifies reaction to outside stimuli and operates "independently" of the animal or primal instincts of survival. Modern psychology seldom makes any mention of animal behavior, and, even in studies of animals, tries to find human characteristics. The use of what we call instinct therapy, assumes the opposite. We are first and foremost animals, and human only because of brain complexity. As mentioned above, hierarchy may be the single most powerful instinct in all of us that may produce unwanted behaviors and lead to abnormal action. It is important to remember that hierarchy may not always act alone. Other primal instincts may intertwine and lead to extremely bizarre behavior, but the hierarchical instinct is certainly the most powerful in its influence over our thinking and our behavior. We have devised a series of questions that involve daily hierarchical situations. They are certainly not scientific in any sense, but tell us a lot about our self-esteem and our need to control others in the environment. Answer them to the best of your ability and as quickly as possible. Do not spend time thinking about the question. Choose the answers that best describes what comes to mind and then move on to the next. There is no right or wrong answer. Be sure to include actions or feelings from your past experiences, even if you just fantasized them or actually participated at any point in your life.

Read the following scenarios and circle as many answers as would best describes how *you* would behave. You may circle all answers if necessary.

1. I am at a party. I discover that there is no one there that I know. No one is making the effort to talk to me, even after considerable time.
A) I feel angry and sad, so I leave, they're just a bunch of stuck ups.(nr)
B) I feel OK, so I reach out and make friends. (ir)
C) I feel angry, but I reach out anyway and try to mix in. (ir)
D) I feel angry and worthless; I do whatever it takes to be the center of attention. (nr)
E) I feel completely worthless, so I pick an argument or damage property. (sr)

2. I am at work. I just heard that one of my co-workers is in trouble with the boss.
A) I felt tired, but now my energy level is back and my work improves. (nr)
B) I feel OK, but can't help wondering what happened. (ir)
C) I'm angry at the boss, and try to comfort my co-worker. (ir)
D) I begin joking about my co-worker to others. (nr)
E) I comfort my co-worker, but emphasize how I'm not in trouble. (sr)

3. I am at work. My boss is pointing out some mistakes that I made.
A) I feel hurt and defend myself vigorously. (nr)
B) I feel worthless and decide to call in sick the next day. (sr)
C) I feel bad but I take it and go on working. (ir)
D) I feel OK, this happens a lot and no body cares. (ir)
E) I get angry and point out the boss's shortcomings. (nr)

4. I'm on the freeway. A driver cuts me off nearly causing an accident.
A) I finger the idiot and continue on my way. (ir)
B) I finger the idiot and speed up so he can see it. (nr)
C) I feel angry and insignificant and take it out on my family later. (nr)
D) I follow the driver as far as I can so he knows I'm tailing him. (sr)
E) I take down his license number and report him to the police later. (nr)

5. I just bought a new vehicle.
A) I take it to work and show it off to my friends. (ir)
B) I peel out on to the street every chance I get. (nr)
C) Even though the car is new, my best friend just bought a new Mercedes, and I feel angry and jealous. (nr)
D) I don't really care what others drive, I just like my car. (ir)
E) I would love to remove the muffler and race on the main drag. (sr)

6. I am at a party with lots of people I know. Some, but not all, are doing drugs and drinking.
A) I join in on the activity but make no decisions about doing drugs. (nr)
B) Even though I don't like beer, I like the people, so I pick up a drink. (nr)
C) I decide not to drink or do drugs, but I try to dominate the conversations. (sr)
D) I quietly involve myself with friends regardless of their activity. (ir)
E) I get wasted and lead my friends to the nearest bar. (sr)

7. I just moved in to a new place. I discover my neighbors are racially mixed.
A) I avoid these people as much as possible. (sr)

B) When my neighbors talk to me, I think of it as just small talk, and leave quickly. (nr)

C) I join in conversations and use lots of big words. (nr)

D) I join in conversations and talk like them. (nr)

E) I don't care one way or the other. (ir)

8. I have come into a sum of money. I have been asked to join a local organization.

A) I am honored and attend the functions regularly. (ir)

B) I feel proud and donate some funds anonymously. (ir)

C) When asked to give money, I never hesitate. (sr)

D) I feel proud and donate funds with my name involved. (nr)

E) I volunteer to lead various groups, taking time off of work. (nr)

9. I am at a restaurant with a friend and see a well known celebrity at the next table.

A) I go over to get an autograph in the middle of my meal. (nr)

B) I do whatever it takes to shake hands and get an autograph. (sr)

C) I sit for a while, and comment to my friend about getting an autograph. (ir)

D) I'm not paying attention to my friend's conversation, I just watch the celebrity. (sr)

E) I talk endlessly to my friend about what I know about this celebrity. (nr)

10. I'm standing in line at the bank. A poorly dressed person in front of me looks confused about what to do.

A) I politely ask the person to step aside so I can move on. (nr)

B) I wait my turn even though I'm impatient and angry. (ir)

C) I help the person as much as I can. (ir)

D) I'm impatient and angry, and I move to another line. (nr)

E) I tell the person to hurry up, then I feel better. (sr)

Now that you have answered the questions, look for the symbol at the end of each response and record the total number of responses you circled for each category.

(ir) ....

(nr).....................

(sr).....................

Each symbol stands for a level of response. (ir) refers to insignificant response. (nr) is a noteworthy response, and (sr) is a significant response. Again, while this is not a scientific measure of behavior, it is meant to be an awareness mechanism that may show an individual the influence that hierarchical instinct has on overall behavior in daily situations. Naturally, the greater the number of responses in the insignificant category, the greater the tendency for that individual to use the intellect in everyday life. If there are more noteworthy responses, it is probable that hierarchy is very dominant in the individual, and may tend to overshadow intellect in many cases. If significant response shows a high number of choices, there is a high probability that the individual is prone to aggressive and seriously damaging behavior. Please remember that this is not a scientific study. It must pass the rigors of a controlled experiment and must be given to several thousand participants in order to establish norms and parameters. As of this writing, that has not been done, but it can be an interesting reflection of the response mechanism to challenges to the primal hierarchical instinct. It is important to remember that any primal instinct is the culmination of complicated, but exquisite chemistry deep in the primitive structures of the brain. Tremendous challenge bombards us all on a daily basis and the intellect must sort out the various conscious options, but only after the primal brain pathways fire. In other words, it is our nature to respond through primal animal mechanisms first, and temper our behavior with conscious intellect choices second. There are millions of examples of this in everyday life from every person in every culture. Abnormal behavior is more common than we would like to admit, and it is the metaphor for a great deal of unhappiness. Remember that the R-complex and the limbic system are several hundred million years old, and the neocortex in humans is only about 850,000 years old (and still evolving?) The often heard phrase "use your head" is literally a plea to the intellect to intervene over the primal instincts before serious faulty behavior has a chance to inflict damage on an otherwise orderly society. Conversely, the phrase "follow your instincts" is not always good advice. In this context, "using your head" does not appear to be the main thinking mechanism, and the results are often hurtful or disastrous. When the hierarchical instinct is involved, and restoring self-esteem is the issue, it is clear that the satisfaction cycle, and its powerful brain chemistry, needs a great deal of assertive action to restore the balance. Most of us have a choice; to use the intellect and refrain from abnormal response. This takes longer, and feelings of anger, sadness, rage, and even hate stick around awhile until the brain chemistry resets itself.

When small children are heard to say "I'm better than you are" we are looking at pure animal instinct using the hierarchy mechanism to better their position in the environment. One would think this is a part of growing up, and it is. It's harmless on the surface, but over an extended period of time, if the child is not taught to temper that behavior with intellect, the chances of that behavior becoming abnormal as an adult are high. Learning morals and ethics and how to treat our fellow man with respect is a difficult intellectual exercise, and requires many years of practice. Remember it is not about 'intelligence'. It is about 'intellect'. That is to say: that part of our conscious neocortex that recognizes the difference between right and wrong. (Adolph Hitler was intelligent, but had "no" intellect.) Hierarchical behavior is very evident in everyday society. Case in point: young college and NFL football players. Time and time again, the news is full of examples of players involved in bar fights, battering, sexual assault, armed robbery, and a host of other bad behavior. When confronted, the usual response is "I'm sorry, I didn't mean for it to happen, I just can't control my anger," followed by so-called anger management classes and so called therapy. This should be a red flag to any anthropologist that animal instincts are at work here and standard counseling is not going to alleviate the situation. Traditional therapy doesn't work; the same behavior repeats again. The emotions become the issue, but the core instinct that precipitated the behavior is never dealt with. It is clear that 'instinct counseling' is necessary. By simply adding 'primal awareness' to standard therapy can go a long way in changing behavior. It is imperative that the individual be made aware of the complex brain chemistry at work here. If that sounds over-simplified, it isn't. No one can change unless change is accompanied by the fullest understanding of why this is happening is explained. If one knows that one has cancer, the disease cannot be effectively treated until one knows how it is progressing. The same holds true for abnormal behavior. If one knows why one behaves that way, there is at least a sporting chance of changing it. Psychobabble and 'how are we feeling today?' does not address the problem. We all have the capacity to learn, and that must be incorporated into standard counseling. One can easily see that 130 years of standard psychology has not worked well and a newer approach through forensic behavioral anthropology is needed. While hierarchy is the most prevalent instinct, others play equally important roles in our behavior. Remember that no one instinct is exclusive in determining an individual's actions. We are, all of us, animals first, and apparently, foremost. Let us take a look at the instinct of territorialism, and how that affects our behavior.

The instinct of territorialism is, by definition, a very real and driving force in a living organism's control of the environment. Naturally, if one has more room, then it follows that one has more access to the resources available. This instinct has evolved through natural selection to allow organisms to survive over less adapted organisms, giving them the greater share of the riches. Nature seems to be very "imperialistic". In short, them thats got…gets more. The economic structures of humanity seem to be patterned after this behavior, and our societies have practiced this behavior throughout recorded history. It is fair to assume that even prehistory was filled with this patterned "capitalism". On an individual level, the chemistry is quite elegant. The amount of information needed to drive this type of behavior cannot be stored adequately by DNA, therefore, the repository of the brain is necessary. Earthworms and snails do not have brains beyond simple autonomic functions, and, not coincidentally, do not exhibit any instincts more than reproductive and self-preservation. This fact suggests that territorialism, as well as hierarchy and ritualism, are functions of the brain. All three of these abstract instincts produce behaviors only in higher evolved organisms. When we look at the brain structure, and MacLean's triune description, i.e. R-complex, limbic system, and neocortex, it becomes apparent that this very old and highly evolved behavior originates in the lower levels of the R-complex. Since this ancient gray matter evolved around the Cambrian period, most organisms were able to proliferate quickly. The often described Cambrian Explosion accounts for the great diversity of life that led, eventually, to *Homo Sapiens*. New approaches to domination of the environment were a necessity due to the ever expanding development of new species. Since the planet was wide open to new life forms, enormous competition must have necessitated the growth of survival techniques beyond simple 'eat and reproduce' behavior. The brain is composed of neuropathways inundating all levels. This electro-chemical structure allows for ample information storage and seems to operate below the conscious level. That follows that these pathways are deep in the R-complex and the limbic system, and since that is at a level below consciousness, the perceived effect is automatic and, therefore, a pure instinct. In higher life forms, territorial instincts manifest themselves in a behavior pattern that compels the organisms to acquire territory, any way that they can. Let us take a look at how this powerful instinct affects *Homo Sapiens*.

Acquisition of territory is not a bad thing. As stated, it is a natural and primal instinct. The purpose of this discussion is to look at abnormal behavior, and how this instinct motivates humans to irrational and dangerous practices. Anywhere you look in nature, living organisms are engaged in the process of acquisition. That may include many items other than just living space. Birds acquire building material for nests, insects collect sap for living quarters, and humans build homes and place address numbers on them. All of these examples equate to the instinct of territorialism. Naturally, these are normal expressions of the instinct and do not require discussion. What, then, does abnormal behavior look like in nature. A pride of lions in the wild experiences the inclusion of a new member; a male lion from outside the territory. His primal instincts initiate a series of behaviors that define his acquisition of new territory. He will immediately kill some of the newborn cubs of the females in the pride. This establishes his hierarchical position and brings the females into heat more quickly in order for their reproductive instincts to include his genetic material in the coming generation. The male will then mark the boundaries of the new territory with spraying to signal to other males his new acquisition. This behavior includes many of the primal instincts, such as hierarchy and reproductive, but it is important to note that the primary motivation here was territorialism. In nature there are no laws or written policy to prevent this behavior. If there were, that would be a product of the intellect, and lions, as well as most of nature, do not have sufficient neocortex material to develop such intricate social controls. Only *Homo Sapiens* practices sociological control mechanisms due to the size and complexity of human neocortex brain tissue. In other words: we enact laws to prevent members of our species from taking what doesn't belong to them. This is a purely intellectual exercise and we define this as civilized behavior. What happens when territorial instincts overrule human intellect? It is no different than other organisms. We just take what we want and ignore the intellectual conscious levels of the brain. It is called stealing. It takes many forms in our society. Armed robbery, burglary, and even simple uses of another's property without permission. What is occurring at the level of brain chemistry? A.W. Deckel, in his paper *Hemispheric Control of Territorial Aggression*, talks about the effects of mild stress as a mechanism. To an extent, that is true. Is stress not indicative of challenge? Remember the cycle of challenge and satisfaction that alternately controls the emotions associated with our lower brain primal functions. Challenge to our instincts, any one of them, at any time, can cause stress. The challenge to an instinct requires satisfaction. That leads to a behavior of some type that will cycle the brain chemistry back to a level playing field. The example of the lion includes no intellectual intervention mechanism, and, therefore, he satisfies the challenge in a way that humans find shocking and repugnant. But, yet, some humans do behave this way with great regularity. Is brain chemistry involved? And what mechanism occurs that allows for abnormal behavior?

For the vast majority of humanity, the intellect intervenes when challenges to primal instincts occur. We are taught the rules by society, and we know the difference between normal expression of territorial gain and abnormal behavior. Remember that this is intellect at work and not primal instinct. It is acceptable to place our names and other identification on items that we own. It is not acceptable to take an item that is clearly marked by others. Why are the defining lines between those two types of behavior so routinely violated by our species? The answer partly appears to be in the neocortex. Since the neocortex is the most recent level of the brain to evolve, it is still young by comparison to the limbic system and the R-complex. Therefore, the neurosynaptic pathways of the cortex are still in their infancy, and periodic lapses may occur in transmission. Gregory Fischer has coined a term called *synaptic impasse*. This may be defined as a neocortex transmission that fails to reach full depolarization of the complete neuropathway. In other words, an incomplete thought in a state of consciousness. It can be interpreted as not knowing the difference between right and wrong, or knowing the difference and ignoring the attempt by the intellect to suppress the challenge. If either of these two possibilities is in play, primal behavior is the result and the individual will proceed to satisfy the primal instinct. Society will define this as abnormal and take action accordingly. Synaptic impasses may occur with great regularity in some and the psychology community often refers to this as a type of insanity. The legal community refers to the criminal mind quite often also. The above explanation is a hypothesis of possible mechanisms. This is supported by the fact that medically treated individuals seem to have this behavior under more control, but the challenge to satisfy primal instincts remains. That is why repeating abnormal behavior is common in spite of treatment. No one has figured out a way to alter the pathways of the neocortex, or, for that matter, the pathways of the primal brain levels. Medication and therapy can help, but it appears that instinct therapy with its 'why this happens' approach is also necessary. 'Training' is a function of a conscious neocortex and must be included in any attempt to alter abnormal behavior. As previously mentioned, if one knows why one behaves that way, there is a sporting chance of correcting this behavior. Even a lion can be trained not to kill newborn cubs and spray. Working with a human should be easier. How do we deal with territorial challenges in everyday life? The following is a list of behaviors that exemplify challenges to the territorial instinct. Some are simple and others are extreme. It will be clear to the reader that this is a powerful primal instinct.

Each of the following examples displays a situation where the territorial instinct is in play following a challenge. As you read each one, remember that the focus is on abnormal behavior and there is no pre-emption by the intellect. You may use your intellect to find a more civilized solution.

A car cuts in front of you while you are driving and road rage sets in. You can't stand the thought of losing your place. Anger and rage makes you drive faster and you cut someone else off finally causing an accident.

You get your paycheck and go cash it immediately. Even though you have bills to pay, you rush off to the mall and 'shop till you drop'.

You are talking on a public phone and a person comes up behind you. After a few minutes, the person begins looking at his/her watch, indicating the need to use the phone. You look away and continue talking, knowing full well your conversation is actually over.

Your spouse tells you about plans to meet with friends. You argue that you are suspicious that something is going on and you end up screaming that 'you belong to me'. The argument escalates until violence ensues.

You and co-workers share equipment and facilities at your job. You systematically tell others not to 'use' your stuff until relationships are damaged to the point where you are ready to quit.

Your hometown team has just won a championship. You drink a few beers and climb up a water tower, spray painting victory slogans on public property.

Your neighbors are having a garage sale, so you back your car out of the driveway and park on the public street in front of your house so no one else can park there.

You are having trouble paying your debts. You discover that someone at work has left open the safe and it is full of cash. You grab a handful of bills when no one is around.

Your ex girlfriend (boyfriend) has become engaged to someone you don't know. When you discover this, you go to her (his) house and assault her (him), saying that 'if I can't have you, no one else will either'.

A popular doll has gone on sale opening the Christmas season at a local store. You push your way through people, trampling on some who have fallen, to get the last few available.

In all of the above examples, it is important to note that abnormal territorial behavior does not limit itself to acquisition of just space or objects. As one can see, this unfortunate behavior also includes the perceived acquisition of people. The psychology community refers to this as possessiveness; however, it is still motivated by poorly wired neuropathways that make up the territorial instinct, and, perhaps, synaptic impasses in the conscious neocortex. It is apparent in cases of possessive behavior, particularly where violence occurs, that very little intellect is being used. Territorialism is not just an individual action. Collective territorialism applies its destructive behavior to entire populations as well. That is the primary motivation behind the act of war, aggression, and invasion of countries by other groups or countries. The failure to find intellectual resolutions to global conflicts is due to the territorial instinct of our species, an instinct that predate us by hundreds of millions of years, hence the enormous difficulty of negotiating. The weight of evolution on an "immature" species is, indeed, frustrating for those with the desire to use intellect to find peace. Normal expression of territorial instincts are healthy and beneficial for each of us, as they give us curiosity, inquisitiveness, and inventive spirit. Primed, then, by good intellect, we can make intelligent choices about what we acquire to better our lives in a complex environment. It is lack of application of the intellect and overly developed primal instincts that creates abnormal behavior. How does one come to terms with a complex environment? That is the subject of my next discussion: The instinct of ritualism.

It has been said "we are creatures of habit". When that phrase was coined, no one can say for sure, but one thing is clear. The author must have had some insight into behaviors that we all share. Indeed, the repetitive action living organisms practice seems to serve no other purpose than to help adjust to a new or challenging environment. By definition, ritual behavior is exemplified by repetitive motion; a constant recycling of the same action, over and over again. The following discussions will move from simple to ever more complex behaviors. There are many examples of harmless ritualism in nature. Birds move side to side while perching as they rest or contemplate their next flight. Insects move their anterior appendages back and forth as if washing their faces when they rest. Mammals are certainly more striking in their motion, sometimes making it easier to associate with some form of identifiable activity. Is this repetition of design? Or is it coming from deep within the lower brain centers of the R-complex and limbic system? Since this behavior is so common throughout the animal kingdom, including *Homo Sapiens*, it is easy to study and observe. By looking at ritual behavior in man, conclusions may be drawn that help explain animal behavior in general. Humans have a propensity for exposure to new experience. Higher mammals are curious due to the influence of territorial and hierarchical instincts. Self-preservation and reproductive instincts play a significant role as well. With all this adventurous activity going on, the environment continuing to offer great challenges, and brain chemistry changing by the microsecond, some mechanism must have evolved to deal with all the changes. It appears that a potent subconscious instinct evolved to help living organisms adapt to spontaneous challenge from environmental sources. What mechanism is it that helps to align the intellect when faced with a new or unfriendly environment? It would have to be something that allows the brain's conscious intellect time to adjust, but in friendly, recognizable circumstances. That mechanism may be repetition, a process involved in learning and mimicry itself. That mechanism is ritual. The biological basis for this instinct is fairly simple. Personality traits dictated by genetic sequencing already are known to influence hierarchical and territorial behaviors. Studies by Dr. A. Benis, et al., involving narcissism, perfectionism, and aggression prove conclusively that behavior is a complex response to the environment, but genetically coded from conception. Ritualism is most certainly a complex and abstract behavior, in that it shows up very early on, even in the youngest of a species. Without this important brain function, a living organism can be observed to be disoriented, detached, and even totally separated from the outside world. Poorly developed pathways may even produce a high dependence on this instinct to help the organism cope, even to the point of complete detachment.

Remember that the definition of ritualism is repeating the same motion, over and over again. Let's take a look at human ritual, keeping in mind that this instinct is common throughout most higher life forms. It is important to note that powerful emotions are present in ritual, as well as all primal instincts, and that it is a lower brain function that operates in tandem with these emotions. The most fundamental and simple form of human ritual is 'twiddling your thumbs' or variations of that motion. It is most certainly subconscious, and, therefore, a pure instinct. Why do so many people do it so often? It is usually found in situations when a person is ill at ease or nervous in a new situation. Look around a meeting room or a public event of some type and try to observe the number of people wringing their hands, twiddling their thumbs, or motioning some form of repetitive movement. A sporting event is a great place to observe. If the game is tight, this activity increases among the fans. If the game is easy, there is noticeably less activity. If this is an instinct, it must follow the challenge and satisfaction cycle. As fans get nervous about the score, it is a challenge, and the ritual behavior initiates. This helps the individual cope with nervous "energy" in a temporarily challenging environment. As the score eases up, satisfaction initiates a more comfortable environment, and the ritualistic activity subsides. Certainly, a very simplistic example, but adequate to describe a fundamental behavior. Looking at something a bit more complex, the so-called daily routine we all take for granted, is a good example of satisfaction and challenge. Each thing that we do on a regular basis, from getting up in the morning till we retire at night, or vice versa for some, is partly controlled by the ritual instinct. We are, all of us, creatures of habit, and with good reason. Imagine how strange and frightening the day would be without our ability to perform simple tasks, over and over again, day in, day out. For many, this is diagnosed as a mental disability. More will be discussed about this when we look at abnormal behavior. But this is a graphic example of how important ritual is when we face an environment in flux and change. We put our shoes on the same way and follow the same routine without thinking about it. This activity is not intellect. It is primal instinct. It follows that if you don't think about it, and it's automatic, then it is driven by neuropathways deep in the R-complex and limbic system of the brain. Is ritual behavior common in other species? Most certainly. Observe caged mammals at your next trip to the zoo. If they're in open areas, there is little challenge and, therefore, little ritual. When caged animals are present, they pace. Back and forth. Sad to say, this is still the case in most zoos, and, as humane as this may seem, it is enormously challenging to the animal. They are most certainly unhappy, trying to cope with a stressful environment. This example is not meant to raise an issue of animal rights or controversy, it is meant to point out the biological activity of ritual and how it applies.

Humans appear to have the same behavior patterns when confronted by challenging atmospheres. Pacing is not uncommon in even the least stressful situations, as many people practice this ritual as a way of relieving an uncomfortable exposure. Our species is very aware of time frames, and any challenge to our impatience may lead to pacing, hand wringing, or other repetitive motion, exhibiting our frustration. Indeed, a challenge is present, and the lower brain centers initiate the instinct best able to deal with finding satisfaction. That appears to be ritual. Believe it or not, primal ritualism surfaces in even pleasant circumstances. Our species, as well as other higher mammals, seem to be drawn to activities that soothe and excite our senses. Music and dance are prime examples. These activities are, in themselves, perfect examples of repetitive action, designed to satisfy some perceived challenge. They delight and entertain. They are expressive and rich. As rituals, they seldom produce unwanted emotions. In fact, they are instrumental in converting negative or destructive emotions to desirable ones. As Shakespeare said, 'music to soothe the savage breast' (often corrupted to say 'beast'). The meaning, though, is clear. Music and dance, both, are repetition by nature, and, therefore, are ritualism by definition. Do these rituals originate in primal instinctive pathways in the brain? To answer this, consider the opposite. Many people report annoying music 'in their head' that they cannot eliminate. A song or melody fragment can find its way into everyone from time to time. One that 'won't go away'. Statements such as "I hate that song, and I've been hearing it all day in my head" are common complaints from many. Dangerous, no. Annoying, yes. There are examples of dangerous 'head' noise in schizophrenic patients, but more on that later when we look at abnormal behavior. The point here is that if repetitive sound is present in a person's memory, then it is controlled by a neuropathway deep in the lower brain centers, and surfaces in the neocortex as conscious music awareness. Very often, and this can be tested adequately, the music heard is in the actual musical key the song was written in originally, even in tone-deaf individuals. Proof, once more, that ritualistic neuropathways are at work here.

What about tone deafness versus musical genius? The vast majority of human kind is pleasantly somewhere in the middle. Listen closely to a chorus of 'happy birthday' by a group of people and you will hear several different keys being sung. This is the norm, as each individual has a different diversified ritual pathway, and each 'hears' it in a different key. A small percentage of the population have poorly developed ritual instinct, and cannot carry a tune, so to speak. An even smaller percent are the opposite. They are described as having perfect pitch. Properly trained or encouraged, they become our greatest creative individuals, and go on to add significant contributions to our culture. The same can be said for dancing, and other forms of repetitive expression.

Moving up the scale in complexity is another level of ritualism. This is the area of primal instinct and intellect together creating a product that seems greater than the sum of its parts. It is called religion. Since the advent of our earliest forms of civilization, various cultures have devised ways of dealing with the concept of a universal creator. A discussion of theology would be inappropriate here. The purpose here is to define the mechanisms by which our species practices its various belief systems, and proceed from a cultural standpoint through neurophysiological anthropology. There is no doubt that religion is endowed with great cultural richness, regardless of the belief system involved. Each part of our diversified civilization practices a system that encompasses individuals as well as the masses, and contributes greatly to man's ever changing spectrum. Though hierarchical instincts play an enormous role in the development of religious structure, such as how an individual or group fits into the so-called scheme of things, the primary component in religious practice is ritual. Every culture and faith adorns their participants with symbols, clothing, and ornaments that express meaning and identification. The common denominator, though, is repetitive motion, song, dance and verbiage. There can be no doubt that the ritual instinct is being satisfied. People engaged in prayer or serious worship may be transfixed, almost hypnotically, indicating activity deep within the limbic system of the brain, and even the R-complex itself. The behavior involved in seeing visions, wailing, singing, and crying, indicates a high emotional level, which only lends credibility to the idea of control by neuropathways. Since the resulting behaviors are repetition and more repetition, primal ritualism seems to be the best mechanism to describe this. In short, ritual instinct demands satisfaction, and the practice of religion seems to admirably accommodate.

When environmental influences fuel these practices, individuals tend to melt into the group dynamics. This is where we enter the realm of abnormal behavior. Most mainstream religions are designed to be peaceful expressions of relationships with our creator, but often, political agendas driven by hierarchy and territorial instincts elevate this ritual to dangerous proportions. Most of the planet's conflicts are fueled by the group dynamics of religious extremism. Fundamentalists of all faiths tend to justify their hate and violence through a complex mixture of religious ritual, hierarchical, territorial, and self-preservationist behaviors. The justification for abnormal responses is ignored by the intellect, and, primal behavior tends to be encouraged. Human conflict is usually the result. It must be remembered that this behavior is very ancient. The intellect is young by comparison. Very often, primal behavior is given validity by political expedience, moral righteousness, and generalizations of group dynamics.

The spectrum of group dynamic instincts is a wide one. Blowing up abortion clinics, violence in Ireland and the Middle East, revolution in the Far East, attempts to infuse religious belief systems into American public institutions, and encroachments on the territories of others, are all extreme examples of primal behavior without the discipline of intellect. The high degree of emotional content is prime evidence that this type of behavior is controlled by primal instincts. This discussion is not an attempt to find solutions to the world's problems, but it is clear that the neocortex and its capacity for intellect is the place to start. Moving up again on the ladder of complexity is another form of ritual behavior; the abnormal response of ritual out of control, beyond the ability of the intellect to perceive: obsessive compulsive disorders. By their very nature, they are identified by a wide variety of behaviors. There is, as we will see, a common thread that binds these disorders together. Looking at some examples we can see that ritualism plays an enormous role in the behavior. A man collects baseball cards. This is a normal expression of ritual satisfaction. A man collects spiral notebooks, never making a single entry in them, letting them pile up around the house. This is abnormal behavior. Psychologists may refer to this as obsessive compulsive behavior. Looking at this through the perspective of primal instincts, this is poorly developed neuropathways that control the instinct of ritual, leading to outwardly abnormal behavior. The idea of collecting something that has no apparent use is most definitely abnormal. People who wash their hands 100 times a day, or people who can't bear to throw anything away are also in this group. It is clear that their suffering is deep within the lower brain centers and intellect seems powerless to help. Therapy should also include 'instinct awareness' that may help the individual understand the mechanism involved. If the intellect can be 'trained' it cannot do so without a fundamental knowledge of the behavior. What motivates a serial killer to destroy life in the manner he/she does? Is ritual involved? Most certainly. A serial killer collects, and seems to fit that reasoning. There are, of course, other instincts in play here in this complex behavior. Hierarchy and territorial instincts are also poorly developed, and self-preservation adds to the perception of paranoia the killer must feel. It is doubtful that intellect 'training' alone or standard therapy will alter this behavior. The neuropathways are far too complex and require medication, incarceration, and intense work medically. All of this behavior, as bizarre as it is, is still within the diversified spectrum of the human species. Our society labels this as abnormal because it is behavior without discipline, in other words, contrary to the right vs wrong understanding of the neocortex.

Autism is, or rather was, defined as 'absorption in self centered mental activity, withdrawal from reality'. However, autistic children (and autistic adults) are *mind-blind: their specific instinct for attributing minds to others is damaged*. But observing an autistic individual, one sees rocking motion to and fro, repetitive sounds, and a complete or partial detachment from the world around. There needs to be little discussion about the involvement of the ritual instinct here. The point about autism that makes it such a dynamic example of ritualism is the success stories in treatment. A special type of success story is the ability of autistic individuals to respond to music. Instructions on tying your shoes can be sung, and the response is phenomenal. They can be taught many normal functions in life if they are sung to. Why does this work so well? Music is ritual, as stated earlier. This is satisfaction of the instinct just as they do in their dysfunctional state. They respond because it is the same thing, easy to communicate in the language of ritualism. Therapists know how to do this but they don't know why. Paralleling instinct is why. Transferring activity from abnormal behavior to the real world via the same instinct. Is this instinct therapy? Of course. It is interesting to note that many elderly people behave in ways that exemplify pure instinctive behavior. As a person gets older, a sort of reverse evolution occurs. Since the intellect is the latest part of the brain to evolve it is "obvious" that this is the first functional level to deteriorate. Dementia, forgetfulness, and even Altzheimer's disease display the same end product. The intellect degrades and the instincts blossom into full view. Many elderly cannot function well when intellectual pursuits are involved, but childlike behavior is predominant and extremely consistent. They do the same thing every day. Can't bare to throw anything out. Talk about the same subjects over and over. They display growing needs to be recognized and acknowledged. They hold on to personal belongings no longer needed. They increase their relative control over family. They become easily frightened and sometimes paranoid. Do any of these behaviors sound familiar? Naturally, they are all primal instincts surfacing, and controlling their thoughts and actions. Newborn children behave the same way until their little intellects begin to grow through maturation, training and knowledge. The reverse happens to the elderly as the neuropathways of the intellect fall away and well rooted primal instinct pathways surface. Primal instincts are millions of years old. High intellect is roughly 850,000 years. Not much of a contest by comparison. All the above examples reflect the predominant instinct of ritual, but other primal instincts play a great role in all these behaviors. Combinations of primal behavior inundate all of us to some degree. Many of us are creatures of habit. When any primal instinct is powerful enough, it is possible to cross that line to abnormal behavior. Territorialism plays a role, and the powerful influence of hierarchy dominates our relations with others. Our personalities are complex mechanisms, created by genes and driven by neuropathways in the brain. Our intellect is that saving grace, the diffuse border between the mind of the animal and the "logic" of human expression. All of the abstract instincts, hierarchy, territorialism, and ritual, play roles in normal as well as abnormal behavior. Two instincts have been with us far longer than these. They predate man and other mammals by 750 million years. These are the primal instincts of self-preservation and reproduction. We shall discuss those next.

Chapter 6 The primal instincts of self-preservation and reproduction

by
Mitch C. Bronston

"Real life consists of bluffing, of little tactics of deception, of asking yourself what is the other man going to think I mean to do."

John Von Neumann

"All instincts are survival instincts."

N.K.O.

Much has been discussed already as to how the abstract primal instincts of hierarchy, territorialism, and ritualism affect human behavior. These instincts, and the neural pathways that control them, play important roles in survival, and they add their complex resultant behaviors to the overall personality of the individual. It has also been discussed that these influences are not specific to just *Homo Sapiens*, but inundate most of the wide spectrum of life, to one degree or another. It must be remembered that a combination of several instincts may play a role in the outward observed response an organism will display when confronted by environmental challenges. Two other instincts lend their influence to the mix and add extremely complex variations in behavior. Those the basic primal instincts of self-preservation and reproduction. Both self-preservation and reproduction are as old as life itself. They are, both, most certainly primordial, and development of brain pathways that enhance outward behavior appear early in the life cycle. That fact alone can be demonstrated in even the simplest life forms, i.e. organisms without highly developed brains still display protective behaviors when threatened, and know when and how to reproduce without instruction. For the purposes of this discussion, we will concentrate on the behavior associated with *Homo Sapiens* with only passing references to other organisms when appropriate. First, taking a look at self-preservation, we find a behavior that defines life in its most fundamental description. There is no question that for someone to stay alive, and negotiate the perils of the environment, one must somehow know how to survive. Is this taught to the individual from birth? If so, that would indicate instruction from someone else, and that would imply outside environmental influence Newborn humans instantly display suckling behavior and feed without organized instruction. Consequently, the first hint of self-preservation, the need to take nourishment, surfaces immediately. This is information supplied by a well developed neural pathway in the primitive brain-levels. These levels developed their pathways during gestation and originated in genes encoded in DNA. The rapid display of this behavior indicates pure instinct and only the type of refinements added later are environmental influence. A two year old toddler can eat with a fork, indicating a learned behavior; however, it is still taking nourishment and the overall behavior is based on a learning instinct. Learned behavior is situational and may be a result of learning intellect and/or learning basic instinct (all instincts are learning instincts (= instincts can learn)). That involves the neocortex and its associated training. As we can see here, it is only the method of indulgence that defines intellectual training; the self-preservation behavior itself is still primal instinct behavior. Instincts can learn, as the heritablitiy coefficient demonstrates, and this becomes part of the overall behavior and action.

The need to eat to survive is clearly a challenge, and the act of eating is the behavior associated with satisfaction of the instinct. This mechanism applies to all instincts, but here it refers to basic survival, and, therefore, helps define self-preservation as one of the primal instincts. This differs from abstract instincts in that the neural pathways are already mature even from birth. To see how this applies, consider the reverse. Many elderly people and those with anorexia exhibit the "exact same" behavior when faced with the challenge of hunger. They both exhibit avoidance of food. This could indicate poorly developed self-preservation pathways, i.e. the challenge to this instinct is ignored as unimportant, leaving the individual without a priority to satisfy. This is a very complex situation involving other instincts and perhaps a poorly trained intellect needed to intervene, but the primary behavior is identical in both cases. Both cases show different perception of the environment, but it is clear that the self-preservation instinct itself is damaged or undeveloped, and this is physiological, part of the brain structure, in other words. Treatment is often approached through intellectual channels and is not too effective. This behavior will repeat when subjects are left to their own devise. Perhaps the challenge to another instinct, that of, say, ritualism, might help in channeling challenge and satisfaction cycles in parallel fashion. Taking food on their own accord by habit alone, through repetitive behavior, might offer a solution. The behaviors here are abnormal and need to be approached through primal instinct, not intellect alone. What about other challenges to self-preservation? We all run from fire instinctively. We all dodge flying objects and retreat from danger instinctively. This is self-preservation. Remember that there are a host of emotions that accompany any instinct, but emotions are particularly graphic in self-preservation. Not surprisingly, they are involved with life threatening challenges. Some anthropologists see fear as the most glaring emotion, a barometer indicative of severe challenges to self-preservation. It may be real or perceived, but very active brain chemistry is occurring during the initial challenge. Fear reactions, according to forensic anthropology, fall into three distinct types. Fear of falling, fear of predators, and fear of closed spaces. Falling is as old as primate evolution. To understand this, picture the world nearly 20 million years ago in the Pleistocene epoch. Primates were beginning to evolve and diversify into many species. Those that could move freely in the treetops did so with many accidents, leading to evolutionary pressure that changed brain chemistry to a less risky amount of activity. Natural selection weeded out the risk takers, leaving a variety of species that developed a hesitation neuropathway. These species went on to develop into ground dwellers, leading to *Homo Sapiens.* Other factors, such as the conversion of jungle into savannah also contributed greatly, but it is easy to see how many events gave us this natural fear mechanism that saved many a life. Fear of falling is a common self-preservation emotion that we all experience when we look down from a height. It is more intense in some than others, while some have little fear at all. Our instinct tells us to get down as soon as possible. The chemistry is so powerful that we even dream about it. No wonder, these neuropathways have been with us for millions of years. Fear of predators is the easiest to understand. Natural selection gave us this part of the self-preservation instinct long before primate evolution. It is interesting to see how many people are afraid of snakes and other reptiles. Carl Sagan speculated in *Dragons of Eden* that because reptiles are the primary survivors from post Cambrian periods, that they represent the quickest neural images of a predator. If you are a mammal, and we are, of course, then you carry genetic memory of being hunted by their ancestors. The reaction to a snake is a swift one, and humans recoil instinctively. Our literature, including the Bible, is awash in stories of dragons, snakes, and other mythical tales of these beautiful creatures unfortunately representing all that is evil. Our dreams, again, are full of images of being hunted by monsters, and small children vividly describe these events consistently, without being taught by any adult. How can this behavior be so wide spread in our species? Genetic memory and self-preservation instinct, no doubt. Fear of predators, expressing challenge to self-preservation instinct, may be intensified greatly in some, leading to what is referred to as paranoia. Mixed in with hierarchical instincts that may be damaged, a situation develops that leaves an individual afraid of almost anything and everything. This behavior is multiplied again when certain neuro-active drugs are used. Cocaine and methamphetamine are such examples. Hallucinogens also contribute to this behavior. The common pharmacology here is changes in neurotransmitter brain activity. Depleted norepinephrine and dopamine levels from consistent use of the drugs will easily alter even normal intellects and allow primal pathways to predominate. Self-preservation and hierarchical instincts alter perceptions of the world and emotions such as fear and anger result in bizarre activity. The subjects actually feel threatened and behave accordingly. Fear of closed spaces makes no sense initially. Most organisms feel safety in closed areas and it seems contradictory to self-preservation to have a fear of such a safe place. But this is a very common behavior by many humans. Claustrophobia seems to defy logic when we define primal self-preservation, but looking a little closer, we can see the chemistry of this strange activity. The key word in closed spaces is 'space'. That would lead us to think that territorial instincts are involved here. If you agreed with that, you would be right. Territorialism is indeed part of the equation. A very real and fearful loss of territorial integrity on a primal instinctive level, combined with self-preservation challenge, and the perception by the intellect is one of extreme danger. There is no magic to this diagnosis. Simple understanding of primal instincts and their resultant behaviors can adequately describe the causes of such anomalies. It is interesting to note that highly territorial people in everyday life tend to be the best candidates for claustrophobia. In other words, if an individual behaves possessively toward objects or people, he/she will have problems having a CT or MRI scan, and may panic inside the device's enclosure. Self-preservation instincts are part of the behavior as well, and it must be one of the components. Simple 'shop till you drop' people are not this reactive, but combined instincts of territorialism and self-preservation may produce unrealistic fears and behaviors.

There are many other aspects of self-preservation, and it would take volumes to describe it all. This discussion was intended to enlighten the reader about a powerful and ancient drive deep in the primitive centers of the brain. We now turn to the primal instinct of reproduction. It is important to point out that reproduction does not only refer to sex. If it were that simple, there would be a glaringly obvious lack of emotion involved with this instinct. On the contrary, reproduction is highly emotional and produces in humans, as well as many other organisms, observable and animated emotional activity. A great deal of chemistry is necessary for this instinct to initiate mating, and that can be documented right down to the DNA level. Even a virus has that capability. But emotion is involved in organisms with brains and complex neurotransmitter and hormonal capabilities. Here, challenge and satisfaction cycles are evident, and easily understood. Anyone who ever became attracted to another knows what challenge is, and, certainly, also knows what satisfaction is. Stepping aside of emotion for the moment, let's just look at the basic process first. Mating, naturally, is the goal. The agenda is to pass one's genetic material to the next generation. Without that simple fact, life would never have evolved beyond one-celled organisms. Evolution by random mutation and natural selection takes a long time to occur successfully. The trial and error method is even displayed in our behavior. Advanced life forms have elevated this instinct to a fine art, but many other instincts play a role in the mating process. This is where emotion comes in, and the chemistry of selection. Mating does not occur spontaneously in higher species. It is not just a simple exchange of genetic material. That simple exchange was invented more than 800 million years ago when simple cell division was not adequate in multicellular organisms. Exchange of DNA became very efficient: sex was invented. It is interesting to observe that the more complex the organism, the more complex the mating behavior. In the case of higher mammals, and especially humans, many abstract instincts are also involved. When two people meet, the reproductive instinct usually sets off a chain reaction of behaviors. This is normal, but, as we will see, abnormal behavior may result in some. The basic urge to mate is the first obvious development. This may be underscored by some territorial behavior in the urge to acquire that person. Hierarchy rears its influence in the subsequent moments as both individuals begin to display how dominant they are by comparison to others. This is a powerful instinct and many variations in behavior are displayed. The primitive idea here is that my DNA is as good or better than anyone else. Then the ritualism develops, and the two individuals maneuver into the games that precede mating.

So far, we have been talking about people, but these steps are followed by a surprising number of other species throughout the spectrum of life. Many emotions surface during this process, and, with that many instincts involved, they cover a wide area. Not all are pleasant. This is where abnormal behavior can influence the process. Challenges occur to many of the basic instincts when the process fails. Rejection by one party or the other challenges not just reproductive instincts but territorial and ritual as well. The most dangerous instinct, if challenged sufficiently, is hierarchy. Rejection is a challenge that reduces one of the parties to a level below the perceived hierarchical structure, and emotions of anger, jealousy, and even rage, are common. Well adjusted people, that is, those with sufficient intellect, can recover quickly, and go about their lives normally. Those with immature intellect, such as young people, and those with consistently miswired instincts, react with outward anger, destructive rage, and even violence. This may seem overly simplistic and does not have the literary draw of *Men Are From Mars, Women Are From Venus*, but it is plain that many fascinating things are happening when reproductive instincts are challenged. Abnormal behavior may be even more diverse than the above example. Rape, serial sex offences, age inappropriate attractions, and perhaps even infidelity, are all situations that reveal miswiring of the reproductive instinct. The abstract instincts may also be miswired because these behaviors have hierarchical, territorial, and ritualistic components as well. Intellect seems to be a missing ingredient in the above cases; there simply isn't much intellect there. Individuals that behave in this manner cannot effectively interpret the basic instinctive drives involved, and social boundaries placed on them in the real world are often ineffective. Repeat behavior is almost certain. Remember that intelligence is not the same as intellect. Even a rapist or child molester can be intelligent. These unfortunate humans have no real way to suppress the primal instincts. They simply behave in the only manner that is normal for them. As stated earlier, reproductive instinct is not just about mating and sex. This well seated and powerful mechanism has a broad construct. It is also responsible for our behavior associated with parents, siblings, and offspring. Caring for members of our family, and the tightly knit loyalties we display, are no accident. The emotions we experience with this component help to define behaviors such as love and affection. Note that these are behaviors and not traditional feelings as we are led to believe. Poets, philosophers, and even scientists have tried for centuries to define the nature of love. Perhaps they were looking in the wrong place. Love is a behavior based on the emotions that accompany the reproductive instinct. If that were not the case, we would have one set of rules and definitions for humans and a different set for the rest of creation. Our society and our religions try to do just that. But the truth is, this is powerful chemistry in the brain: neuropathways that drive primal instinctive behavior, and the equally powerful neuropathways of emotion that accompany it.

The complex behaviors associated with what we define as 'the relationship', are most certainly a combination of many instincts. Traditional psychology tries to salvage the broken and troubled pairings, usually without much success. The air waves are inundated with 'therapists' and 'counselors' of all types, trying to bring two individuals together. Never, though, do you see anthropologists in this equation. Perhaps there should be. The problems that occur in 'relationships' are, more often than not, the result of poor primal instinct wiring, and poor interpretation by immature intellect. Instinct therapy, as mentioned many times throughout these chapters, can add important knowledge to the efforts to repair these volatile and explosive situations. The overall nature of a 'relationship' is usually twofold. First and foremost is the reproductive instinct, and the associated behaviors of love and affection. Second, a powerful instinctive component that manages the day to day interaction, but has nothing to do with love or affection: hierarchy and its overwhelming drive for satisfaction. Most relationship problems occur when one individual, or both, become overwhelmed by hierarchical challenges. The need to be 'equal to or better' often leads to the so-called 'power game' and 'control issues'. The poor intellectual management of hierarchical challenge and satisfaction cycles ruins more 'relationships' than anything else. Remember that hierarchy is an abstract instinct and, because of its dominance in our overall behavior, it can easily overwhelm and diminish reproductive instincts, negating emotions of love and affection. In their place comes the need to be accepted, the need to be liked, the need to be respected, and the need to be in charge of the situation. Normally these are good qualities, but often they overwhelm and dominate, moving normal behavior into the realm of abnormal. The lack of application of intellect to control these situations often is overlooked, and relationships are damaged beyond repair. Once again, traditional psychology overlooks the importance of primal instinctive behavior, treating this situation as a strictly human enterprise, forgetting the animal component. Maybe that is why this approach is so ineffective. As all instinctive behavior is a combination of many factors, so are self-preservation and reproduction. The control mechanism is intellect, and how it perceives the world, and how we learn to manage our animal passions. Control and suppression by the intellect is part of the mechanism of learning instincts, and how adaptation to situational forces amends behavior. Only when intellect is properly applied, and well trained, can maturity teach our primal instincts to re-route their pathways and graduate, so to speak, from the college of hard knocks.

Chapter 7 How the intellect can intervene and suppress primal abnormal behavior

by
Mitch C. Bronston

"If we are anything, we must be a democracy of the intellect. We must not perish by the distance between people and power."

Jacob Bronowski

"The voice of the intellect is a soft one, but it does not rest until it has gained a hearing. Ultimately, after endless rebuffs, it succeeds. This is one of the few points in which one may be optimistic about the future of mankind."

Sigmund Freud

Much has been discussed about the five primal instincts that contribute to our behavior, but the influence of our *intellect* has remained secondary in the discussion. An appropriate discussion about our intellect is necessary because the intellect plays an ever increasing role in our species. It must be remembered that the intellect is *function* per say, not a structure, of the neocortex, the most recent part of the brain to evolve. It is a *part* or *mechanism* of our overall intelligence. It has been defined previously as that part of the "conscious" intelligence that has the ability to determine the difference between primal and moral behavior. It is "separating us from the animals." It is the manager, the processing unit that balances choices in situational triggering. It moves along the learning process for all instincts, and, is, in itself, innate.

Can intellectual behavior be called *altruistic behavior?* Altruism is defined as unselfish interest in the welfare of others. Most certainly we seem to be "evolving" in this direction as we behave as a collective species through individual action for the betterment of the group. That helps to guarantee our survival as a species, as well as individuals. Often, what's good for all, is what's good for the person, and vice versa. The evolution of *cooperation* is not unique to *Homo Sapiens*, however. John Stewart's book *Evolution's Arrow,* argues that evolution seems to organize itself in ever increasing levels of cooperation and management. Chemicals organize themselves into living cells, cells into organisms, and organisms into societies. This helps to derive a mechanism that allows adaptations to progress to genetic and cultural levels that bypasses random changes that could lead to extinction. All successful species have some built-in cooperative behavior that affects the overall society. This is extremely beneficial for survival. Could this adaptation be altruism? This type of behavior would seem to be the antithesis of primal instinctive behavior, in that it is unselfish rather than selfish. Many species practice altruistic behavior, without motivation, and without much neocortex. If this is true, then we may be allowed to make two conclusions. First, intellect is *not* intelligence, just a function of it. And, second, intellect acts as a defensive line against the intrusion of primal instinctive behavior that may be damaging to the individual.

With all that has been discussed about primal instincts and abnormal behavior, we must be reminded that the perception of what is *abnormal* is dictated by the definitions we apply as a species, and how that behavior compares to society as a whole. Our civilization is, as stated above, a collective adaptation. A list, if you will, of rules, regulations, policies, laws, procedures, and *predefined* behaviors. How we are *expected* to behave for the good of all. Any behavioral deviation outside this narrow boundary is perceived as *abnormal.* It has been our contention throughout these discussions, that abnormal behavior is often motivated by primal instincts, rather than intellect. In other words, selfish design is the product of very primitive pathways in the limbic and R-complex levels of the animal brain. Altruistic behavior, on the other hand, is often the child of a well-developed intellect. (However, the human instincts are *not* more selfish than unselfish, and the human intellect is *not* more unselfish than selfish. Both 'pure' instincts and intellect are balanced. Empathy, sympathy, unselfishness, etc are ordinary discrete instincts.)

A well developed intellect does not happen overnight. This is where *training* becomes the paramount mechanism in the development of the individual and, ultimately, the entire species. If training is defined by repetitive tasks as part of the learning process, why is this necessary in the intellect and how is this different from ritual? It may be recalled that ritual is a prewired instinct that resides in the lower brain centers. It operates in challenge and satisfaction cycles as do the other instincts. Training has an environmental triggering and is imposed from the *outside*. In other words, we must to a certain extent be *taught* through repetition to learn and acquire a behavior that is acceptable to society and/or our peer group. The purpose of training is to develop a type of altruistic behavior that gains us social acceptance. Once this is accomplished, our *intellect* perceives the result as new information and proceeds to develop a new neuropathway, this time in the neocortex. We may now ask the question why is this necessary? The answer is twofold. First, primal instincts are prewired pathways in *older* brain tissue. We are born with them. This can be demonstrated in infants who freely behave with pure instinctive action. These pathways have a history that date back several hundred million years among many species. They are "mature", and, therefore, will fire first. Neocortex tissue is relatively new, only millions of years, and pathways here must be "artificially" developed into *new learning experiences and memories*. Behavior must, partly, be molded and taught. Second, there is much evidence that we are social creatures because we are evolved to be that way. That requires a new set of standards beyond the realm of the animal primal instincts. Social evolution requires collective management as stated earlier. We must continue to learn and develop new behaviors that benefit not only the individual, but the group as a whole. Our intellect is the best adaptation we have.

Social adaptation and peer acceptance appear to be intellectual pursuits, and, to some extent, they are. It must be remembered that the instinct of hierarchy is the dominant driving force. The hierarchical instinct demands our inclusion in a group or with another individual. While the drive is to dominate, the intellect usually perceives the experience as empowerment and the challenge is satisfied. In some, however, there is little or no controlling action by the intellect and these individuals will either try to control others, compete inappropriately, become violent or abusive, or just leave the group in search of another. In others, the challenge of social empowerment has little or no influence on their perceived needs. They may have "poorly developed" hierarchical instincts or/and a well-trained intellect that allows them to acquiesce to more aggressive people. The self-preservation instinct may demand an immediate retreat, and individuals such as this tend to be portrayed as the 'followers' of society. The fact that intellect is intervening here with great regularity among many is, perhaps, an indication that we are "evolving" in a direction that steers toward altruistic social adaptation.

How do we define altruistic behavior, as convened by the intellect? The best way to approach this is by looking at the ultimate altruistic expression and working back.

We might define the ultimate as the man who throws himself on the grenade to save his buddies. This is pure intellect, without the constraints of primal instincts. It should be remembered that the primal instinctive behavior surfaces first, because it is "mature", and the intellect follows, because it is "immature". If this is true, then why doesn't self-preservation demand that this individual save his own life? It does. And the challenge is indeed great, perhaps greater than any comparative primal challenge imaginable. He does not do this to impress his comrades; that would be hierarchical behavior. He does not do it because the grenade is his own;

that would be territorial. There are also no apparent ritualistic or reproductive reasons for this act. What remains is the conclusion that the intellect has triumphed over pure instinct. In other words, through a lifetime of training the intellectual "portion" of the neocortex to recognize a behavior that is beneficial to the group, even at the cost of one's own life, he saves the group by sacrificing his. This *training* comes in the form of an ideal or a value. But is altruistic behavior unique to *Homo Sapiens*? No. All higher life forms perform altruistic acts. Birds sacrifice their lives to lead others to migration routes. Cats rescue their kittens from raging fires, even dogs rescue humans and other animals in dire circumstances. Bees will sting an attacker to save the hive, dying in the process. Examples are plentiful. What mechanism drives this behavior and why does it come in so many different forms?

The intellectual "portion" of the neocortex is a "conscious" one. Intellect, is paramount to altruistic behavior in *Homo Sapiens*. Although altruistic behavior is a complex mechanism, and usually involves some primal instincts, the overall motive is the betterment of the group. This requires a fundamental understanding of the group makeup and a prioritizing mechanism. That mechanism is called the intellect. As stated above, many species, but especially man, may be intelligent, but that does not guarantee that an intellect is present. Human individuals that depend primarily on their primal instincts to accomplish a goal, are behaving without the benefit of sufficient intellect to do what is good for the group. The oldest evolutionary mechanism for survival is primal instincts, but as intelligence and intellect grow, and awareness of group need becomes a focus, the intellect gains importance and "drives" behavior. Remember that the intellect needs *training* to work well. Intelligence and knowledge are not sufficient. No one automatically throws them self on a grenade without deep understanding of morals, ethics, and the priority of the group at the forefront.

Following is a list of primal behaviors. Opposite is a similar list of behaviors that exemplify the intellect at work. Note that the goal in the first list is the survival of the individual and the goal of the second list is the survival of the group. This is not a scientific comparison. It was meant to show how intellect can intervene to alter primal behavior.

Primal behavior:	**Altruistic behavior:**
Stealing money	Giving to charity
Teasing	Complimenting
Refusing to change	Trying new things
Race hatred	Tolerance
Butting in	Waiting your turn
Running from fire, ignoring others	Saving others from fire
Panic at another's heart attack	Giving CPR
Driving recklessly	Following the traffic laws
Cheating on your income tax	Paying your fair share
Dominating a conversation	Listening to others
Shooting rabbits in your back yard	Adopting a pet
Painting graffiti	Cleaning a neighborhood
Assaulting a person for a verbal threat	Discussion and debate
Win at all costs	Compete with vigor but fairly
Complaining about what others make at work	Living within your means
Thinking you're always right	Giving others credit
Lying to protect your position	Admitting you are wrong
Imposing your belief system on others	Living in peace with others
Cheating on your spouse	Staying monogamous
Blaming someone	Protecting another's honor
Playing hooky from work or school	Being dependable and on time

This list could go on endlessly; however, it is clear that the primal behavior is the easier of the two lists. It takes work and training to achieve the altruistic ideals and requires the use of the intellect to intervene. There is no question that these lists are familiar to all of us. We have been exposed to them since the second grade. Remarkably, most cultures around the planet have some form of education, no matter how primitive, with the ultimate goal of 'doing good unto others'. This similarity among such diverse peoples indicates a "predilection" of our species to "evolve" toward a group survival. It may be one of the reasons that *Homo Sapiens* has survived. Perhaps it wasn't just language or larger brains that allowed us to proliferate. It could have been a trend toward altruistic behavior for the good of the whole as well.

When the neocortex is exposed to a new learning situation, the perception is to react instinctively. Many do, and with negative results in many cases. It takes time and repeated exposure to a *new* thought process that requires choice. A choice based on easy response from age-old primal instincts, or a choice based on humanitarian (altruistic) ideals formulated from the rule of law. We need training imposed from the outside to suppress potentially harmful behaviors originating in the primal brain. This is where morals and ideals come into play. Without these altruistic choices, we would still be clubbing each other to death over water holes in East Africa. In a sense we still do. The art of warfare has reached a point of total genocide because of advances in technology, but the behavior is still the same. If we have clear choices and understand the nature of our behavior, there is a good chance that we can continue to "evolve" toward collective adaptation.

It must be remembered that the intellect is just a *function* of our overall intelligence. It is not a structure in the brain or a physical level recognizable on a CT scan. Though it resides in a structure called the neocortex, it is "diffuse and nebulous." The intellect is more noticeable when it is *not* there than when it *is*. To see how this works, just add the mix of mind altering substances most commonly found in our society and observe the suppressing effect on the intellect followed by the exaggeration of primal instincts. Alcohol and drugs act on the "recently" evolved neocortex and seldom on the limbic system or R-complex of the brain. With the intellect effectively minimized, primal behavior becomes the paramount factor in outward action. A trip to any bar in town will demonstrate this adequately. People are rowdy and inconsiderate, even violent. Hierarchical behavior is the most noticeable, with individuals trying to dominate others. Territorialism gains ever- increasing potential as more alcohol is consumed. Behaviors range from aggression to depression in wild swings of mood in the context of challenge and satisfaction cycles. Self-preservation and reproductive instincts dominate as morals and ethics are discarded in favor of ancient needs. It is interesting to note that *intelligence* is "not" affected when an individual is using drugs or alcohol. It may even be enhanced. It seems that the *intellect* along with conventional motor skills are the "only" neuropathways affected, and leave the individual behaving as a simple, but intelligent animal with primal challenge and satisfaction cycles.

What, if anything could we call an irregularity of the intellect. A clue has already been advanced by Gregory Fischer in which the intellect seems to have periodic lapses of transmission even in normal situations. It has been referred to as a *synaptic impasse.* Therefore we must conclude that any periodic loss of integrity of the intellect pathways, however temporary, could demonstrate consistent behaviors that are abnormal. According to Mr. Fischer, this could be called *synaptic impasse syndrome.* In other words, a collection of symptomatic primal behavior without the intervening effect of the intellectual pathways. This syndrome may explain a great deal of human abnormal behavior.

Synaptic impasse syndrome, or SIS, may be applied to almost any circumstance from the simplest daily occurrence to the most severe behavior in man's arsenal. 'Simplest' would include rudeness and inconsiderate behavior. 'Severe' would include genocide, murder, rape and a host of other destructive abnormal behaviors. The key may be SIS: the inability of the individual to employ the intellect, or the conscious choice not to. When a person is referred to as an 'animal', it usually means that this individual has committed some form of crime or behavior that is diametrically opposed to civilized behavior as the group interprets it. In other words, those who are *using* their intellect can recognize those who *don't.*

As we "evolve" toward collective adaptation and our society becomes more 'global' in nature, as it is in this era, we probably employ the intellect more often than at any time in our species history. The rule of law, as it influences the institutions of our species, reflects our drive toward intellectual control and away from primitive instinctual control of our behaviors. The group is "guaranteed" survival by civilized behavior of the individual. In other words, our species is capable of deflecting the hammer of exctinction by individual and collective acts of altruism, and in doing so, help preserve the group survival as a whole.

What kind of conclusions can we make about the ability of the intellect to suppress abnormal behavior? And how does this apply to the ability of instincts to learn? It must be remembered that all instincts are situaltional and extremely flexible. If given proper training by the intellect, even abnormal or damaged instincts may produce actions and behavior that is acceptable to the collective adaptation of our society. Cycles of abnormal challenge and satisfaction can be reduced in frequency, and instincts can be remolded. Instincts can learn. That is the key to behavior. Choice and learning instincts. Below are listed basic principles of how intellect and primal instincts act biologically. One of the hopes of *The New Synthesis* is the new application of *instinct therapy*.

Principles of a biological basis for behavior:

1. **Behavior is an organism's response to its environment, determined by the physiological processes of neurosynaptic pathways and/or genetic nucleic sequencing**
2. **Organisms with neurophysiology respond by two mechanisms: the primary use of neuropathways supporting primal learning instincts, and the secondary use of neuropathways supporting innate learning intelligence and intellect**
3. **The chemistry of primal instincts originates in the lower animal brain tissues of the R- complex and the limbic system. The chemistry of intellect originates in the neocortex**
4. **Primal instincts are of five basic types: self-preservation, reproductive, hierarchical, territorial, and ritual. These types, and their combinations, appear to account for almost all behavior perceived as normal and abnormal**

5. Behavior of the intellect is of one basic type: altruism. This type appears to account for almost all behavior perceived as civilized, and dictates collective adaptation

6. Primal instinct behavior operates unconsciously through cycles of challenge and satisfaction, accompanied by high levels of emotional response. These behaviors surface first, and are often perceived as abnormal

7. Much altruistic behavior operates consciously through the intellect, but only as a component of overall intelligence. This behavior surfaces secondarily, and is partly a learned behavior, imposed from the environment, and perceived, mostly, as normal

8. The primary function of the intellect is intervention and suppression of the primal instincts allowing "freedom" of choice in individual behavioral response.

Chapter 8   The Debate

by
Nils K. Oeijord

"I think the impulse to censor is one of the worst of all human instincts."

Camilla Paglia

"A new theory doesn't win over its opponents, but waits for its opponents to die off."

Anonymous

Robert Chambers, a Scottish publisher and naturalist, was the secret author of *Vestiges of the Natural History of Creation* (1844), an anonymous book that sparked hot controversy. *Vestiges* took the ambitious theme of the development of the universe from a nebulous mass of gas, moving through the history of the Earth and the fossil record as an evolutionary sequence, up to the evolution of apes into human beings. It sold and sold, reaching near 40 000 copies in 1890.

In his book *The Descent of Man*, published in 1871 (2nd ed., 1874, Ch. 3), Charles Darwin put forward his thesis of the continuity of man and animals as follows: "It has … now been shewn that man and … especially the Primates, have … instincts in common. All have the same senses, intuitions, and sensations,—similar passions, affections, and emotions, even the more complex ones, such as jealousy, suspicion, emulation, gratitude, and magnanimity; they practise deceit and are revengeful; they are sometimes susceptible to ridicule, and even have a sense of humour; they feel wonder and curiosity; they possess the same faculties of imitation, attention, deliberation, choice, memory, imagination, the association of ideas, and reason, though in very different degrees. The individuals of the same species graduate in intellect from absolute imbecility to high excellence. They are also liable to insanity, though far less often than in the case of man." This enormously talented and wonderful understanding and insight are simultaneously advanced primatology, advanced anthropology, advanced human ethology, advanced sociobiology, advanced evolutionary psychology, advanced behavioral genetics—the conclusions of a human genius. (Naturally Darwin didn't know that the great apes have a language module and that they can learn the American Sign Language, but he certainly understood that the great apes too are situational warriors and situational peacemakers, situational violent and situational non-violent.)

Darwin had intended to discuss thoroughly the human emotional instincts in *The Decent of Man*, but saved his theories of emotional instincts for his *Expression of the Emotions in Man and Animals* (1872). This book is the foundational document for evolutionary psychology and human sociobiology.

Darwin introduced evolution, but it was Francis Galton (1822-1911) who elevated the studying of human behavior to the level of modern science; inventing modern statistics, psychometrics, and behavioral genetics in the process. He discovered the existence of extremely bright children in dull families, and the existence of dull children in bright families. These facts totally contradicted both the traditional theory of 'blended inheritance' and the theory of environmentally created intelligence (and intelligence differences). Besides, the old theories did not explain how different levels of intelligence could have emerged in the first place. But Galton understood that with his new theory of 'particulate inheritance', the existence of bright children/dull parents or dull children/bright parents are anomalies we should anticipate.

John Hughlings Jackson published his important research on the evolution of the nervous system between 1881 and 1887.

The next great researcher of human behavior was William James. His *The Principles of Psychology* (1890) is the foundational document for psychology. Chapter XXIV INSTINCT of *Principles* is marvellous.

The term "evolutionary psychology" has been in use for well over a century and consequently doesn't refer only to the works of Leda Cosmides and John Tooby. The best guide to the early works in and about evolutionary psychology is R. J. Richards (1987): *Darwin and the emergence of evolutionary theories of mind and behavior*. Chicago, IL: University of Chicago Press. Here are some early works (books) in evolutionary psychology:

G. J. Romanes: *Mental Evolution in Man* (1888)

H. M. Stanley: *Studies in the evolutionary psychology of feeling* (1895)

C. Lloyd Morgan: *Habit and Instinct* (1896)

L. T. Hobhouse: *Mind and evolution* (1901)

Helen Bradford Thompson: *The Mental Traits of Sex: An Experimental Investigation of the Normal Mind in Man and Women* (1903)

C. J. Patten: *The passing of the phantoms; a study of evolutionary psychology and morals* (1924)

J. H. Bradley: *The will to live; an outline of evolutionary psychology* (1931)

In the 1920s the 'instinct psychology' of William McDougall and others explored more than 1000 different human instincts. Sigmund Freud partly understood human behavior, but his enemy, Gustav Jung (1875—1961) was more talented and fully understood the human instincts. He called them archetypes (= "eternally repeated behaviors among human beings"). Behaviorism, generally credited as beginning with Watson's paper in 1913, didn't understand instincts at all, and therefore broke down. The psychology books of today are collections of competing theories partly contradicting each other. (See: Leslie Stevenson: *Ten Theories of Human Nature* 3rd ed. (1998).)

Nikolaas Tinbergen's book *The Study of Instinct* (1951) and Konrad Lorenz's *Studies on Animal and Human Behavior* (1935), *On aggression*

(1963) and *Animal and Human Behavior* (1965) were important contributions to the growth of ethology. The first use of the term (human) sociobiology likely dates to the work of Warder C. Allee, Alfred E. Emerson, and their associates in their 1949 book *Principles of Animal Ecology*. Human sociobiology developed from the studies in population biology and genetics. William D. Hamilton ("Darwin II") explained in the 1960s the evolution of altruism instincts. This (the kin selection theory) was a key contribution to human sociobiology. A gene exists not just in one individual, he understood, but also in others, closely related. Consequently, an action that endangers the individual but promotes the survival of closely related individuals would nonetheless be genetically advantageous. The kin selection theory was expressed in mathematics and published in the *Journal of Theoretical Biology* in 1964. In the 1960s Noam Chomsky rediscovered Darwin and James' insight that we are born with the apparatus for learning language (= language instincts). One of Chomsky's observations was that children are able to learn from impoverished input. (However, Chomsky resolutely refuses to include human language within an evolutionary framework of natural selection!) Fortified with new terminology, the study of human instincts was revived in the 1960s. The kin selection theory became the backbone of Richard Dawkins's revolutionary book *The Selfish Gene* (1976)—an enormous leap forward for the theory of evolution, called the selfish gene revolution. Dawkins has contributed to the important application of information theory to evolutionary theory. His 1971 book *The Extended Phenotype* is also an important contribution to the theory of evolution (including human evolution). Richard Dawkins is our most radical Darwinian thinker and our best science writer.

Edward O. Wilson's books *Sociobiology: The New Synthesis* (1975) and *On Human Nature* (1978) added new publicity to human sociobiology, but not new insight and knowledge. Desmond John Morris (1928 -), an extraordinary talented English anthropologist, published *The Story of Congo* [a chimpanzee] (1958), *The Biology of Art* (1962) *Men and Apes* (with Ramona Morris, 1966), *Primate Ethology* (ed, 1967), *The Naked Ape* (1967), *The Human Zoo* (1969), *Patterns of Reproductive Behaviour* (1970), and *Intimate Behaviour* (1971)—*prior* to Wilson's famous *Sociobiology*. The New Synthesis belongs to Morris et al. (including Darwin and James). Desmond Morris is "The man who made science sexy". Morris has changed the science of human behavior via behavioral research, 52 books, and eight TV Series.

The Adapted Mind (1992), edited by Jerome H. Barkow and the husband-and-wife team Leda Cosmides and John Tooby, is the most important work in evolutionary psychology since the 1930s. Cosmides and Tooby's 1997 paper *Evolutionary Psychology: A Primer* is the best paper ever written about human behavior and human instincts, I think.

Robert Wright's *The Moral Animal* (1994), Steven Pinker's *The Language Instinct* (1995) and *How the Mind Works* (1997), and David M. Buss' *Evolutionary Psychology* (1998) are extremely important for our understanding of human behavior.

In 30 years behavior genetics, evolutionary psychology, and human sociobiology have come from being small fields to being recognized as central to an understanding of human behavior. And the dogma of environmental determinism has relaxed in recent years.

A common view held by scientist and philosophers before and after Darwin's *The Origin of Species* (1859) says that the human mind resembles a blank slate until written on by the hands of experience. Examples:

"There is no human nature" (Jean-Paul Sartre).

"We are the being whose essence lies in having no essence" (Simone de Beauvoir).

"Any genome can give rise to any kind of person" (Martine Rothblatt).

"Anyone has the potential to develop virtually any identity within the spectrum of humanity"(Richard C. Lewontin).

"... the dream of the human genome and other illusions" (Richard C. Lewontin)

"... the organism is not specified by its genes" (Richard C. Lewontin).

"Schizophrenia is socially determined" (Leon J. Camin et al.).

"Schizophrenia is caused by racism" (Steven Rose).

"There exist no data which should lead a prudent man to accept the hypothesis that IQ test scores are in any degree heritable" (Leon J. Camin).

"...average IQ increases in some nations since the Second World War equal to the entire fifteen-point difference ..." (Stephen Jay Gould) [Gould believes intelligence is created by the environment]

"The human brain must be bursting with *spandrels* [= accidental by-products]" (Stephen Jay Gould).

"Wright presents no neurological evidence of a brain module for sweetness, and no paleontological data about ancestral feeding" (Stephen Jay Gould) [Gould rejects that humans have an instinct for sweetness!]

There is no need to go on. Undoubtedly there exist two distinct categories of scientists and philosophers: Those who understand human behavior spontaneously, and those who never understand human behavior. (I think both categories agree!)

Stephen Jay Gould and Richard C. Lewontin are the leading living environmentalists.

They are attacking everything: the Millennium, the genome, genomics, behavioral genetics, adaptation, modularity, gradual change, the human instincts, the existence of physical traits, the existence of behavioral traits, IQ-testing, testing in general, factor analysis, natural selection, "Darwinian evolution", human sociobiology, evolutionary psychology, the superiority of black runners, sex differences, individual genetic differences, genetic disorders, that homosexuality is inborn, the USA ("crazy country"), the democratic parts of the world, animals (lack of consciousness), Neanderthals ("they had low intelligence"!), living persons (Wilson, Dawkins, Cosmides, Tooby, R. Wright, Pinker, and others), dead persons (See: Reviews of Stephen Jay Gould: *The Mismeasure of Man*).

"Evolutionary psychology is the attempt to understand our mental faculties in light of the evolutionary processes that shaped them. Stephen Jay

Gould [NYRB, June 12 and June 26] calls its ideas and their proponents "foolish," "fatuous," "pathetic," "egregiously simplistic," and some twenty-five synonyms for "fanatical." Such language is not just discourteous; it is misguided, for the ideas of evolutionary psychology are not as stupid as Gould makes them out to be. Indeed, they are nothing like what Gould makes them out to be" (Steven Pinker).

Gould and Lewontin do not provide any alternative ideas to improve evolutionary psychology, and only act as an overly critical source. Example: Gould says that features like language are accidental by-products of a large brain size plus culture. But Steven Pinker has amply demonstrated that language is one of the most highly designed adaptations imaginable. Language is a mechanism with a very specific pattern that develops in children without instruction. The problem for environmentalists is not only to demonstrate that "there is no good reason to think that genetics overwhelmingly determines behavior." They need to make a positive case for strong environmental determination of human behavior, but they don't. Unfortunately, for the environmentalists, the latter conclusion doesn't directly follow from the first. Steven Rose says "the heritability of human traits cannot be determined because human cannot be selectively bred." But every textbook on human genetics describes methods for heritability estimation! Steven Rose says that our memory span is entirely "culture-bound". (He confuses the five-item-constraint instinct and the chunking instinct. The five items can be five chunks, e.g. five chunks of numbers.)

"Our brains, hands and tongues have made us independent of any single features of the external world… Thus it is our biology that makes us free." Clearly this is an argument against environmentalism, but it was written by S. Rose, L. J. Kamin, and R. C. Lewontin as an argument for environmentalism! "Organisms not only determine what aspects of the outside world are relevant to them by peculiarities of their shape and metabolism, but they actively construct, in the literal sense of the word, a world around themselves." Obviously this is an argument for "biological determinism", but it was written by R. C. Lewontin as an argument against "biological determinism"!

Many reviewers say Gould prefers to deal with scientifically very old history. Example: His most significant book is *The Mismeasure of Man* (1981). Though practically all the studies of brain size and intelligence cited in *The Mismeasure of Man* are more than 100 years old, he meticulously points out their errors and biases. He is attacking a straw man! Gould's reissue of his 1981 edition was not revised in light of new evidence: All the chapters of the initial edition have been repeated. *The Mismeasure of Man* tells us that human intelligence is determined by environmental factors, and that factor analysis is a worthless technique. Gould even attacks the science of mathematics. Factor analysis, he says "is, to put it bluntly, a bitch."

The Mismeasure of Man concludes that the measurement of intelligence is immoral and unscientific because, as he believes, all healthy human individuals and all healthy ethnic groups of people are born with exactly the same capabilities. Gould's attack on IQ-testing is the strongest since Adolph Hitler banned IQ-testing in 1937 to prevent the much above-average IQ's of the Jews from being advertised. Gould also concludes that genetically different groups don't exist. This is very dangerous because people from different groups may have genetic variations that affect the way they respond to medicines. For example, if you give the Saami people the same medicines as you give Norwegians you are a potential murderer. Gould's conclusions are not only dangerous and erroneous, they are directly stupid. If you want to find a man to beat Michael Johnson's 19.32 (in the 200 meters) you would be very stupid if you look for a white man. And if you wanted a white man to knock out Mike Tyson (at the top of his career) you had to be stupid too. To look for the best long-distance runners you must go to certain regions of northern Africa. And so on. Instincts can learn, yes! But the learning itself has certain genetically based limitations. 10.00 in the 100 metres is a failure for hundreds of black runners, but only a wild dream for all white runners. But Gould insists that in the area of behavior (running is behavior), genetic differences are non-existent or should be ignored. Remember that genes come in several forms—*alleles*—and these give rise to different variants of a protein. A genuine Eskimo from Greenland and a genuine Pygmy from Africa probably have few alleles in common even if they have more than 99.9 percent of their genes in common. Genes are theoretical constructs, while alleles are entities.

By the way, on three adjacent pages of an issue of *Science* we are led to believe that genetically different populations do not exist, but that it is important to assess the genetic diversity of remaining native populations, and that a black scientist at a black university should be funded to investigate the black genome as a route to appropriate treatment of diseases of blacks!

The illegitimacy of inferring "ought" from "is" (and "is" from "ought") has been a matter of virtual consensus in both science and philosophy for a century. But Gould is reading right-wing messages into "conventional" ideas about how evolution works! Gould also often infers "is" from "ought". Example: Innate disposition is "is", and Gould rejects hypotheses about innate dispositions because innate disposition "fobs off responsibility for our violence and sexism upon our genes" (See: Stephen Jay Gould: *Ever Since Darwin*).

Strangely, Gould and Lewontin even object to ordinary natural selection and to the division of organism into independent or semi-independent traits, each of which can separately respond to selective forces. But they cannot do that, because these views make evolution absolutely impossible.

Gould and Lewontin reject the adaptational approach. They call it the "Panglossian" paradigm, recalling the optimistic doctor of Voltaire's *Candide*: Dr. Pangloss, who found a function subserved for every distinct structure we could identify (e.g. the nose has its shape to enable us to wear glasses). Well, the human eye are absolutely "Panglossian"! And why do we have wrinkled, asymmetrical ears? Because they filter sound waves coming from different directions in different ways. The sound shadow tells the brain whether the source of the sound is above or below, in front of or behind us. Obviously certain seeing and hearing instincts (adaptations!) must also exist! The information in the famous *Gray's Anatomy*, and the information from the science of human physiology contradict Gould and Lewontin. The fact that the human genome contains "only" 30 000 active genes gives no room for non-adaptive active genes. Human brain research and human behavior research have so far contradicted the anti-adaptational view. There is no need to go on. We have already proved that Gould and Lewontin are wrong about the adaptational approach. Adaptationalist approaches have proven essential to discovery. Look at the journals! Gould and Lewontin have no alternative research program to offer. Nevertheless Gould says: "The human brain must be bursting with *spandrels* [accidental by-products]" He has no proofs at all.

To support their criticism of the adaptational approach, Gould and Lewontin in 1979 devised, in the paper *The spandrels of San Marco and the Panglossian paradigm: A critique of the adaptationist programme*, an analogy rooted in historical architecture. But even the analogy itself was ill chosen (and Gould and Lewontin's other example from architecture was ill chosen, as well, as it turns out). Strictly speaking, the tapering, roughly spherical surface in between the dome and the four round arches is a *pendentive*, not a *spandrel*. The "spandrels" of San Marco aren't spandrels even in Gould's extended sense. They are adaptations for largely aesthetic reasons. Their primary adaptive function is to provide a showcase for Christian symbols. (Humans have aesthetic and religious instincts.) Their secondary adaptative functions are to strengthen the physical structure of the building, to be a part of the walls of the building, and to protect the people as well as the building itself against the forces of nature, such as rain, wind, sunlight and gravitation.

Stephen Jay Gould has nearly made a career of claiming that modern evolutionary biologists suffer from a tendency to uncritically overattribute adaptation. However, the revolution in evolutionary biology (including evolutionary psychology) that began in the 1960s was rooted exactly and specifically in a widespread reaction against and rejection of the practice of overattributing adaptation. . "I object to Gould's tendency to visit the alleged sins of early investigators on present day investigators" (John B. Carroll, University of North Carolina). Another example: Gould says: "All organisms evolve as complex and interconnected wholes." (He is attacking the modularity of physical and behavoral traits.) If we take it literally, then evolution is totally impossible. As a former plant breeder I perfectly know that Gould is wrong. All plant and animal breeders know that we can change one particular trait (physical or behavioral) without changing the other traits. "Gould is uninformed when he repeats the cliché that evolutionary reasoning is just cocktail-party speculation ["just so" story]. The standards of the field require a good empirical fit between the engineering demands of an adaptive problem and the facts of human psychology. The former is grounded in game-theoretic and other optimality analyses, in artificial intelligence and artificial life simulations, and in relevant sciences such as genetics, physiology, optics, or ecology. The latter is based on converging evidence from experiments with children, adults, and neurological patients and from survey, historical, ethnographic, paleoanthropological, archeological, and economic data" (Steven Pinker).

The fascinating nature of the discoveries of "adaptationists" can be illustrated with the following example. Gould rejected the possibility of adaptive sexual suicide attributed to the male redback spider. Irritated at Gould 's attempt to declare an interesting puzzle out of bounds, Maydianne Andrade went ahead and explored the life and evolution of the redback spider. Andrade found that if the female spider does consume the male, his sperm will fertilize *more* eggs than if he fails to become a sexual suicide. Of course Gould rejected that the female orgasm is adaptive. But researchers found that muscular contractions associated with the female orgasm pull sperm from the vagina to the cervix, boosting conception chances. Besides, after climax, you're more likely to lie down, thus increasing sperm retention, again boosting your chances of conception.

The distinguished evolutionary scientist John Maynard Smith has noted, in the *New York Review of Books*, November 1995: "Gould occupies a rather curious position, particularly on his side of the Atlantic. Because of the excellence of his essays, he has come to be seen by non-biologists as the preeminent evolutionary theorist. In contrast, the evolutionary biologists with whom I have discussed his work tend to see him as a man whose ideas are so confused as to be hardly worth bothering with, ... he is giving non-biologists a largely false picture of the state of evolutionary theory." The flaws in the argumentation of Gould and Lewontin are so serious that their works are now studied by rhetorical theorists as a model of sophistical rhetoric in science.

The list of false accusations made by Gould, Lewontin, Rose, and Kamin (and other leading environmentalists) is long. The most untalented accusation is the accusation of genetic determinism (= biological determinism = "the details of present and past human social arrangements are the inevitable manifestations of the specific action of genes"). Their accusation is false because the system of a large number of competing situational learning instincts is an enormously flexible, statistical system; it is not a deterministic system. "Cyril Burt went to the extreme length of faking numerical data, but it can be argued that what lay behind his crime was an eagerness to give ideology priority over truth. If this is so, who are the Cyril Burts of today?" (Richard Dawkins). "Off the hook" is an expression often used by environmentalists (including Gould and Lewontin) when they attack behavioral sciences and scientists. Example: "Wilson blames genocide on human nature and overpopulation to let imperialists...off the hook" (Steve Rosenthal). Don't imperialists have a human nature? How old is imperialism? What is stone age imperialism? Who killed 66 million in the USSR? An evolutionary explanation and a political explanation are totally different, and largely independent, systems of explanation. The evolutionary explanation is a basic explanation, and might be used for long-term prediction. A political explanation is often better than an evolutionary explanation for short-term prediction. Both systems are statistical systems.

If the concept of gradualism in evolution can be badly shaken and the alternative revolutionary ideas of sudden leaps can be established, it would become easier to argue against the existence of adaptations (instincts). Therefore Stephen Jay Gould and Niles Eldredge published a paper in 1972 entitled *Punctuated Equilibria: an Alternative to Phyletic Gradualism.* However this hypothesis was not an alternative to gradualism, but only a supplement (see below). Besides, their leap model is argued from the standpoint of negative evidence and hence is exceedingly vulnerable to annihilation by new discoveries. Recent researches on early primates and other mammals have established incontrovertible evidence of gradual evolutionary changes through time, including the gradual evolution of new species both by changes within a single population, phyletic evolution, and by splitting or speciation. Gould and Eldredge were wrong. By the way, Gould is one of the few scientists who still think of natural selection as working only at levels higher than the individual organism!

Sometimes Gould and Lewontin seem to endorse radical evolutionary holism, sometimes not. They reject "Darwinian evolution", the claim that evolution proceeds by continual selection over small variations at a constant rate. But that is not Darwinian evolution. "The periods, during which species have undergone modification, though long as measured by years, have probably been short in comparison with the periods during which they retain the same form" (Charles Darwin). Clearly, the idea of punctuated equilibria belongs to Darwin and to the Darwinian theory of evolution. Ernst Mayr, Gould's mentor, insists that any plausible version of punctuated equilibrium is completely consistent with the modern Darwinian synthesis, and that the engine of change in punctuated equilibrium is natural selection. Mayr should know. He created the theory of punctuated equilibria, decades before Gould gave it that title!

Many environmentalists (including Gould and Lewontin) don't understand the selfish gene revolution. Example: "According to the selfish gene hypothesis, the winners in the game of reproduction were those individuals who selfishly and single-mindedly acted to breed the most. As a result their offspring inherited those characteristics of individual selfishness" (Keith Rankin). This is absolutely wrong and absolutely meaningless. The "selfish" genes produce you and me. The "selfish" genes produce unselfishness too. And empathy, sympathy, goodness, and cooperation. "The metaphor of the selfish gene must be taken seriously: people don't selfishly spread their genes; genes selfishly spread themselves. They do it by the way they build our brains. By making us enjoy life, health, sex, friends, and children, the genes buy a lottery ticket for representation in the next generation, with odds that were favorable in the environment in which we evolved (because healthy, long-lived, loving parents did tend, on average, to send more genes into the next generation). Our goals are sub-goals of the ultimate goal of the genes, replicating themselves" (Steven Pinker). Marvelous! Simply fantastic!

The Nature versus Nurture formula is the concept of heritability (= fractionation into genetic and environmental components). The concept of (broad) heritability has now almost completely replaced other views. But David Lykken has found a better formula: The Nature via Nurture formula. He says: "… genetic effects on human psychology are often distal in the causal chain while the proximal causes are environmental, just as those reactionary Lockians have always claimed. A better formula than Nature versus Nurture would be Nature via Nurture. But, distal or not, the genetic influences are strong and most of us develop along a path determined mainly by our personal genetic steersmen. It is often possible to intervene, but it is seldom easy." Dawkins explicitly states that the environment will always modify the effect of genes. Obviously Dawkins' view is Nature via Nurture.

Steven Pinker: "… what's innate about language is just a way of paying attention to parental speech, carving it into specific units like nouns and verbs and adjectives and objects. If you didn't have a learning device focusing on those things, you'd never get it to work." However, the language instincts don't need parental speech. Proof: Spontaneous private language in twins or other children. Undoubtedly all instincts are learning instincts, more or less. Even reflexes ("little instincts") can learn.

Certainly, an instinct has two "parts": A directly innate part and an innate learning part. Both parts may (or may not) need development/maturation after birth. The relative "size" of these parts is innate and vary from instinct to instinct, and from individual to individual. Obviously instincts are situational (situational triggering of actions and learning). Note that both learning and triggering are indirectly innate because all learning is specialized, content-dependent, domain-specific, and functionally distinctive, as experience, reasoning and research tell us. So behavior is not innate, even instincts are not totally innate. What is innate is our situational learning instincts.

Even though we clock up more unique experiences as we age, evidence amassed over the past seventy-five years suggests that the "genetic contribution" to mental achievement and emotional characteristics *increases* with age!!! Example: The (broad) heritability coefficient of IQ is about 0.4 (= 40 %) when measured in children, about 0.6 (= 60%) in adolescents, and about 0.8 (= 80%) in later maturity. More learning causes *more* genetic determinism!?

Can we quantify how well a particular instinct can learn? Yes. This problem was solved by my co-author Mitch C. Bronston. His solution is to use the (broad) heritability coefficient, but let the "environmental" part of the coefficient (= of the variance) quantify how well an instinct can learn. The *Bronston heritability coefficient* directly explains the paradoxes above. It tells us that a behavioral trait's genetically determined specific learning ability/capacity is *decreasing* with age. But, fortunately, this coefficient also tells us that the other parts of the total ability/capacity of a behavioral trait are *increasing*, so that the total ability/capacity is pretty *constant* with age.

Even if environmentalism was only *partly* correct, the Bronston coefficient had to *decrease* with age. Clearly, the *increasing* Bronston coefficient for human behavioral traits *proves* that human *behavior is*

instinctive, and is *not* created by the chaotic and poverty-stricken environmental factors. But remember: 1) all instincts are learning instincts, and 2) all instincts are situational. Obviously, human intelligence(s) and intellect(s) depend on our having *more* instincts, not fewer.

The environmentalist Alan Wolfe calls for a return to the works of Karl Marx and Margaret Mead as a means of understanding human behavior. But Marx incorporated in his later work an idea of an invariant human nature which cannot be changed! Marx (in his later work) understood the human instincts! Marx even admired Darwin's work and saw his science of human history eventually being built on Darwin's ideas (the human instincts)! But, believe it or not, Richard C. Lewontin and Richard Levins wrote: "There is nothing in Marx ... that is or can be in contradiction with the particular physical facts and processes of a particular set of phenomena in the objective world." (Lewontin and Levins totally reject evolutionary psychology and human instincts.) Margaret Mead sided with Edward O. Wilson's human sociobiology! She has even published ideas on the biological basis of social human behavior. One was that each society contains an array of people genetically predisposed toward different tasks. She even invited Wilson to have dinner with her to discuss human sociobiology.

History tells us that scientific disciplines are always riddled with internal disagreements and verbal violence, even physical violence. Example: Edward O. Wilson was physically attacked by environmentalists. But scientific argument often leads to greater knowledge. Example: Gould said: "At the very most, biology might help us to delimit the environmental circumstances that tend to elicit one behavior rather than the other." Undoubtedly, this blank-slate statement motivates behavioral geneticists and others to find still more genetic behaviors. This dooms Gould et al. to constant nay saying, and they therefore now feel an obligation to produce "some positive program for understanding life." We are promised "dialectical biology" because "interactionism" is not quite "dialectical"... and interactionism supposes the "alienation" of organism and the environment ... (There is no need to go on. They communicate nothing.)

For a hundred years, guilty parents have endured the environmentalist blaming them for causing schizophrenia, autism, anorexia, homosexuality, etc. The same environmentalists dismiss genetic and physical diseases as "psychological reaction", "false consciousness", etc. Environmentalists in organizations like Science for the People are persecuting our best scientists. Environmentalists in *Scientific American* transform important articles into insane ones: An article on behavior genetics is doctored into "Eugenics Revisited", an article on evolutionary psychology is doctored into "The New Social Darwinists", and so on. Dawkins said of the genes: "They created us, body and mind." But Lewontin, Rose, and Kamin quote it repeatedly as "They *control* us, body and mind." In the USSR Lenin and Stalin tried to create "a new human mind" using the environmentalist's denial of the inborn human mind. The well known result was more than tragic. Hitler used environmentalism (youth organizations, propaganda films, threats, violence, etc) to create a nazi mind. He even banned IQ-testing. Needless to say, he failed. Later several other mass killers have misused environmentalism, for example Pol Pot in his Killing Fields, to transform the human mind. Aleksandr Etkind, a professor of humanities from St. Petersburg says "Trotsky shed rivers of blood in order to get rid of the power of human instincts."

Chapter 9   Synopsis

by
Nils K. Oeijord and Mitch C. Bronston

"When intellect triumphs over pure instinct, it is not only the mark of a man, but the triumph of a civilization."

M.C.B.

Instincts are often thought of as the opposite of learning and reasoning. However, the reasoning and the learning neuropathways have all the characteristics of an instinct: natural, effortless, automatic, reliable, precise, fast, economical, unconscious, innate, and requires little or no instruction, even though they reside in the neocortex. So behavior is not caused by instincts or learning (alone), because learning is caused by instincts. We don't have to learn to learn because we have learning instincts. Human behavior is often more flexible intelligent than that of other species because we have more instincts than they do, not fewer. (See the A to Z list of human instincts in the Appendix.)

The human instincts work so well that quite a lot of scientists don't realize that they exist. Even reflexes can learn, so, of course, all instincts are learning instincts (= instincts can learn). Moreover, all instincts are situational (= situational triggering of learning and actions). **The system of a large number of competing situational learning instincts is an enormously flexible, statistical system; it is not a deterministic system**. Obviously, human intelligence(s) and intellect(s) depend on our having more instincts, not fewer. In a sense, the intellect has to be, by definition, more innate than "lower" instincts because it must be **more** buffered against both the inner and the outer environments than the lower instincts are.

The list of normal and abnormal human behavior is long, but it is important to note that just about all human activity can be explained by the five primal instincts: 1) the reproduction instinct, 2) the self-preservation instinct, 3) the territorial instinct, 4) the social-hierarchy instinct, and 5) the ritual instinct. Our *Synthesis* explains how the primal instincts contribute to abnormal (and normal) human behavior. This is a new approach to forensic anthropology without psychologically confusing platforms.

It is possible to quantify how well a particular instinct can learn. We may use the (broad) heritability coefficient, but let the "environmental" part of the coefficient (= of the variance) quantify how well an instinct can learn. This new coefficient was discovered by Mitch C. Bronston in May 2001.

Even though we clock up more unique experiences as we age, evidence amassed over the past seventy-five years suggests that the "genetic contribution" to mental achievement and emotional characteristics increases with age. Example. The (broad) heritability coefficient of IQ is about 0.4 (= 40%) when measured in children, about 0.6 (= 60%) in adolescents, and about 0.8 (= 80%) in later maturity. More learning causes more "genetic determinism".

The **Bronston heritability coefficient** (see above) directly explains the paradoxes above. It tells us that a behavioral trait's genetically determined specific learning ability/capacity is **decreasing** with age. But, fortunately, this coefficient also tells us that the other parts of the total ability/capacity of a behavioral trait are **increasing**, so that the total ability/capacity is pretty **constant** with age. **Even if environmentalism was only** *partly* **correct, the Bronston heritability coefficient had to** *decrease* **with age. Clearly, the** *increasing* **Bronston heritability coefficient for human behvioral traits** *proves* **that** *human behavior is instinctive,* **and is** *not* **created by the chaotic and poverty-stricken environmental factors. But remember: 1) all** instincts are learning instincts, 2) all instincts are situational, and 3) human intelligence(s) and intellect(s) depend on our having *more* instincts, not fewer.

The data collected prove that genuinely identical MZA twins (see Chapter 4) living in different genuine free-choice environments have identical wills (= they live parallel lives). Note that this finding is the strongest support for free will that it is logically possible to imagine. Here the will is extremely independent of environmental factors (including other peoples' wills).

"Psychological conditions" are typically accompanied by an array of other medical problems. This fact alone suggests that these "conditions" are not "psychological conditions". However, the existence of situational learning instincts, and the logic of the Bronston heritability coefficient, tell us that therapy (especially the use of what we call instinct therapy) works. Therapists reading about new specific results emerging from behavioral genetics have (specifically) switched from trying to treat their clients' problematic behavior to make them content with their innate pre-dispositions. They have found that it works. Far from being a sentence, the realization of innate personality is often a release.

Every week, it seems, a new gene is discovered that controls some aspects of the human situational learning instincts. Behavior is not innate, but learning instincts are innate. In recent decades it has become clear that the environmentalists' view of the human mind is untenable. Human nature (= the human situational learning instincts, including intelligence and intellect) is beginning to appear while the traditional "psychological" views are fading away. *The New Synthesis* will give us a new way of thinking about who we are and how we can improve ourselves, and it may make us more understanding of others.

In defining a new way to look at behavior, we have attempted to move away from standard approaches through psychology, and simplify the way we classify an organism's response to the environment. That response is the only visible and quantifiable evidence that an organism is indeed interacting with the immediate surroundings. In other words, behavior is a direct reaction an organism makes when confronted by external change. Reaction, or behavior, may be produced two ways: by basic learning instincts, and by innate learning intellect. In the context of our previous discussions, we have concluded that all behavior is controlled by biological processes; primarily neurosynaptic pathways in organisms with brains and/or direct genetic control by DNA in simple life forms. The chemistry of neuropathways and nucleic sequencing is not always visible, but the effects are. That effect is what we call behavior.

We have repeatedly stated that no scientific studies have been performed that map out behavior by this classifying method. It may be considered a new way to look at what we already know, but with new conclusions. No one has ever seen a neuropathway or charted its depolarization sequence. No one has ever seen a black hole either, but astronomers can prove its existence by the way it behaves when it leaves synchronic radiation trails and high energy x-rays of degraded matter. So too with brain tissue, leaving a wake of evidence in the form of outward individual behavior. Like the gravitational vortex of a black hole, the response a living organism makes to its environment is adequately verifiable.

Though there is much yet to learn about our nature, and the instincts we possess, the purpose of this book was to simplify. It appears that we, all of us, have evolved with a unique and splendid biology, capable of preserving our life, passing our genetic information to the next generation, and interacting with our fellow humans in ways that define our unique qualities as individuals. Satisfying our basic instincts occupies almost all of our human activity, often to the detriment of others. The predominant factor that makes us human is our capacity for intellect. In the mass of neurons and neuropathways of the neocortex, lies our humanity, our compassion, and our creative genius. We can use our intellect for moral, ethical and valued pursuits that benefit our species, as well as all life on this planet. Race hatred once used to satisfy the hierarchy instinct can be massaged into peaceful bliss with intellectual choices of behavior. The insanity of nuclear threat or genocide, once used to satisfy our territorial and hierarchical instincts, can be replaced by intellectual processes, and human values. The key is choice. This is the main thing our intellect gives us, and the true hope for human continuance on this planet. Psychotherapy can deal with the emotions associated with challenges and satisfaction, and the abnormal responses that accompany them. Improved medical treatment can alter poor 'prewiring' and balance neurotransmitters. Nature is nature, and we must accept what we are, but we can also grow with understanding and compassion, and our species can reap the rewards as we move toward the distant future.

About the Authors

BLURB:

The New Synthesis consists of 1) a new understanding of heritability, 2) a new interpretation and understanding of the broad heritability coefficient, 3) a new understanding of the human instincts, 4) a new understanding of normal and abnormal behavior, 5) a new interpretation and understanding of intellect and free will, 6) a new understanding of the behavior of genuinely identical MZA twins in different genuine free-choice environments, and 7) a new list of the human instincts.

Mitch C. Bronston was born in Sioux City, Iowa and is 52 years old. He is a graduate of Drake University, and currently a science writer and facilitator of abnormal human behavior. His recent papers on *Primal Instincts and Their Effect on Human Behavior* appear widely on science websites. Mitch C. Bronston's first book was *A Dictionary of Human Instincts* (with Nils K. Oeijord, 2001). Previously, he has taught neuro-electrophysiology at a St Louis technical school, and now lives in Sioux City. Mitch and his wife Sydney have four grown children.

Nils K. Oeijord was born in Norway in 1947. A graduate of the Agricultural University of Norway, he also studied mathematics at the University of Trondheim, in Norway as well. He is a former assistant professor of mathematics at Tromsoe College, Norway, and is the author of several scientific works in Norwegian. He is currently a full time science writer. Nils K. Oeijord's first book in English, *Human Instincts Explained*, was published in 2000 (Vantage, New York). His second book in English, *A Dictionary of Human Instincts*, was published in 2001 (iUniverse.com).

Note: The Appendix: *A Dictionary of Human Instincts* is also published as an independent book.

Appendix

(Note: A Dictionary of Human Instincts is also published as an independent book)

A DICTIONARY OF HUMAN INSTINCTS

by
Nils K. Oeijord and Mitch C. Bronston

"Life never occurs in main effects."

Abbott

"Nothing but the heart can change the heart."

Carroll O'Connor

"You cannot hold back a good laugh any more than you can the tide. Both are forces of nature."

William Rotsler

"Imagination is more important than knowledge."

Albert Einstein

"Curiosity has its own reason for existing."

Albert Einstein

Introduction

This dictionary is thorough, but not complete. It contains many pairs, triples, etc of synonymous entries. Therefore a particular instinct, or a particular minimal unit of behavior, may appear several times in the list.

The entries are 1) a normal, ordinary instinct, 2) a normal variant of an instinct, 3) an abnormal instinct, 4) a certain aspect of an instinct, 5) a reflex ("little instinct"), 6) the learned/learning part of an instinct (but it's nevertheless an innately specified behavioral trait), 7) a group of instincts, 8) an unclassified genetic minimal unit of behavior, or 9) a non-instinctual innate element of behavior.

The list of normal and abnormal natural behavior is long, but it is important to note that just about all human activity can be explained by the five primal instincts 1) the reproduction instinct, 2) the self-preservation instinct, 3) the territorial instinct, 4) the social-hierarchy instinct, and 5) the ritual instinct.

Even though we clock up more unique experiences as we age, evidence amassed over the past seventy-five years suggests that the "genetic contribution" to mental achievement and emotional characteristics increases with age!!! Example: The (broad) heritability coefficient of IQ is about 0.4 (= 40 %) when measured in children, about 0.6 (= 60%) in adolescents, and about 0.8 (= 80%) in later maturity. More learning causes *more* genetic determinism!?

Even reflexes can learn, so, of course, all instincts are learning instincts (= instincts can learn). Moreover, instincts are situational. Can we quantify how well a particular instinct can learn? Yes. This problem was solved by Mitch Bronston. His solution is to use the (broad) heritability coefficient, but let the "environmental" part of the coefficient (= of the variance) quantify how well an instinct can learn. The *Bronston heritability coefficient* directly explains the paradoxes above. It tells us that a behavioral trait's genetically determined specific learning ability/capacity is *decreasing* with age. But, fortunately, this coefficient also tells us that the other parts of the total ability/capacity of a behavioral trait are *increasing*, so that the total ability/capacity is pretty *constant* with age.

Even if environmentalism was only *partly* correct, the Bronston coefficient had to *decrease* with age. Clearly, the *increasing* Bronston coefficient for human behavioral traits *proves* that *human behavior is instinctive*, and is *not* created by the chaotic and poverty-stricken environmental factors. But remember: 1) all instincts are learning instincts, and 2) all instincts are situational. Obviously, human intelligence(s) and intellect(s) depend on our having *more* instincts, not fewer.

A

a, the-a-speech-sounds instinct (The a speech sounds are the minimal units of instinctual speech sounds that correspond roughly to the letter a of the alphabet)

aback, you-are-taken-aback instinct (if you are taken aback, you are so surprised or shocked that you have to pause for a moment and cannot think or do anything)

abandon, to-abandon-oneself-to-an-emotion instinct

abandon, to-do-something-with-abandon instinct

abandoned, an-abandoned-way-of-behaving instinct

abase, to-abase-oneself instinct

abashed, to-be-abashed instinct

abhor, to-abhor-something instinct

abhorrence, abhorrence-of-evil instinct

abide, you-can't-abide-something instinct

abject, to-be-abject instinct (remember: instincts are situational)

ablaze, people's-eyes(-or-faces)-are-ablaze instinct

abnegation, abnegation instinct

abnormal, abnormal instincts (e.g. phobias, philias, manias, perversities, mental disorders)

above, to-be-above(-doing)-something instinct

above, to-be-above-someone (be in a position of emotional authority over them) instinct

abrasive, to-be-abrasive instinct

abreaction, abreaction instinct

abrupt, to-be-abrupt instinct

absent-minded, to-be-absent-minded instinct (or genetic, but non-instinctual, behavior?)

absent, to-be-absent (they are not paying attention to something because they are thinking about something else) instinct

absenteeism, absenteeism instinct (yes, genetic behavior!)

absorbed, absorbed-concentration instinct

absorbs, something-absorbs-someone (it interests them very much and takes up a lot of their time) instinct

abstracted, to-be-abstracted instinct

abstract, abstract-intelligence instinct

abstract, abstract-problem-solving instinct

abstract, abstract-reasoning instinct

abstract, abstract-thinking instinct

abstraction, abstraction (forming abstract ideas and concepts) instinct

absurdity, a-feeling-of-absurdity instinct

abuse, abuse-of-someone (cruel and violent treatment of them) instinct

abusive, to-be-abusive (say or write rude, offensive, or unkind things) instinct

academic, to-be-academic (be interested in studying) instinct

acarophobia, acarophobia (fear of mites/small insects or animals) instincts

acceptance, acceptance instinct

acceptance, feeling-of-acceptance instinct

acclamation, acclamation instinct

accommodate, to-accommodate-someone instinct

acculturation, acculturation instinct

accusation, accusation instinct

accustomed, to-be-accustomed-to-something(-or-to-something-happening) instinct

acerbity, acerbity instinct

achieve, the-will-to-achieve instinct

achievement, need-for-achievement instinct

acquire, to-acquire-a-taste(-or-habit) instinct

acquisitive, to-be-acquisitive instinct

acrid, acrid-words-or-remarks instinct

acrophobia, acrophobia (dread of or in high places) instinct

act out, act-out-your-feelings-or-ideas instinct

acting, acting-on-the-spur-of-the-moment instinct

actions, to-fear-the-actions-of-strangers instinct

activity, activity instinct (general-activity instinct)

activity, the-level-of-activity instinct

actor/actress, actor/actress instinct

actualization, self-actualization instinct

acumen, acumen instinct

acumen, inferential-acumen instinct

adamant, to-be-adamant-about-something instinct

adaptability, adaptability-to-change instinct

addicted, to-be-addicted-to-something instinct

addled, to-be-addled (confused and unable to think properly) instinct (yes, genetic behavior!)

adhere, to-adhere-to-a-particular-opinion-or-belief instinct

admiration, admiration instinct

admiration, a-warm,-passionate-admiration-for-fine-deeds instinct

admiration, smiles-of-admiration instinct

admired, we-want-to-be-admired-by-others instinct
admonition, admonition instinct
adoration, adoration instinct
adoring, to-look-at-someone-in-a-loving-and-adoring-way instinct
adornment, adornment instinct
adornment, bodily-adornment instinct
adornment, the-adornment-of-females instinct
adulation, adulation (very great and uncritical admiration and praise) instinct (Hitler's Germany!)
adventure, to-enjoy-adventure instinct
adventure, to-seek-adventure instinct
advertisement, self-advertisement instinct
advertisement, sexual-advertisement instinct
advice, advice instinct
aesthetic, aesthetic-pleasure instinct
aesthetic, aesthetic-talking instinct
aesthetic, the-desire-for-aesthetic-expression instinct
affectation, affectation instinct
affection, affection-and-sense-of-mercy-towards-others instinct
affection, a-need-for-affection instinct
    affection, seeking-affection instinct
affectionate, to-be-affectionate instinct
affective, affective-fixation instinct
affiliation, the-need-for-affiliation instinct
aflame, someone's-face-is-aflame instinct
afraid, to-be-afraid instinct
after, after-dinner-nap instinct
afterthought, afterthought instinct
against, to-be-against-someone instinct
against, to-do-something-against-someone-or-something instinct
agape, to-be-agape (your mouth is open, because you are very surprised

by something) instinct

aggression, aggression-between-rival-females instinct

aggression, aggression-between-rival-males instinct

aggression, aggression-induced-by-a-desire-to-control-others instinct

aggression, aggression-induced-by-a-desire-to-push-forward-one's-own-ideas-or-interests instinct

aggression, anger-induced-aggression instinct

aggression, counter-attack-aggression instinct

aggression, displaced-aggression instinct

aggression, fear-induced-aggression instinct

aggression, frustration-induced-aggression instinct

aggression, hostile-aggression (where the sole aim is to harm another) instinct

aggression, impulsive-aggression instinct

aggression, instrumental-aggression instinct

aggression, interfemale-aggression instinct

aggression, intermale-aggression instinct

aggression, irritable-aggression instinct

aggression, moralistic-and-disciplinary-aggression instinct

aggression, parental-aggression (protects the young) instinct

aggression, people-who-are-frustrated-react-with-anger-and-aggression instinct

aggression, predatory-aggression instinct

aggression, sadistic-aggression instinct

aggression, sexual-aggression instinct

aggression, stress-induced-aggression instinct

aggression, territorial-aggression instinct

aggression, the-baby's-aggression instinct

aggression, verbal-aggression instinct

aggression, violent-aggression instinct

aggression, wanton-aggression instinct

aggression, weaning-aggression instinct

aggressive, aggressive-intention-movements instinct

aggressive, aggressive-redirection-activity (e.g. a wife smashes a vase to the floor) instinct

aggressive, aggressive-responses-to-members-of-rival-groups instinct

aggressive, aggressive-sweating instinct

aggressive, scaling-of-responses-in-aggressive-interactions instinct

aggressiveness, aggressiveness instinct

aggrieved, to-be-aggrieved instinct

aghast, to-be-aghast (filled with horror and surprise) instinct

agitated, to-be-agitated instinct

agitation, agitation instinct

agnosticism, agnosticism instinct

agog, to-be-agog instinct

agonize, to-agonize-over-something instinct

agonized, the-agonized-grimace instinct

agonized, to-be-agonized (showing by what you say or do that you are in great pain, either physically or mentally) instinct

agony, to-scream-in-agony instinct

agony, you-are-in-agony (or in agonies) instinct

agony, you-are-piling-on-the-agony instinct

agoraphobia, agoraphobia (dread-in,-and-of,-open-spaces) instinct

agreeableness, agreeableness instinct

a-ha, a-ha-experience instinct

aha, 'Aha!'-response-involving-an-up-and-back-tilt-of-the-head instinct

aichmophobia, aichmophobia (fear of pointed instruments) instinct

ailurophobia, ailurophobia (fear of cats) instinct

aim, the-human-urge-to-aim-at-something instinct (there are more aiming sports today than all other forms of sport together)

airs, someone's-airs-and-graces instinct (they behave in a way that shows that they think that they are more important than other people)

alacrity, alacrity instinct

alarm, an-alarm-cry(or scream)-in-moments-of-fleeing-or-panic instinct

alarmed, to-become-alarmed-or-frightened instinct

alert, the-sound-of-rustling-leaves-is-enough-to-alert-us-when-we-are-walking-in-the-woods instinct

alertness, alertness instinct

algophobia, algophobia (abnormal fear of pain) instinct

alienation, alienation (a-feeling-of-strangeness-or-separation-from-others) instinct

alignment, alignment instinct

allegiance, allegiance instinct

alliances, making-alliances instinct

aloneness, feeling-of-aloneness instinct

aloud, fear-of-speaking-aloud instinct

altruism, heightened-altruism-toward-closest-kin instinct

altruism, reciprocal-altruism instinct

altruistic, altruistic-behavior-toward-non-relatives instinct

amathophobia, amathophobia (fear of dust) instinct

amaxophobia, amaxophobia (fear of riding in a vehicle) instinct

amazement, amazement instinct

ambiguity, tolerance-of-ambiguity instinct

ambition, ambition instinct

ambition, competitive-ambition instinct

ambivalence, ambivalence instinct

amble, to-amble (walk slowly and in a relaxed manner) instinct

amiability, amiability (being friendly and pleasant) instinct

amok, amok (an acute, murderous frenzy) instinct (to-run-amok instinct)

amorous, amorous-feelings-and-behavior instinct

amuse, infants-amuse-themselves-and-their-families instinct

amuse, to-amuse-oneself-and-others instinct

amusement, amusement instinct (to-be-amused-by-something instinct)

anal, anal-eroticism instinct

analogical, analogical-reasoning instinct

analyze, to-analyze-something instinct

anathematization, anathematization instinct

androphobia, androphobia (fear of man (the species)/the male sex) instincts

anemophobia, anemophobia (fear of wind/air) instincts

anger, feelings-of-anger instinct

anger, gestures-of-anger instincts

anginophobia, anginophobia (fear of suffocation or being suffocated/fear of an attack of angina) instincts

angry, angry-crying instinct

angry, angry-outbursts instinct

angry, the-angry-face instinct

angry, to-be-angry-that-you-cannot-make-others-as-you-wish-them-to-be instinct

anguish, anguish instinct

animal, the-interest-in-the-animal-world instinct

animated, to-be-animated (lively and interesting) instinct

animosity, animosity (a feeling of strong dislike and anger) instinct

annoyance, annoyance instinct

answering, answering instinct

antagonism, antagonism (hatred or hostility) instinct

anthrophobia, anthrophobia (fear of man (singly)/society) instincts

anti, anti-contact-behavior instinct

anti, anti-stare instincts (covering the eyes with the hands, burying the face in the crook of the elbow, closing the eyes, etc)

anticipation, nervous-anticipation instinct

anticipation, the-feeling-of-anticipation instinct

antipathy, antipathy instinct

anxiety, anxiety-at-the-presence-of-strangers instinct

anxiety, the-feeling-of-anxiety instinct

anxiousness, anxiousness instinct

aphephobia, aphephobia (fear of being touched by another person) instinct

apiphobia, apiphobia (fear of bees) instinct

apologetically, apologetically-hug-and-kiss-the-child instinct

apology, to-make-an-apology instinct

appeased, to-be-appeased-by-submissive-gestures instinct

appeasement, a-sensation-of-appeasement instinct

appeasement, appeasement instinct (e.g. to appease the mountain)

appeasement, appeasement-signals instincts

appetite, appetite instinct

appetite, the-general-appetite-for-life instinct

applaud, to-applaud-someone-after-a-good-performance instinct (applause instinct)

apply, apply-your-mind-or-attention-to-something instinct

appreciation, appreciation instinct

apprehension, apprehension-span instinct

apprehensions, apprehensions (feelings of worry or fear about the future) instinct

approaches, to-play-with-novel-approaches instinct

approval, moral-approval instinct

approval, the-feelings-of-approval-and-disapproval instinct

approving, approving-gesture-or-expression instinct

aquaphobia, aquaphobia (fear of water/swimming) instincts

arachneophobia, arachneophobia (fear of spiders) instinct

arbitration, arbitration instinct

arch look, arch-look-or-expression (is mischievous or cunning) instinct

ardent, ardent-about-something instinct

argue, to-argue(-fiercely) instinct
arguments, to-like-to-pick-arguments instinct
arithmetic, arithmetic instinct
aroma, aroma instinct
arousal, arousal (the state of being alert or excited) instinct
arousal, emotional-arousal instincts
arousal, sexual-arousal instinct
arrogance, arrogance instinct
arrogate, you-arrogate-something instinct
art, art instinct
artistic, artistic-creation instinct
ascendance, ascendance instinct
asceticism, asceticism instinct
ashamed, to-feel-ashamed instinct
ashen, to-be-ashen instinct (someone who is ashen looks very pale because they are afraid or shocked)
ask, to-ask-someone-something instinct
asleep, falling-asleep instinct
asperity, asperity instinct (asperity is impatience and sternness that you express in your tone of voice)
aspiration, aspiration instinct
aspiration, the-thrill-of-aspiration instinct
assault, assault instinct
assault, assault-on-someone's-beliefs-or-attitudes instinct (also often an attempt to change them!)
assertion, assertion instinct
assertion, self-assertion instinct
assertive, to-be-assertive instinct
assertiveness, assertiveness instinct
assimilate, assimilate-new-ideas instinct
association, association instinct
association, free-association instinct

associative, associative inhibition instinct

assumption, to-make-an-assumption instinct

assurance, assurance (a feeling of confidence and lack of doubt) instinct

assurance, self-assurance instinct

astonishment, astonishment instinct

astound, something-or-someone-astounds-you instinct

astraphobia, astraphobia (fear of lightning/thunderstorms) instincts

astringent, astringent-behavior (behavior in which you criticize someone or something severely) instinct

at ease, feeling-at-ease-with-someone instinct

at ease, feeling-not-at-ease-with-someone instinct

at-homeness, 'at-homeness' instinct

atheism, atheism instinct

athletic, an-interest-in-athletic-skills instinct

atonement, atonement instinct

atonement, a-gesture-of-atonement instinct

attachment, attachment-bond (e.g. between an infant and its mother) instincts

attack, attack-someone (use violence against them) instinct

attack, personal-attack instinct

attack, physical-attack instinct

attack, political-attack instinct

attack, verbal-attack instinct

attacker, the-attacker-suddenly-explodes-with-a-rapid-series-of-blows-and-kicks instinct

attention, attention instincts

attention, attention-getting-feat instinct

attention, attention-seeking instinct

attention, attention-span instinct

attention, selective-attention instinct

attention, something-catches-your-attention instinct

attention, to-focus-your-attention instinct

attention, to-summon-parental-attention instinct

attentiveness, attentiveness instinct

attraction, attraction (feeling of liking someone very much) instinct

attractive, dominance-in-a-man-is-considered-attractive-by-women instinct

attractive, tall-men-are-considered-more-attractive-by-women-than-short-men instinct

attractive, to-make-oneself-seem-attractive instinct

attractive, poise,-self-assurance,-optimism,-efficiency,-perseverence,-courage,-decisiveness,-intelligence,-and-ambition-are-things-women-find-attractive-in-a-man instinct

audacious, audacious-behavior instinct

audacity, audacity instinct

audition, audition instinct (audition=the sense of hearing)

auditory, auditory-imagery instinct

auditory, auditory-localization instinct

aunt, aunt-behavior instinct

authoritarian, to-be-authoritarian instinct (authoritarianism instinct)

authority, the-readiness-to-abandon-private-judgement-for-some-external-authority instinct

autoeroticism, autoeroticism instinct

autohypnosis, autohypnosis instinct

automatized, automatized-behavior (e.g. cardriving) instinct

autophobia, autophobia (fear of oneself/being alone) instincts

avenge, avenge-a-wrong-or-harmful-act instinct

avenging, avenging instinct

aversion, aversion instincts

aversive, any-aversive-event-may-trigger-off-violence instincts

avert, to-avert-one's-eyes-or-gaze-from-someone-or-something instinct aviophobia, aviophobia (fear of flying) instinct

avoidance, avoidance instincts

avoiding, avoiding-pain instinct

avowed, you-are-an-avowed-believer-in-something instinct

awareness, a-conscious-perceptual-awareness-of-the-thing-that-is-important-right-then-and-an-unawareness-of-things-that-are-not-important instinct

awareness, awareness-of-other-people's-feelings instinct

awareness, conscious-awareness instinct

awareness, unconscious-awareness instinct

awareness, unconscious-awareness skills instincts

awareness, visual-awareness instinct

awe, awe instinct

awkwardness, feelings-of-awkwardness instinct (instincts are situational!)

B

b, the-b-speech-sounds instinct (The b speech sounds are the minimal units of instinctual speech sounds that correspond roughly to the letter b of the alphabet)

babble, idle-babble instinct

babble, to-babble instinct

babies, babies-babble instinct

babies, male-babies-like-male-babies-better-than-female-babies,-but-female-babies-do-not-show-any-preference-for-either-sex instincts

baby, the-baby-can-swim instinct

babyface, the-babyface-signal-release-protective-feelings instinct

baby's, baby's-general-smile instinct

baby's, baby's-parental-recognition-gurgle instinct

baby's, baby's-reflex-smile instinct

baby's, baby's-specific-smile instinct

baby's-sucking instinct

baby's-weeping instinct

baby talk, baby-talk instinct (the baby talk that adults use with infants may help them learn to speak)

bacillophobia, bacillophobia (fear of bacilli (germs)) instinct

back-away,   to-back-away-from-someone-or-something   (walk slowly backwards and away from them because you are frightened or nervous) instinct

backbiting, backbiting instinct

backs, backs-to-the-wall instinct (no one ever voluntarily selects a center table in an open space)

      bad-tasting, bad-tasting-food instincts

      bad-tempered, to-be-bad-tempered instinct

      badger, to-badger-someone instinct

bafflement, bafflement instinct

bah,   to-say-'bah'-in-order-to-express-scorn,-disappointment,-or-irritation instinct

balance, balance instinct

balky, the-balky-age instinct

ballistophobia, ballistophobia (fear of thrown objects/missiles) instinct

bandinage, bandinage instinct

banging, banging-things instinct (both chimps and children like banging things)

banter, banter (teasing or joking talk that is amusing and friendly) instinct

barbarism, barbarism instinct

bare, people-bare-their-teeth-when-enraged instinct

baresthesia (the sense of pressure and weight), the-emotional-aspects-of-baresthesia instinct

barracking, barracking instinct

barrage, a-barrage-of-questions,-complaints,-criticisms,-etc instinct bashfulness, bashfulness instinct

basiphobia, basiphobia (fear of walking/standing erect and walking) instincts

bated breath, to-wait-for-something-with-bated-breath instinct

bathing, bathing instinct

bathophobia, bathophobia (dread of depths) instinct

bathyesthesia, bathyesthesia (deep sensitivity), the-emotional-aspects-of-bathyesthesia instinct

baton signals, baton-signals instinct

batter, to-batter-someone instinct

battle, battle-cry instinct

battle, the-cheer-excitement-of-battle instinct

bawl, to-bawl instinct

beaming, a-beaming-smile instinct

bear, bear-hug instinct

beasts of prey, to-fear-beasts-of-prey instinct

beat, 'It-beats-me' instinct

beat time, the-speaker-beat-time-to-his-words-with-small-head-jerks-or-hand-movements instinct

beat time, to-beat-time-to-a-piece-of-music instinct

beat up, to-beat-up-someone instinct

beautiful, beautiful-women-smell-nice instinct

beauty, appreciation-of-beauty instinct

beauty, universal-aspects-of-beauty instincts

beckoning, beckoning instinct

bedroom, make-bedroom-eyes-at-someone instinct

begging, begging instinct (apes and dogs beg!)

begging, begging-or-pleading-gesture:-palms-turned-upwards instinct

begging, the-begging-or-imploring-posture instinct

begrudge, to-begrudge-someone-something instinct

beholden, to-be-beholden-to-someone instinct

belief, belief (a feeling of certainty that something exists or is good) instinct

belief, belief-perseverance instinct

belittle, to-belittle-someone-or-something instinct

belligerence, belligerence instinct

bellowing, bellowing instinct

belly, belly-laugh instinct

belonephobia, belonephobia (fear of sharp, pointed objects) instinct

belongingness, the-need-for-belongingness-and-love instinct

bemoaning, bemoaning instinct

benevolence, benevolence instinct

berating, berating instinct

bereavement, bereavement instinct

berserk, to-go-berserk instinct

beseeching, beseeching instinct

beside yourself, to-be-beside-yourself-with-a-particular-feeling-or-emotion instinct

besmirching, besmirching instinct

besotted, to-be-besotted-with-someone-or-something instinct

bestiality, bestiality instinct

betrayal, fear-of-betrayal instinct

bewail, to-bewail-something instinct

bewilderment, bewilderment instinct

bewitched, to-be-bewitched instinct

bias, bias instinct

bibliophobia, bibliophobia (fear of books/irrational hatred of books) instincts

bickering, bickering instinct

big-hearted, to-be-big-hearted instinct

bigotry, bigotry instinct

biofeedback, biofeedback instincts

biological, biological-clocks instincts
biological, biological-intuition instinct
biological, biological-rhythms instincts
biophilia, biophilia instinct (the secure biophilic pleasure from the nearness of animals and growing plants)
birds, "birds of a feather flock together" instinct
birds of prey, children-fear-birds-of-prey instinct
birth, birth-cry instinct
bisexuality, bisexuality instincts
bitching, bitching instinct
biting, biting instinct (there is perhaps a slight sex difference here)
bitterness, bitterness instinct
black-despair, to-feel-black-despair instinct
black humor, black-humor instinct
black mood, to-be-in-a-black-mood instinct
blame, blame-avoidance-need instinct
blame, to-blame instinct
blame, to-blame-oneself instinct
blame, to-try-to-avoid-blame instinct
blank, your-mind-goes-blank instinct
blase´, to-be-blase´ instinct
blind obedience, blind-obedience instinct
bliss, bliss instinct
bliss, love-bliss instinct
bloated, to-be-bloated-after-eating-a-meal instinct
bloating gorges, bloating-gorges instinct
blood, blood-and-injection-phobia instinct
blood, dread-of-the-sight-of-blood instinct
blood lust, blood-lust instinct
bloodthirsty, to-be-bloodthirsty instinct
blow, the-overarm-blow instinct
blow, to-blow-your-nose instinct

blows, to-come-to-blows instinct
blue, to-feel-blue instinct
bluffing, bluffing instinct
blunt, being-blunt instinct
blurt, to-blurt-out-something instinct
blush, blush instinct
bluster, bluster instinct
boast, boast instinct
bodily activity, bodily-activity instincts
body, the-brain-places-its-body instinct
body adornment, body-adornment instinct
body contact, body-contact (skin-contact) instinct
body contact, body-contact-tie-signs instincts (e.g. a hand on the shoulder is experienced as a sign of friendship, touching the adult head is experienced as condescending or sexual, touching the elbow emphasizes something)
body fragrance, after-only-forty-five-hours-the-newborn-can-tell-its-own-mother-from-other-mothers-purely-by-her-body-fragrance instinct
body language, body-language instincts
body privacy, body-privacy-and-contact-taboo instincts
body sag, body-sag-as-defeat-signal instinct
body senses, body-senses instincts
body shape, the-perception-of-desirable-body-shape instinct
body stress reactions, body-stress-reactions instincts
body stroking, body-stroking-and-caressing instincts
boldly, looking-boldly-head-on-at-someone instinct
boldness, boldness instinct
bonhomie, bonhomie instinct
boo, to-boo-someone instinct
boohoo, to-boohoo instinct
boost, to-boost-someone-or-something instinct
bored, to-be-bored instinct

boredom, reactions-to-boredom instincts

boredom, repetition-begets-boredom instinct

bosom, to-take-someone-to-your-bosom instinct

bossiness, bossiness instinct

bottle up, bottle up, to-bottle-up-a-strong-emotion-that-you-feel instinct

bound, to-feel-bound-to-do-something instinct

bow down, to-bow-very-low-in-order-to-show-great-respect instinct

box, to-box-a-child's-ears instinct

boy or girl, children-have-a-stable-concept-of-what-it-means-to-be-a-boy-or-girl instinct

brace, to-brace-oneself instinct

brachiating, brachiating instinct

bragging, bragging instinct

brain, to-have-something-on-the-brain instinnct

brainstorm, brainstorm (a sudden insightful idea, usually accompanied by a compelling emotional reaction) instinct

bravado, bravado instinct

brave, to-be-brave instinct

bravely, to-fight-bravely instint

bravery, bravery instinct

bravery, bravery-on-the-field-of-battle instinct

bravura, bravura instinct

brawl, brawl instinct

breath, holding-my-breath,-not-daring-to-move instinct

breath, something-takes-your-breath-away instinct

breathless, breathless-suspense instinct

bridle, to-bridle instinct

brilliant, a-brilliant-smile instinct

brisk, to-be-brisk instinct

broadly, to-smile-broadly instinct

brontophobia, brontophobia (fear of thunder) instinct

brood, to-brood-about-something instinct

broody, to-get-broody-when-you-see-small-babies instinct

brow, sweating-brow instinct

brows, to-knit-one's-brows instinct

brush by, to-brush-by-someone instinct

brush off, to-brush-someone-off instinct

brusqueness, brusqueness instinct

brutality, brutality instinct

bubbling, bubbling-over-with-joy,-happiness,-etc instincts

bubbling, bubbling-with-a-good-feeling instinct

buffeted, you-are-buffeted-by-something instinct

buffoonery, buffoonery-makes-you-laugh instinct

bullied,   people-who-look-confident-are-less-likely-to-be-bul-lied instinct

bullies, most-kids-fear-and-dislike-aggressive-bullies instinct

bullying, to-enjoy-bullying instinct (an individual may enjoy bul-lying, but think poorly of himself for acting in this way)

buoyancy, buoyancy instinct

burn, something-burns (it gives you a painful hot feeling) instinct

burning, burning-face-or-cheeks instinct

burning, to-be-burning-to-do-something instinct

burst in, to-burst-in-on-someone instinct

burst into, to-burst-into-laughter instinct

burst into, to-burst-into-tears instinct

burst out, to-burst-out-crying instinct

bury, to-bury-a-particular-feeling-of-something instinct

bury, to-bury-a-particular-memory-of-something instinct

bury, to-bury-your-face-in-your-hands instinct

bust-up, bust-up (serious quarrel which ends a relationship) instinct

busy, to-busy-yourself-with-something instinct

butchery, butchery instinct (the cruel killing of a lot of people/great apes)

butterflies, to-have-butterflies-in-one's-stomach instinct

bystander, bystander-effect instinct

C

c, the-c-speech-sounds instinct (The c speech sounds are the minimal units of instinctual speech sounds that correspond roughly to the letter c of the alphabet)

cackle, to-cackle (laugh in a loud unpleasant way) instinct

cainotophobia, cainotophobia (fear of novelty/new things/new ideas) instincts (also called cenotophobia)

call, to-call-someone-names (to insult someone by using offensive words) instinct

callousness, callousness instinct

calm, a-feeling-of-calm instinct

calm, a-sense-of-calm instinct

calm, you-calm-down intinct

camaraderie, camaraderie instinct

candidness, candidness instinct

candor, candor instinct

cannibalistic, cannibalistic-tendencies instinct (our closest relatives, chimpanzees, are not averse to eating their own, and research suggests cannibalism has a long history among humans)

canniness, canniness instinct

canny, a-canny-smile instinct

caper, caper (a light-hearted practical joke or trick) instinct

caper, to-caper instinct

caprice, caprice instinct

capriciousness, capriciousness instinct

captivate, someone-or-something-captivates-you instinct

cardiophobia, cardiophobia (fear of heart problems) instinct

care, care (a feeling of concern, anxiety, or worry about something) instinct

care, involvement-of-male-in-parental-care instinct

care, medical-care instinct

care, prolonged-maternal-care instinct

care, to-care-about-others instinct

carefulness, carefulness instinct

caressing, caressing instinct

careworn, to-look-careworn instinct

caring, caring (loving or affectionate behavior, or affectionate feelings) instinct

carnage, carnage instinct

carnal, carnal-desires/feelings instincts

carnival, carnival instinct

carsick, carsick instinct (yes, genetic behavior!)

castigation, castigation instinct

catcall, catcall instinct

catch, something-catches-your-attention instinct

catch, to-catch-oneself-doing-something instinct

categorization, categorization instinct

catharsis, catharsis (emotional release) instinct

catotrophobia, catotrophobia (fear of mirrors/breaking of a mirror) instincts

causality, innate-given-knowledge-of-causality instinct

cavil, to-cavil instinct (= cavilling instinct)

cavorting, cavorting instinct

celebrate, celebrate, to-celebrate-lavishly-and-joyfully instinct

celebration, celebration instinct

celebration, victory-celebration instinct

cenotophobia, cenotophobia (fear of novelty/new things/new ideas) instinct (also called cainotophobia) censure, censure (a strong disapproval and condemnation of something that has been done, or of the way it was done) instinct

censure, moral-censure instinct

ceremony, ceremony instinct

certainty, a-feeling-of-certainty instinct

certitude, certitude instinct

chagrin, chagrin instinct

challenge, to-like-a-challenge instinct (If skill is too little in relation to the task, people become anxious. But something easily achieved is boring. An experience where there is a balance between skill and the difficulty of a task evoked joy even if dangerous.)

chanting, chanting instinct

character, admiration-for-character instinct

charade, charade instinct

charismatic, charismatic-authority instinct

charity, charity-towards-strangers instinct

charm, charm instinct

charm, charm-offensive instinct

charm, to-charm-and-seduce-the-sex-object instinct

charming, finding-someone-to-be-charming instinct

charmingness, charmingness instinct

chary, to-be-chary instinct

chase, the-thrill-of-the-chase instinct

chasten, you-chasten-someone instinct

chastity, chastity instinct

chat, chat instinct

chatter, chatter instinct

chatter, feeling-the-need-to-keep-up-a-stream-of-cheerful-chatter instinct

chauvinism, chauvinism instinct

cheap, to-feel-cheap instinct

cheated, to-feel-cheated instinct

cheater, to-know-a-cheater-when-you-see-one instinct

cheating,　catching-people-who-are-cheating-on-a-social-bargain instinct

cheating, cheating instinct

cheating, our-cheating-hearts instinct

cheer, to-cheer instinct

cheerful, cheerful-mood instinct

cheerfulness, cheerfulness instinct

chemical-sense, sense instincts

cherish, you-cherish-something

cherophobia, cherophobia (fear of fun/gaiety) instincts

chest, men-thrust-out-their-chest instinct (gorillas pound their chest)

chewing, chewing instinct

child-parent fixation, child-parent-fixation instinct

children, to-place-his/her-children-above-all-else instinct

chilly, you-feel-chilly instinct

chirp, to-chirp instinct

chivalry, chivalry instinct

choice, choice instinct

choice, feelings-of-choice instinct

choke, something-chokes-you instinct

choke, to-choke-back-a-strong-emotion instinct

choleric, to-be-choleric-with-rage instinct

chortle, to-chortle instinct

chortle, to-chortle-to-oneself instinct

christen, to-christen-someone-or-something instinct

chromaesthesia, chromaesthesia (to perceive sounds as colors) instinct (colored-hearing instinct)

chuckle, to-chuckle instinct

chuckles, loud-play-chuckles instinct

chunking, chunking instinct (chunking is the organization process whereby distinct 'bits' of information are collected together perceptually and cognitively into larger, coordinated wholes, or 'chunks')

cicatrization, cicatrization instinct

circadian-rhythms, circadian-rhythms instincts

circumspection, circumspection instinct

civilian catastrophe reaction, civilian-catastrophe-reaction instinct

clairvoyance, clairvoyance instinct

clamor, clamor instinct

clapping, clapping-your-hands instinct

clarion, clarion-call instinct

clash, two-or-more-colors-clash instinct

clash, two-or-more-styles-clash instinct

classical, classical-conditioning instincts (Note: All instincts are learning instincts; "classical conditioning" is only a kind of instinctual learning. Example: Humans have many fear instincts; perhaps all instincts are fear instincts. The number of possible phobias is perhaps limited only by the number of normal instincts. Fear instincts cause fear; "classical fear conditioning" does not cause fear, as traditional psychology believes.)

classification, a-genius-for-verbal-classification instinct

classification, classification instinct

classify, the-urge-to-classify-the-elements-of-the-environment instinct

classify, to-classify-people-into-friends-and-aliens instinct

claustrophobia, claustrophobia (fear of closed spaces) instinct

clean, the-urge-to-keep-ourselves-clean instinct

clear, to-clear-one's-throat instinct

clench, to-clench-your-fist-because-you-are-angry instinct

clench, to-clench-your-teeth-because-you-are-angry instinct

climb, the-urge-to-climb-trees instinct

cling, infants-(often)-cling,- grasp,-grab,- and-do-whatever-else-they-can-to-stay-close- to-their-parents instinct cling, the-cling-and-feed-reaction-of-the-newborn instinct

clinging, clinging instinct (children is running to the parent and clinging)

clinging, clinging-response instinct (the baby's body movements are remains of the ancestral primate clinging response)

clique, clique instinct

clocks, biological-clocks instincts

closeness, closeness (intimacy, supportiveness, etc) instincts

closure, the-principle-of-closure instinct (= the-viewer-perceives-incomplete-figures-as-complete-wholes instinct)

clustering, clustering instinct

coaxing, coaxing-voice instinct

cocktail party phenomenon, cocktail-party-phenomenon instinct

coddle, to-coddle-our-friends instinct

coercion, coercion instinct

cogitating, cogitating instinct

cognition, cognition instincts

cognitive, cognitive-map instinct

cognitive, cognitive-reflex instincts (= reflexive-mental-process instincts, as opposed to reflective-mental-process instincts)

coin, to-pay-someone-back-in-their-own-coin instinct

cold shoulder, to-give-someone-the-cold-shoulder instinct (Psychologists have found that the cold shoulder (social ostracism) is much more common than anyone supposed. 75 per cent of respondents said that they had been ostracized by a loved one, while 68 per cent admitted ostracizing a close friend or relative. Men and women are equally likely to be both perpetrators and victims. Ostracism usually involves not talking and avoiding eye contact.)

cold stare, to-give-somebody-a-cold-stare instinct

cold sweat, the-cold-sweat-of-fear instinct

cold, to-feel-cold instinct

coldness, coldness instinct

coldness, coldness-in-one's-voice instinct

coldness, the-sensing-of-coldness instinct

collecting, collecting instinct

color, a-strong-preference-for-foods-with-colors-of-ripe-nuts,-fruits-and-roots instinct

color, color-experiences (colors, hue, saturation, luminance, etc) instincts

color, the-emotional-aspects-of-normal-color-vision instincts (e.g. color fascinates all of us)

colors, to-judge-blue-and-green-as-'cold'-colors instinct

colors, to-judge-red-and-yellow-as-'warm'-colors instinct

combat, combat instinct

combat, the-passions-aroused-by-combat instinct

combat fatigue, combat-fatigue instinct (gross-stress-reaction instinct)

combination tone, combination-tone instinct

come hither, 'come hither'-look instinct

comedy, comedy instinct

comfort, comfort instinct

comfort, to-comfort-someone instinct

comfortable, to-feel-comfortable instinct

comforting, comforting-movements (e.g. swaying rhythmically from side to side) instinct

comforting, comforting-vocalizations instinct

comic, comic instinct

commiseration, commiseration instinct

commitment, commitment instinct

committed, the-more-emotional-the-behavior,-the-more-committed-that-person-is-to-what-is-being-said instinct

common chemical sense, the-emotional-aspects-of-the-common-chemical-sense instincts

common sense, common-sense instincts

communicate, a-general-urge-to-communicate instinct

communicating, communicating-feelings-and-ideas instincts

comparing, comparing instinct

compass, magnetic-compass instinct

compassion, compassion instinct

compassion, compassion-elicits-reciprocal-compassion instinct

compensation, compensation instinct

competent, we-tend-to-be-attracted-to-competent-people instinct

competition, between-group-competition instinct

competition, competition instinct

competitive, competitive-ambition instinct

complacency, complacency instinct

complaining, complaining instinct

compliment, to-compliment-someone instinct

compunction, compunction instinct

computerphobia, computerphobia (fear of computers or using them) instincts (also called cyberphobia)

comradeship, comradeship instinct

concealment, concealment instinct

conceit, conceit instinct

concentrate, ability-to-concentrate-on-things instinct (children with ADHD cannot concentrate for more than a few seconds)

concentration, absorbed-concentration instinct

concentration, deep-concentration instinct

concept, concept-formation instincts

conception, conception instinct

concepts, basic-innate-concepts instincts (e.g. concepts like red, purple, large, small)

concern, concern instinct

concern, genuine-concern-for-others instinct

concerned, a-concerned-facial-expression instinct

concession, concession instinct (normal behavior needs to be explained!)

conciliation, conciliation instinct

concord, concord (harmonious relationship between tones sounding together) instincts

condemnation, condemnation instinct

condescending, to-be-condescending instinct

condescending, to-be-theatrically-condescending instinct

conditioned, conditioned-learning instinct

confabulate, confabulate instinct

confidence, confidence instinct

confined, confined spaces, dread-of-confined-spaces instinct

conflict (serious disagreement), the-emotional-aspects-of-a-conflict instinct

conflict, to-solve-conflict-by-aggression instinct

conform, humans-conform-to-their-culture instinct (conformity is decided by a desire and a desire is an instinct)

conformity, a-predisposition-to-conformity-and-consecration instinct

conformity, conformity instincts

confrontation, confrontation instinct

congratulation, congratulation instinct

conjure, to-conjure-something-up instinct

connectedness, desire-for-social-connectedness instinct

conquering, conquering instinct (instincts are situational!)

conscience, conscience instinct

conscientiousness, conscientiousness instinct

conscious, conscious-self-awareness instinct

consciousness, consciousness instincts (There is nothing we know about more directly than consciousness, but it is extraordinarily hard to reconcile it with everything else we know. However, all instincts have a conscious component) consciousness, divided-consciousness instincts (Example: driving and thinking about sex)

consciousness, focused-consciousness instinct (=directed-consciousness instinct)

consciousness, loosely-drifting-consciousness instinct (= flowing-consciousness instinct)

consciousness, normal-waking-consciousness instincts

consciousness, the-immediate-experience-that-consciousness-is-a-singular instinct

consecration, consecration instinct

consent, consent instinct (normal behavior needs to be explained!)

conservation, the-concept-of-conservation instinct

conservatism, conservatism instinct

considering, considering instinct (reflection instinct)

consolation, consolation instinct

consonance, consonance (harmonious blending or fusion of tones) instinct

constancy, the-principle-of-brightness-constancy instinct

constancy, the-principle-of-color-constancy instinct

constancy, the-principle-of-shape-constancy instinct

constancy, the-principle-of-size-constancy instinct

consternation, consternation instinct

contact comfort, contact-comfort instinct

contagion, behavioral-or-emotional-contagion instinct (e.g. one child may faint when dissecting in a biology lesson, promptly followed by numbers of others)

contemplation, contemplation instinct

contempt, to-have-contempt-for-someone-or-something instincts

contention, contention instinct

contentment, contentment instinct

contest, contest instinct

continuity, the-principle-of-continuity instinct (the viewer tends to perceive continuity in lines and patterns)

contra-suggestibility, contra-suggestibility instinct (a tendency (seemingly possessed by all children) to take a position counter to or opposite to one which has been suggested)

ontrol, desire-to-control-others instinct

control, keeping-self-control instinct

control, to-control-one's-impulses instinct

control, to-control-one's-own-feelings instinct

control, you-are-in-control:-palms-turned-downwards instinct

controlling, controlling-motor-activity instincts

convergent, convergent-thinking instinct

conversation, to-enjoy-conversation instinct

conversion, a-moment-of-religious-conversion instinct

conviction, firm-convictions-and-established-beliefs instinct

conviction, ideological-convictions instinct

cooing, cooing-voice instinct

cool, a-color-that-is-cool instinct

Coolidge effect, Coolidge-effect instinct (= following intercourse, males will have intercourse again with the same receptive female some time after the refractory period has elapsed)

cooperation, cooperation-based-on-reciprocity instinct

cooperativeness, cooperativeness instinct

coordination, eye-hand coordination

coprophobia, coprophobia (fear of feces/dirt/filth/contamination) instincts

copulation, copulation instincts (privacy is sought, kissing, licking, sucking, biting, soft nibbling, gentle nipping, lubrication, increasing pulse rate, increasing blood pressure, erection, penis insertion, sexual flush, gasping, moaning, grunting, fighting for air, climax: the face may be contorted, with mouth wide open and nostrils expanded, ejaculation, exhaustion, relaxation, rest, sleep)

coquetry, coquetry instinct
cosiness, cosiness instinct
count, we-all-want-to-count-for-something instinct
counter, counter-attack instinct
counter, counter-threat instinct
counteraction, counteraction-need instinct
counterphobic, counterphobic-character instinct
courage, courage instincts
courage, mental-courage instincts
courage, physical-courage instincts
courtesy, courtesy instinct
courtliness, courtliness instinct
courtship, courtship-and-pre-copulatory-sequence instincts (a distinctive vocalization tone, murmuring sweet nothings, hand-to-hand, arm-to-arm, mouth-to-face, mouth-to-mouth, embracing, running, chasing, jumping, dancing, juvenile play patterns, courtship feeding ...)
covetousness, covetousness instinct
cowardice, cowardice instinct (may sometimes be a survival instinct!)
cowed, to-be-cowed instinct
cowering, cowering instinct
coyness, coyness instinct
cradle, mothers-cradle-their-infants-in-their-left-arm,-next-to-their-hearts instinct (left-handed mothers behave in the same way)
craft, craft instinct
crawling-walking, , crawling-walking instincts
creasing, creasing-the-forehead-when-you-are-puzzled instinct
creation, artistic-creation instincts
creation, creation instincts
creative, to-be-happy-about-creative-activity instinct
creativeness, creativeness instincts

creativity, creativity instincts (It is possible to be highly creative without being highly intelligent, and vice versa)

credulity, credulity instinct ("Credulity is the man's weakness, but the child's strength" Charles Lamb.)

creed, creed instincts

creep, to-creep instinct (people and animals creep)

cringe, to-cringe instinct

critical, critical-thinking instinct

criticism, criticism instinct

criticism, indignant-criticism instinct

criticism, the-need-to-defend-oneself-from-criticism instinct

criticize, to-criticize-heartlessness instinct

criticize, to-criticize-someone-or-something instinct

criticizing, the-pleasure-of-criticizing instinct

crooked, the-one-sided-crooked-smile instinct

crouch, to-crouch-down-because-you-are-frightened-or-are-hiding-from-someone instinct

crouching, the-basic-submissive-response-of-crouching-and-screaming instinct

crow, to-crow-about-or-over-something instinct

crowd, to-crowd-someone instinct

crowded, to-feel-crowded instinct

cruelty, cruelty instinct

crushed, to-be-crushed instinct

cry, a-frantic-cry instinct

cry, to-cry instinct (when you cry, you produce tears)

cry, to-cry-out instinct

cry, to-cry-with-laughter instinct

crying, baby's-crying instinct (newborn babies cry but they do not weep)

crying, crying-fearfully instinct

cuddle, a-baby-must-be-cuddled-a-lot instinct

cuddle, we-want-to-cuddle-an-infant instinct

cues, to-interpret-social-cues instincts

culture, the-capacity-for-culture instincts

cunnilingus, cunnilingus instinct

cup, to-cup-one's-ear-to-hear-better instinct

cupidity, cupidity instinct

curb, to-curb-someone instinct

curiosity, curiosity instinct

curiosity, to-show-curiosity-toward-strangers instinct

curse, to-curse-someone instinct

curse, to-curse-something instinct

cursed, to-be-cursed instinct

cursory, a-cursory-glance instinct

curved, the-sight-of-a-slender-curved-shape-lying-flat-on-the-path-ahead-of-us-is-sufficient-to-elicit-defensive-fear-responses instinct

cussedness, cussedness instinct

custom, attachment-to-custom-and-tradition instinct

customary, customary-behavior instinct

cut off, cut-off instincts (e.g. 'nervous breakdown', eye-screening at moments of deep concentration, he/she shuts his/her eyes tightly as he/she searches his/her memory, looks away for unusually long periods, keeps glancing away and then back again rapidly, struggling to open and shut his/her eyes at the same time (the stuttering eye))

cutaneous senses, the-emotional-aspects-of-cutaneous-senses-for-contact,-pressure,-cold,-warmth,-and-pain instincts

cutting, a-cutting-remark instinct

cyberphobia, cyberphobia (fear of computers or using them) instincts (also called computerphobia)

cynically, to-smile-cynically instinct

cynicism, cynicism instinct

cynophobia, cynophobia (fear of dogs) instinct

cypridophobia, cypridophobia (fear of venereal disease/sexual activity in general) instincts

D

d, the-d-speech-sounds instinct (The d speech sounds are the minimal units of instinctual speech sounds that correspond roughly to the letter d of the alphabet)

damaged, damaged instincts (due to gene damage) SCIENCE DON'T RECOGNIZE THE GENETIC CATASTROPHE, WHY ???

damn, just-not-giving-a-damn-any-more instinct

dancing, dancing instinct

dancing, dancing-eyes instinct

dancing, dancing-mania instinct

dandyism, dandyism instinct

danger, avoiding-danger instinct

danger, refusing-to-recognize-a-real-danger instinct

danger, to-feel-danger instinct

daredevil, daredevil instinct

dark, dark-and-light-adaptation-of-the-eye instinct (note: seeing is behavior; reflexes are instincts, but instincts are not reflexes)

darkness, fear-of-darkness-or-of-night instinct

dastardly, a-dastardly-action instinct

dawdling, dawdling instinct

day-dreaming, day-dreaming instinct

dazzle, someone-or-something-dazzles-you instinct

death, death-feigning instinct (immobility instinct)

deceit, a-smile-of-deceit instinct

decency, decency instinct

decent, decent-feelings instinct

decentered, decentered-thinking instinct (thinking of more than one thing at a time) deception, calculated-deception instinct

deception, deception instinct

decision, decision-making-and-emotion-go-together instinct

decisions, to-make-calculated-decisions-about-something instinct

decisiveness, decisiveness instinct

declaim, to-declaim instinct

decoration, decoration instinct

decoration, we-are-quite-prone-to-leaping-to-conclusions-about-someone's status,-social-strata,-trustworthiness,-and-overall-character-from-body-decoration instinct

decorum, to-behave-with-decorum instinct

dedication, dedication instinct

deduction, deduction instinct

defamation, defamation instinct (=defaming instinct)

defeat, the-postures-of-defeat (the head is lowered etc.) instinct

defecation, private-defecation instinct

defend, the-need-to-defend-oneself instinct

defend, to-defend-someone-or-something instinct

defending, defending-his/her-own-individual-home-base instinct

defense, defense-mechanisms instincts (projection, denial, reaction formation, regression, rationalization, displacement, sublimation, repression, intellectualization)

defense, defense-reaction instinct

defense, group-defense-of-territory instinct

deference, deference-behavior instinct (to admire and defer to a leader or superior)

defiance, defiance instinct

deindividuation, deindividuation (what often occurs in mobs when individual choice is submerged in mob action) instinct

dejection, dejection instinct

delectation, delectation instinct

deliberation, deliberation instinct

delight, delight instinct

delighted, delighted-when-friends-and-acquaintances-enjoy-good-fortune instinct

delinquency, delinquency instinct

delinquency, juvenile-delinquency instinct

delusion, delusion instinct

demand, to-demand instinct

demean, to-demean-someone-or-something instinct

demophobia, demophobia (dread-of-crowds) instinct

denigrate, our-villingness-to-denigrate-any-group-that-exists-out-side-our-own instinct

denigration, denigration instinct

denunciation, denunciation instinct

depreciation, the-need-to-counteract-depreciation-of-self instinct

depressed, to-be-depressed instinct (= feeling-depressed instinct)

deprivation, a-sense-of-deprivation instinct

depth, depth-perception instinct (is accomplished by using a number of two-dimensional visual cues to create a perceptual distance)

depths, dread-of-depths instinct

derision, derision instinct

derogatory, a-derogatory-remark-or-comment instinct

deserves, "the agent deserves praise or blame" instinct

designs, preferred-visual-designs instinct

desire, you-desire-something instincts (see each individual desire)

desolation, desolation (a feeling of great unhappiness and despair) instinct

despair, despair instinct

desperation, desperation instinct

despondency, despondency instinct

detection, detection instincts

detection, detection-of-cheating instinct

detection, pattern-detection instincts

determination, determination instinct (to-be-determined instinct)
determination, self-determination instincts
deterrence, deterrence instinct
detest, you-detest-someone-or-something instincts
detraction, detraction instinct
devotion, devotion instinct
devotion, devotion-to-duty instinct
dexterity, dexterity instincts
dexterity, manual-dexterity instincts
diction, diction instinct
diet, the-urge-to-seek-a-varied-diet instinct
dietary, dietary-preference instinct
diffidence, diffidence instinct
dignify, to-dignify-someone-or-something instinct
dignity, the-sense-of-dignity instinct
digression, digression instinct (= to-digress instinct)
dilation, pupil-dilation/constriction-signals instincts
diligence, diligence instinct
direction, a-sense-of-direction instinct
dirt, dread-of-dirt instinct
dirty, dirty-jokes instinct
dirty, to-say-and-do-dirty-things instinct
disagreement, disagreement-cause-anger instinct
disappointment, disappointment instinct
disapproval, disapproval instincts
disapproval, moral-disapproval instinct
disaster, disaster-victims-revert-to-behavior-stemming-from-their-infancy instinct
discharge, discharge-of-affect (the diminishing of experienced affect by displaying and expressing it) instinct
discipline, discipline instincts
discomfiture, discomfiture instinct

discomfort, discomfort instinct
discomfort, to-adjust-to-discomfort instinct
discontent, discontent instinct
discourage, discourage instinct
discouraged, to-become-discouraged instinct
discourtesy, discourtesy instinct
discreet, discreet-behavior instinct
discrimination, discrimination instincts
discrimination, pattern-discrimination instincts
discussion, discussion instinct
disdain, to-feel-disdain-for-someone-or-something instinct
disease, dread-of-some-particular-disease instinct
diseases,   the-brain-and-immune-system-continuously-signal-
each-other-and-influence-how-well-we-resist-or-recover-from-infectious-
or-innflammatory-diseases instincts
disgrace, disgrace instinct
disgust, disgust-that-makes-you-spit-out-bad-tasting-food instinct
disgust, to-feel-disgust instinct
dishonesty, dishonesty instinct
dishonor, dishonor instinct
disillusionment, disillusionment instinct
disinclination, disinclination instinct
disingenuity, disingenuity instinct
disinhibition, disinhibition (seeking sensation through social
activities such as parties) instinct
disinterest, disinterest instinct
dislike, dislike instinct
disloyality, disloyality instinct
dismay, dismay instinct
disobedience, genuine-disobedience instinct (exists?)
disparagement, disparagement instinct

displacements-activities, , displacements-activities instincts (Displacement activities appear in almost any situation of stress and tension. Examples: (displacement) feeding, rubbing our chins, rubbing our hands together, licking our lips, scratching our heads, 'washing' our faces with our hands, biting our nails, stroking our ear-lobes, cleaning our ear-passages, rubbing our noses, picking our noses, blowing our noses, sniffing our noses, tugging at our beards or moustaches, fumbling, fiddling, fidgeting, sipping, nibbling, displacement-yawning, tidying, adjusting. Many animals also show displacement activities when in states of conflict)

displacement-sleeping, displacement-sleeping instinct (soldiers experienced an almost overwhelming desire to sleep at the moment they were ordered in to the attack; this is an instinct we share with certain species of birds)

display, sexual-display instinct

dispute, dispute instinct (instincts are situational!)

dispute, indignant-dispute instinct

dispute, voices-raised-in-dispute instinct

disputes, family-disputes instinct (instincts are situational!)

disquiet, disquiet instinct

dissatisfaction, dissatisfaction instinct

dissonance, dissonance (unpleasant effect of two tones sounded simultaneously, which do not blend or fuse) instinct

dissonance, the-reduction-of-cognitive-dissonance instinct

distance, keeping-your-distance (defending your personal space) instinct

distances, to-judge-distances instinct

distortion, systematic-distortion-of-memory-for-past-events-by-defensive-or-repressive-operations instincts

distracted, to-be-distracted instinct

distractibility, distractibility (capable of being distracted) instinct

distraught, distraught instinct

distress, distress instinct

distrust, distrust instinct

divergent, divergent-thinking instinct

diversity, to-enjoy-diversity instinct

divide, to-divide-the-world's-people-into-"us"-and-"them" instinct

divorce, divorce instinct (Helen Fisher has argued that divorce is an adaptation)

docility, docility instinct

dodge, to-dodge instinct

doggedness, doggedness instinct

doggo, to-lie-doggo instinct

dogmatism, dogmatism instinct

dominance, dominance-hierarchy instincts

dominant, males-are-dominant-over-females-in-human-hunter-gatherer-societies instincts

dominant, the-dominant-eye instinct

dominate, you-dominate-a-person-or-a-group-of-people instinct

doodle, to-doodle instinct

dormancy, dormancy instinct

doting, doting instinct

double standard, the-double-standard-of-in-group-morality-and-out-group-ferocity instinct

doubt, doubt instinct

dozing, dozing instinct

drawl, to-drawl instinct

dread, dread instinct

dream, dream instincts (the dream instincts are the ordinary instincts working during sleep!)

dream, to-held-on-to-the-dream-of-something instinct

dreamy, a-dreamy-expression-on-someone's-face instinct

drool, to-drool-over-someone-or-something instinct

drowse, to-drowse instinct

drowsiness, drowsiness instinct

dry mouth, the-dry-mouth-of-incipient-attack instinct

dubitation, dubitation instinct

dubitations, painful-dubitations instinct

dumbfounded, to-be-dumbfounded instinct

dumbstruck, to-be-dumbstruck instinct

duty, a-sense-of-duty instinct

duty, a-sense-of-duty-to-the-group instinct

dysmorphophobia, dysmorphophobia (fear of imagined defects in appearance) instinct

E

e, the-e-speech-sounds instinct (The e speech sounds are the minimal units of instinctual speech sounds that correspond roughly to the letter e of the alphabet)

ear lobe, ear-lobe-stimulation instinct (there are cases on record of both males and females actually reaching orgasm as a result of ear-lobe stimulation)

earnestness, earnestness instinct

ears, to-be-all-ears instinct

ease, to-feel-at-ease instinct

eating, eating instinct

ebullience, ebullience instinct

echo,   to-respond-with-feelings-of-warmth-towards-those-who-echo-our-postures-and-our-body-movements instinct

ecstasy, ecstasy instinct

ecstatic, an-ecstatic-facial-expression instinct

edgy, a-person-gets-edgy instinct

edification, edification instinct

educate, to-educate-someone instinct

effervescence, effervescence instinct

effort, an-investment-of-effort instinct

effrontery, effrontery instinct

egalitarianism, egalitarianism instinct

egocentricity, egocentricity instinct

egoism, egoism instinct (egotism instinct)

egomania, egomania instinct

eh, 'eh' instinct (you say 'eh' when you are asking someone to reply to you or to agree with you)

eidetic, eidetic-imagery instinct

ejaculation, ejaculation-urge instinct

elaboration, elaboration (the process of creating associations between a new memory and existing memories) instinct

elaboration, the-elaboration-of-an-idea instinct

elation, elation (intense joyful excitement) instinct

elegance, the-emotional-aspects-of-elegance instinct

emancipatory, emancipatory striving instinct

embarrassment, embarrassment instinct

embellishment, embellishment instinct

embrace, an-urge-to-smile-at,-touch,-caress,-embrace-and-care-for-the-baby instinct

embracing, embracing behavior instinct

embroider, you-embroider-something instinct

emotional, emotional-sweating (on the palms of the hands, the soles of the feet, the armpits and the forehead) instinct

emotionally charged, so-attuned-are-humans-to-emotionally-charged-events-that-we-eagerly-seek-them-out,-even-if-they-don't-directly-relate-to-us instinct

emotions in others, the-perception-of-emotions-in-others instinct

empathy, empathy instinct

emptiness, a-feeling-of-emptiness instinct

emulation, emulation instinct

enamoured, you-are-enamoured-of-a-person instinct

enamoured, you-are-enamoured-of-something instinct

enchantment, enchantment instinct

encouragement, encouragement instinct

encouragement, giving-cries-of-encouragement instinct

endearment, endearment instinct

endurance, endurance instincts

enervated, to-feel-enervated instinct

enissophobia, enissophobia (fear of criticism) instinct

enjoyment, a-sense-of-self-enjoyment instinct

enjoyment, enjoyment instinct

enjoyment, enjoyment-of-being-with-other-people instinct

enjoyment, enjoyment-of-excitement instinct (this is perhaps only an aspect of the excitement instinct)

enlarged, enlarged-pupils-are-appealing instinct

enmity, enmity instinct

ennui, ennui instinct

ennui, the-mood-of-ennui instinct

ensnare, you-ensnare-someone instinct

entertain, the-need-to-entertain-others instinct

entertainment, self-entertainment instinct

entertainment, to-enjoy-entertainment instinct

enthusiasm, enthusiasm instinct

enticement, enticement instinct

entrepreneurship, entrepreneurship instinct

envy, envy instinct

epistemophobia, epistemophobia (fear of knowledge) instinct

equilibrium sense, the-behavioral-aspects-of-the-equilibrium-sense instinct

erect, erect-posture instinct (postures are behavior)

erection, to-be-aroused-to-erection instinct

eremophobia, eremophobia (fear of solitude/being alone) instincts

ereuthrophobia, ereuthrophobia (fear of blushing) instinct

ergasiophobia, ergasiophobia (fear of work/responsibility) instincts (also called ergophobia)

ergophobia, ergophobia (fear of work/responsibility) instincts (also called ergasiophobia)

erotic arousal, erotic-arousal-pattern instincts

erotic love, erotic-love-play instincts

eroticism, eroticism (sexual excitement arising from areas other than the genitals) instincts

erotophobia, erotophobia (fear of sex) instinct

erythrophobia, erythrophobia (fear of red objects/blushing) instincts

esprit, esprit-de-corps instinct

esteem, esteem instinct

ethical, ethical instincts

ethical, ethical-code instinct

ethical, ethical-conflict instinct

ethnocentrism, ethnocentrism instinct

etiquette, etiquette instinct

euphoria, euphoria instinct (=a-sense-of-euphoria instinct)

euphoria, the-euphoria-of-sudden-love instinct

euphoric, a-euphoric-high instinct

even, to-get-even-with-someone instinct

evil, a-sense-of-the-idea-of-evil instinct

evil, evil-thoughts instinct

evil, to-be-evil instinct (someone who is evil takes pleasure in doing things that harm other people)

exaggerated, exaggerated-strutting-walk instinct

exalt, to-exalt-someone instinct

exaltation, exaltation instinct

exaltation, exaltation-from-discovery instinct

exaltation, religious-exaltation instinct

exasperation, exasperation instinct

excitability, general-excitability instinct

excitable, excitable-runs instinct

excite, the-need-to-excite-others instinct

excitement, excitement-seeking instinct

excitement, nervous-excitement instinct

excitement, the-sheer-excitement-of-vivid-experience instinct

exclamation, exclamation instinct

exclusion, the-automatic-exclusion-of-sexual-bonding-between-individuals-who-have-previously-formed-certain-other-kinds-of-relationship instinct

excuse, to-excuse-your-behavior instinct

exhaustion, a-feeling-of-exhaustion instinct

exhibitionism, exhibitionism instinct

exhilaration, exhilaration instinct

exhorting, exhorting instinct

existential, existential-anxiety instinct

expectancy, expectancy instinct

expectancy, tense-expectancy instinct

expectation, expectation instinct

expectations, to-live-up-to-the-expectations-of-those-around-us instinct

experience, seeking-novel-experiences-through-the-mind-and-senses instinct

expiation, expiation instinct

explanation, explanation instinct

expletive, expletive instinct (an expletive is a rude word or expression which you say loudly and suddenly when you are annoyed, excited, or in pain)

exploratory, exploratory-behavior instinct

exploratory, exploratory-talking instinct

explosions, emotional-explosions instinct

explosive, an-explosive-temper instinct

exposition, exposition-need (need to explain, demonstrate and lecture others) instinct

expostulation, expostulation instinct

expressiveness, expressiveness instinct

extinction, extinction (the process of unlearning) instincts (remember: all instincts are learning instincts)

extravagance, extravagance instinct

extraversion, extraversion/introversion instinct

extremism, extremism instinct

exuberance, exuberance instinct

exultation, exultation instinct

exultation, exultation-of-victory instinct

eye, eye-hand-coordination instinct

eye, eye-movements instincts

eye, something-catches-your-eye instinct

eyebrow flash, the-eyebrow-flash-used-as-part-of-a-friendly-greeting-or-a-flirtation instinct (The eyebrow flash is a rapid raising of the eyebrows lasting about 1/6 of a second. It is a universal sign of either greeting or flirtation.)

eyebrows, elevation-of-the-eyebrows instinct

eyebrows, people-raise-their-eyebrows-at the-center-of-their-forehead-to-duplicate-the-forlorn-look-of-grief-and-distress instinct

eyebrows, raising-eyebrows-in-surprise instinct

eyes, narrowing-the-eyes instinct

eyes, the-automatic-movement-of-the-eyes-to-keep-them-fixed-on-an-object-as-the-head-moves instinct

eyes, the-automatic-movement-of-the-head-to-better-orient-the-ears-to-a-sound instinct

eyes, the-eyes-cast-downwards-when-you-are-upset-or-shy-or-hiding-something instincts

eyes, to-be-all-eyes instinct

eyes, to-lower-one's-eyes instinct

eyes, to-make-eyes-at-someone instinct (you look at them in a way that indicates that you are attracted to them)

F

f, the-f-speech-sounds instinct (The f speech sounds are the minimal units of instinctual speech sounds that correspond roughly to the letter f of the alphabet)

    face, face-recognition instinct

    faces, to-make-faces-at-somebody instinct

    faces, to-remember-faces instinct

    facial, facial-expressions instincts (e.g. a happy face, an unhappy face, a sad face, a serious face, a brave face, a smiling face, a laughing face, a straight face, a shut face, a pulled face, a good face, a puzzled face ... a human has about seven thousand facial expressions)

    facial, 'facial vision' (echolocation) instinct

    facial, the-importance-of-facial-beauty instinct

    facial, to-interpret-facial-expressions instinct

    faction, faction (e.g. political faction) instinct

    faddishness, faddishness instinct

    faeces, dread-of-faeces instincts

    faint hearted, faint-hearted-behavior instinct

    fairness, fairness instinct (= a-sense-of-fairness instinct)

    fairness, judging-the-fairness-of-social-bargains-and-the-sincerity-of-social-offers instinct

    faith, faith (a strong religious belief) instinct

    faith, faith-in-someone-or-something instinct

    faithful, being-faithful-to-our-spouses instinct

    faithfulness, faithfulness instinct

    faithlessness, faithlessness instinct

    fake, a-fake-smile instinct

    fake, people-can-distinguish-a-fake-smile-from-a-real-one instinct fake, to-fake-a-feeling,-emotion,-or-reaction instinct

fall, someone-falls-to-their-knees instinct

fall, to-fall-in-love instinct

fall, to-fall-on-each-other-in-delight-and-tears instinct

fall, to-fall-out-of-love instinct

fall back, to-fall-back instinct (you move quickly away from someone because they have upset or frightened you)

falling asleep, falling-asleep instinct

falls on, someone-falls-on-you instinct (they hug you and embrace you because they are very happy or excited)

fame, a-passion-for-fame instinct

familiarity, familiarity-feeling instinct

families, the-predisposition-to-assemble-into-families instinct

family, family-territory instinct

family, family's-warmth (e.g. cohesion, expressiveness) instinct

famished, to-feel-famished instinct

fan, fan instinct

fan, to-fan-a-feeling instinct

fanaticism, fanaticism instinct

fanaticism, "youthful fanaticism" instinct

fancy, fancy (uncontrolled imagination) instinct

fantasies, sexual-fantasies instinct

fantasize, to-fantasize instinct

fantasize, to-fantasize-when-making-love instinct

fascination, fascination instinct

fashion, fashion instinct

fastidiousness, fastidiousness instinct

fatigue, a-feeling-of-fatigue instinct (feeling is behavior; fatigue is an inborn warning mechanism)

favor, to-do-somebody-a-favor instinct

favoritism, favoritism instinct

fear, ability-to-control-fear instinct

fear, fear instinct

fear, fear-of-failure instinct

fear, the-fear-face instinct

fear, the-infants-fear-of-being-separated-from-their-caregivers instinct

fear, the-infants'-fear-of-strangers instinct

fear, the-scream-of-fear instinct

fearfulness, fearfulness instinct

fearless, apparently-fearless-rage instinct

    fearlessness, fearlessness instinct

feasting, feasting instinct

febrile, febrile-behavior instinct

febriphobia, febriphobia (fear of fever/body dysfunction produced by a rise in body temperature) instincts

fed up, to-be-fed-up instinct

feed, people-gather-together-to-feed instinct

feeding, feeding-behavior instinct (eating instinct)

feeding, feeding-pace instinct

feel bad, to-feel-bad-about-something-that-has-happened instinct

feel bad, to-feel-bad-about-something-that-you-have-done instinct

feeling, feeling-impatient:-tapping-a-foot-on-the-ground instinct

feigning, death-feigning instinct (= immobility instinct)

felicity, felicity instinct

fellatio, fellatio instinct

fellow, fellow-feeling instinct

fellowship, a-feeling-of-fellowship instinct (= fellowship-feeling instinct)

fellowship, fellowship instinct

female beauty, men-desire-women-with-full-lips-and-small-chins instinct

feminine, feminine-coyness instinct

femininity, femininity instincts (all of the women's learning instincts are feminine, more or less)

ferment, ferment instinct
ferocity, ferocity instinct
fertile, to-be-attracted-to-fertile-females instinct
fervent, to-be-fervent-about-something instinct
fervor, fervor-for-something instinct
festivity, festivity instinct
fetishism, fetishism instinct
feud, blood-feuds instinct
feuding, factional-feuding instinct
feuding, feuding instinct
feverish, feverish-emotion instinct
fib, fib instinct
fickleness, fickleness instinct
fiction, the-exquisite-enjoyment-of-fiction instinct
fictionalization, fictionalization instinct
fiddle, to-fiddle-with-something (because you are nervous or bored) instinct
fidelity, fidelity instinct
fidget, to-fidget instinct
fight, intellectual-fight instinct
fight, stand-up-fight instinct
fight, to-fight-an-emotion-or-desire instinct (e.g. to fight the urge to cry)
fight, to-fight-back instinct
fighting, fighting instincts (e.g. using the hands to grasp and squeeze, using the legs to kick, using the body to ram, bump and push, arm-blows and wrestling holds, scratching, tearing of hair, biting, ungainly grappling on the ground, scuffling, killing)
fighting, male-fighting instinct
fighting, play-fighting instinct
fighting, you-are-fighting-with-yourself instinct (this is a special kind of instinct competition)

figure-background,   the-viewer's-figure-background-organization instinct

figure out, the-impulsive-desire-to-figure-everything-out instinct

filial, filial-devotion instinct

find fault, to-find-fault-with-something-or-someone instinct

finger, to-point-a-finger-at-someone instinct

fingers, separate-control-in-the-fingers instinct

firm, to-be-firm instinct

firmness, firmness instinct

first, your-first-reaction-to-something instinct

first sight, the-love-at-first-sight instinct

fist, shaking-a-fist-at-someone instinct

fistfights, the-fistfights instinct

fists,   to-shout-and-shake-our-fists-at-one-another-when-we-are-angry instinct

fixation, fixation (a strong attachment to an idea, theory, another person, etc.) instinct

fixation, the-eyes-maintain-fixation instinct

fixed, fixed-idea instinct (insistent-idea instinct)

flaming, flaming (a mild swear word) instinct

flash, to-flash-a-look-or-a-smile-at-someone instinct

flash, your-thoughts-flash-back-to-something instinct

flashbulb, flashbulb-memories instinct

flashpoint, emotional-flashpoint instinct

flat, to-say-something-in-a-flat-voice instinct

flattery, flattery instinct

flattery, to-be-warmed-by-flattery instinct

flaunting, flaunting-instinct

flaunting, flaunting-his/her-superiority instinct

flavor, sensing-a-flavor instinct (sensing is behavior)

flavor, the-emotional-aspects-of-flavor instinct

flee, ready-to-flee instinct

fleeing, fleeing instinct

flehman, flehman (a lip curl associated with sniffing) instinct

flicker, a-flicker-of-emotion-or-feeling instinct

flicking, the-rapid-flicking-action-of-the-hand-when-ridding-your-self-of-small-creatures-making-contact-with-your-skin instinct

flight, flight-from-reality instinct

flinching, flinching instinct

fling, to-fling-a-remark-at-someone instinct

flirtation, flirtation instinct

flirtatiousness, flirtatiousness instinct

flounce, to-flounce-somewhere instinct (you, usually a woman, walk quickly, with exaggerated movements, in a way which suggests that you are angry or upset)

fluctuations, fluctuations-of-attention instinct

flush, flush instinct

flutter, your-heart-or-stomach-flutters instinct

foaming, foaming-at-the-mouth (because you are very angry) instinct

focal, focal-attention instinct

focus, mental-focus instinct

focus, to-focus-your-attention instinct

foist, you-foist-something-on-someone instinct

follow, to-follow-something-with-your-eyes instinct

follower, to-be-a-follower instinct

fondle, to-fondle-someone-or-something instinct

fondness, fondness instinct

food, finding-food instinct

food, food-gathering instinct

food, food-preferences instinct

food, food-stare instinct (When food is brought to the table, it is met with a food-stare, especially at the moment when it is being placed on the diner's plate) food, getting-food instinct

food, our-perception-of-food-(also-)includes-sensations-from-the-surfaces-of-the-tongue-and-mouth:-touch-and-temperature instinct

food, the-regulation-of-food-intake instinct

food, the-sight-and-aroma-of-food-greatly-affect-our-perception-of-food instinct

food, the-sight-of-food-triggers-a-desire-to-eat instinct

food, the-smell-of-food-triggers-the-desire-to-eat instinct

food, to-get-a-craving-for-a-particular-kind-of-food instinct

food, to-offer-to-share-food instinct

footpath, footpath-routes instinct (When walking on grass you always follow a ready-made track, even if it is not quite direct. Sheep do the same.)

forbearance, forbearance instinct

forbidden, forbidden-fruit-is-sweet instinct

force, the-worship-of-force instinct

forced, a-forced-smile instinct

foreboding, foreboding instinct

foreplay, the-sexual-foreplay instinct

fore-pleasure, fore-pleasure-and-end-pleasure (associated with erotic activity) instinct

foresight, foresight instinct

forethought, forethought instinct

forgetting, forgetting instinct

forgetting, motivated-forgetting instinct

forgiveness, forgiveness instinct

forgiving, to-be-forgiving instinct

forlorn, forlorn-behavior instinct

forlorn, the-forlorn-look-of-grief-and-distress

form, ability-to-recognize-by-touch-the-form-of-solid-objects instinct

forming, forming-a-habit instinct

fortitude, fortitude instinct

forward, to-look-forward-to-something instinct
foul, foul-language instinct
fracas, fracas instinct
fractiousness, fractiousness instinct
fragrance, fragrance instinct
frankness, frankness instinct
frantic, a-frantic-cry instinct
frantic, to-be-frantic instinct
fraternal, fraternal-altruism instinct
fraternity, fraternity instinct
fraternization, fraternization instinct
frazzle, to-be-worn-to-a-frazzle instinct
frazzled, you-are-frazzled instinct
free, free-association instinct
free, the-feeling-of-free-will instinct
free, to-feel-free instinct
free, to-feel-free-in-making-choices instinct
freedom, the-sense-of-freedom instinct
freemasonry, freemasonry instinct
frenetic, frenetic-activity instinct
frenzy, frenzy (violent and disorganized emotional excitement) instinct
friendliness, friendliness instinct
friendly, the-friendly-face instinct
friends, to-partition-other-people-into-friends-and-aliens instinct
friendship, children's-friendship-groups (cliques) instinct
friendship, friendship instinct
fright, fright instinct
frightened, frightened-reaction-against-radical-innovation instinct
frivolity, frivolity instinct
frivolous, someone-is-frivolous instinct
frolic, to-frolic instinct

frostiness, frostiness instinct

frowning, frowning instinct

frozen, to-be-frozen-with-fear instinct (e.g. he heard someone coming and lay frozen)

frugality, frugality instinct

frustrated, people-who-are-frustrated-react-with-anger-and-aggression instinct

frustration, frustration instinct

full throated, full-throated-laugh instinct

full throated, full-throated-shout instinct

fun, fun instinct

fun, fun-laughing instinct

fun, fun-screaming instinct

fun, fun-smiling instinct

funny, to-have-a-funny-feeling instinct

furor, furor (a very angry or excited reaction) instinct

furtive, a-furtive-look-upon-someone's-face instinct

furtive, to-be-furtive instinct

fury, fury instinct

fuss, fuss instinct

futility, the-sense-of-futility instinct (= the-what-can-I-accomplish-anyway-feeling instinct)

G

g, the-g-speech-sounds instinct (The g speech sounds are the minimal units of instinctual speech sounds that correspond roughly to the letter g of the alphabet)

gaiety, gaiety instinct

gallant, to-be-gallant instinct

gallantry, gallantry instinct

gallop, to-gallop-downhill instinct

gamophobia, gamophobia (fear of marriage) instinct

gape, to-gape (to look at someone or something in surprise) instinct

gasp, to-gasp (to take a short quick breath of air in through one's mouth) instinct

gathering/hunting, women-gather,-men-hunt instincts (these genetic traits are limited to man among living primates)

gatophobia, gatophobia (fear of cats) instinct

gaze, a-concentrated-gaze instinct

gazing, gazing instinct

gender, gender-behaviors instinct

gender, gender-identity instinct

generalization, generalization instinct

generosity, generosity instinct

generosity, respect-for-generosity instinct

generosity, to-expect-reciprocal-generosity instinct

generosity, to-return-generosity instinct (reciprocal-generosity instinct)

genital, genital-eroticism instinct

genital, genital-sexual-pleasure instinct

gentle, to-be-gentle instinct

gentleman, be-gentleman/gentlewoman instinct

gentleness, gentleness instinct

geometrical, geometrical-illusions instincts

geometry, innately-given-knowledge-of-the-axioms-of-geometry instincts

gestalt, the-perception-of-gestalt instinct

gesticulations, gesticulations instinct

gesture, gesture-language instincts

get along, get-along-with-other-people instincts

get upset, get-upset instinct

geumaphobia, geumaphobia (fear of tastes) instinct

giddiness, giddiness instinct

gift, gift-giving instinct

gift, to-reciprocate-a-gift instinct

giggling, giggling instinct

gladness, gladness instinct

glamour, glamour instinct

glance, a-scrutinizing-glance instinct

glance, glance instinct

glare, glare (an angry, hard and unfriendly look or expression on someone's face) instinct

glare, to-glare-at-somebody instinct

glee, glee instinct

glee, to-laugh-with-glee instinct

gleeful, gleeful-bashing instinct

glimmering, a-glimmering-of-an-idea-or-emotion instinct

gloomy, you-are-gloomy instinct

glorification, glorification instinct

glory, glory instinct

glum, feeling-glum instinct

gluttony, gluttony instinct

gnash, to-gnash-your-teeth-in-despair instinct

go, let-yourself-go instinct

goals, to-react-according-to-a-set-of-goals-and-values instinct

goals, working-(hard-)toward-one's-goals instinct (= to-realize-your-goals instinct)

God, the-idea-of-God instinct (= the-God(s) instinct)

goo-goo, to-goo-goo instinct (The baby of the host family crawls out to explore, and immediately gets lifted high, to be goo-gooed at, and have its little hands admired, and generally be messed about.)

good, a-sense-of-the-idea-of-good instinct

good, persuasive-calls-to-be-good instinct

gossip, gossip instinct

grace, grace instinct

grainy, to-sense-a-grainy-texture instinct

grammar, the-universal-grammar instinct

grasp, a-neonate-will-reflexively-grasp-anything-that-is-placed-in-its-hand instinct

grasp, to-grasp-objects instinct

grasping, grasping-reflex instinct

gratification, emotional-gratification instincts

gratification, gratification instinct

gratification, sexual-gratification instinct

gratitude, a-feeling-of-gratitude instinct

gravitation, an-innate-bias-in-favor-of-perceiving-things-to-fall-with-gravitational-acceleration instinct

greed, greed instinct

greed, to-find-greed-to-be-repugnant instinct

greediness, greediness instinct

greeting, greeting instinct

greeting, the-greeting-smile instinct

gregariousness, gregariousness instinct (herd instinct)

grief, grief instinct

grieve, to-grieve-our-dead instinct

grimace, grimace instincts

grimace, the-agonized-grimace instinct

grimace, the-grimace-of-fear instinct

grin, a-big-toothy-grin instinct

grin, a-broad-grin instinct

grin, grin instincts

grin, grin-and-bear-it instinct (women have this unique way of blocking out pain)

grinning, grinning-widely instinct

grip, the-power-grip instinct

grip, the-precision-grip instinct

groaning, groaning instinct

groom, groom-each-other instinct (grooming instinct)

groomed, the-need-to-be-groomed instinct (the hairdressing saloon is the perfect answer)

groomed, to-enjoy-looking-smart-and-well-groomed instinct

grooming, grooming-talk instinct (its function is to reinforce the greeting smile and to maintain the social togetherness)

grotesque, something-is-grotesque instinct

grouchiness, grouchiness instinct

group, a-sense-of-duty-to-the-group instinct

group, group-behavior instincts

group, group-cohesiveness instinct

group, group-contagion instinct

group, group-loyalty instinct

group, group-polarization instinct

group, group-size instincts

group, group-spirit instinct (loyalty-to-the-group instinct)

group, openness-of-group-to-others instinct

group, the-upwelling-of-anxiety-from-being-left-out-of-a-group instinct

groupishness, groupishness instinct

groups, our-ability-to-live-together-in-large-groups instinct

groups, our-tendency-to-band-together-in-groups instinct

groupthink, groupthink instinct

groveling, groveling instinct (= you-grovel instinct)

growling, growling instinct

grudge, a-sense-of-grudge instinct

grudging, a-grudging-feeling-or-behavior instinct

gruesome, something-is-gruesome instinct

gruffness, gruffness instinct

grumpy, to-be-grumpy-with-people instinct

grunting, grunting instinct

guesswork, guesswork instinct

guffaw, guffaw instinct
guiding, guiding-idea instinct (guiding-fiction instinct)
guiding, guiding-one's-children-or-grandchildren instinct
guilt, a-twinge-of-guilt instinct
guilt, the-feeling-of-guilt instinct
guilty, infants-act-guilty-after-misbehavior-and-seem-to-feel-ashamed-
after-failure instinct
guilty, to-feel-guilty instinct
gulping, gulping instinct
gummy, a-gummy-smile instinct
gurgle, the-baby-gurgle-when-contended instinct
gustation, gustation instinct (= the-sense-of-taste instinct)
guts, guts instinct

H

h, the-h-speech-sounds instinct (The h speech sounds are the minimal
units of instinctual speech sounds that correspond roughly to the letter h
of the alphabet)
ha, 'ha' instinct (ha is a written form representing a sound that
people make when they suddenly feel surprised or annoyed)
"ha ha ha" sounds, "ha ha ha"-laughing-sounds instinct
habit, habit instinct (to-get-into-a-particular-habit instinct)
habitat, habitat-preference instinct
habituation, nearly-any-constant-stimulus-will-produce-habitua-
tion instinct
hair, hair-erection instinct
hair, the-bristling-of-the-hair-by-terror instinct
hallowed, something-is-hallowed instinct
handedness, handedness instincts
hands, our-hands-move-as-we-speak instinct

haphephobia, haphephobia (fear of being touched by another person) instinct

happiness, facial-expressions-of-happiness instinct

happiness, happiness instinct (= a-sense-of-happiness instinct)

happiness, striving-for-personal-happiness instinct

happiness, to-value-the-happiness-of-others instinct

happy, to-be-happy-with-life instinct

harass, to-harass-the-enemy instinct

harassment, harassment instinct

hardness, hardness instinct

harm, harm-avoidance instinct (danger-avoidance instinct)

hassle, you-hassle-someone instinct (= hassling instinct)

hasty, you-are-hasty instinct

hate, to-hate instinct

hatred, hatred instinct

haughtiness, haughtiness instinct

he-man, he-man instinct

healthy, admiration-for-the-healthy,-vigorous-body instinct

hearing, the-instinctual-aspects-of-normal-hearing instincts (= hearing instincts)

heart, to-take-something-to-heart instinct

heartbeat, the-heartbeat-sound-is-a-soothing-signal instinct

heartbreak, heartbreak instinct

hearted, to-be-warm-hearted instinct

heartless, to-be-heartless instinct

heartlessness, heartlessness instinct

heat, the-behavioral-aspects-of-heat-sensation instincts

heat, the-feeling-of-burning-heat instinct

heat, the-sensation-of-heat instinct (the-feeling-of-heat instinct)

heaving, heaving instinct

heckling, heckling instinct

hedonism, hedonism instinct

hedonistic, hedonistic-delight instinct
heeding, heeding instinct
heedlessness, heedlessness instinct
heliophobia, heliophobia (fear of the sun/sunlight) instinct
help, to-beg-for-help instinct
help, to-give-help-to-someone instinct (helping-behavior instinct)
help, to-help-a-person-in-distress instinct
help, you-shout-'help'-when-you-are-in-danger instinct
helpfulness, helpfulness instinct
helplessness, a-feeling-of-helplessness instinct
helplessness, an-expression-of-helplessness instinct
hematophobia, hematophobia (fear of the sight of blood/blood) instincts (also called hemophobia)
hemophobia, hemophobia (fear of the sight of blood/blood) instincts (also called hematophobia)
hen party, hen-party (a gathering at which only women are present) instinct
herd, herd instinct (gregariousness instinct)
heroism, heroism instinct
hesitancy, hesitancy instinct
hesitation, hesitation instinct
heterosexuality, heterosexuality instinct
heuristic, heuristic-guided-look-ahead instinct
hide, to-hide-behind-their-mother's-skirts instinct
hide, to-hide-one's-feelings instinct
hide, to-hide-oneself instinct
hide, to-hide-something instinct
hidebound, people-are-hidebound instinct
hierarchy, social-hierarchy instinct(s) (see: Introduction)
hierophobia, hierophobia (fear of religion/sacred objects associated with religion/religious rites) instincts

high, the-'high'-that- many-runners-feel-during-and-right-after-endurance-runs instinct

high, to-feel-an-unpleasantly-high-temperature instinct

high, to-hold-one's-head-high instinct

high, your-spirits-are-high instinct

high horse, to-be-on-one's-high-horse instinct

high places, dread-of-or-in-high-places instinct

high-risk, high-risk-behaviors instincts

high spirits, to-be-in-high-spirits instinct

hilarity, hilarity instinct

hit back, to-hit-back instinct

hoarding, hoarding instinct

hoarding, hoarding-is-taboo instinct

hoaxing, hoaxing instinct

hoggishness, hoggishness instinct

homage, homage instinct

home, a-basic-tendency-to-return-to-a-fixed-home-base instinct

home, home-building instinct

homesickness, homesickness instinct

homing, homing-ability instinct

homogamy, homogamy instinct (the tendency for people to select mates who are similar to themselves)

homophobia, homophobia (fear of homosexuality) instinct

homosexuality, homosexuality instinct

honest, to-be-basically-honest-and-reliable instinct

honesty, honesty instinct

honor, honor instinct

honor, personal-honor instinct

honor, the-defense-of-personal-honor instinct

honor, to-honor-someone instinct

hooliganism, hooliganism instinct

hoot, to-hoot-down-someone instinct

hope, hope (a feeling of desire and expectation) instinct

hopping, children's-hopping,-skipping,-throwing,-and-other-motor-behaviors instinct

horror, horror instinct

hospitality, hospitality instinct

hostages, frightened-hostages-often-develop-friendly-feelings-toward-their-captors instinct

hostile, hostile-infantile-signals instincts

hostility, deep,-irrational-hostility instinct

hostility, hostility instinct

hostility, hostility-to-an-idea instinct

hostility, our-occasional-hostility-toward-people-who-look-different-from-ourselves instinct

hotly, to-hotly-debate-a-topic instinct

how things work, to-like-knowing-how-things-work instinct

hubris, hubris instinct

hues, our-discrimination-of-hues instinct

humiliate, to-humiliate-someone instinct

   humiliation, feeling-of-humiliation instinct

humility, humility instinct

humor, black-humor instinct

humor, crude-humor instinct

humor, grim-humor instinct (= sardonic-humor instinct)

humor, the-sense-of-humor instinct

humor, we-often-use-humor-to-deal-with-things-intensely-painful instinct

humor, when-oppressed-peoples-have-no-other-remedy-they-resort-to-humor instinct

hunger, the-feeling-of-hunger instinct

hungry, feeling-hungry-and-starting-to-eat instinct (normal behavior needs to be explained!)

hungry, to-feel-hungry instinct

hunt, the-excitement-of-the-hunt instinct

hunting, hunting-and-prey-killing instinct (Work has become the major substitute for primitive hunting. Sporting activities are modified forms of hunting behavior.)

hurt, to-feel-hurt instinct (= hurt-feelings instinct)

hurtful, to-say-hurtful-things instinct

hyalophobia, hyalophobia (fear of glass) instinct

hydrophobia, hydrophobia (fear of water) instinct

hygienic, hygienic-behavior instincts

hypergamy, hypergamy instinct (Hypergamy is the female practice of marrying men of equal or greater wealth and status)

hyperthymia, hyperthymia (exaggerated emotional excitement) instinct

hypertrichophobia, hypertrichophobia (fear of growth of bodily hair, particularly, excessive amounts) instinct

hypnophobia, hypnophobia (fear of falling asleep) instinct

hypnotic, hypnotic-suggestion instinct

hypocrisy, hypocrisy instinct

hypomania, hypomania (mild condition of overexcitability) instinct

hysterical, hysterical-laughter instinct

I

i, the-i-speech-sounds instinct (The i speech sounds are the minimal units of instinctual speech sounds that correspond roughly to the letter i of the alphabet)

iconicity, iconicity instinct

idea, to-get-an-idea instinct

idea, to-play-with-an-idea instinct

idealism, idealism instinct

idealization, idealization instinct

idealizing, idealizing instinct

ideas, intuitive-ideas instincts

ideation, ideation (the forming of ideas) instinct

identification, the-identification-of-individuals-by-voice-alone instinct

identify, a-mother-is-able-to-identify-her-baby-by-smell-alone instinct

identify, to-identify-with-someone-or-something instinct

identity, identity instincts

identity, self-identity instinct

ideomotor act, ideomotor-act (an overt act initiated by an idea) instinct

idiosyncracy, idiosyncracy instincts (all instincts are such instincts, more or less)

idleness, idleness instinct

idleness, idleness-is-contemptible-and-labor-is-honorable instinct

idolatry, idolatry instinct

idolizing, idolizing instinct

ignore, to-ignore-someone-or-something instinct

illicit, the-sense-of-illicit instinct

illusory, illusory-contour instinct

image, image-making instinct

imageless, imageless-thought instinct

imagery, pleasant-imagery instinct

imagery, visual-imagery instinct

imagination, imagination instinct

imagination, the-child's-imagination-is-very-active instincts

imitate, boys-are-more-likely-to-imitate-the-men,-and-girls-are-more-likely-to-imitate-the-women instinct

imitate, neonates-can-imitate-the-facial-expressions-of-adults instinct

imitation, imitation instinct

immobility, immobility instinct (death-feigning instinct)

immorality, immorality instincts

impatience, impatience instinct
imperious, to-be-imperious instinct
impertinence, impertinence instinct
impervious, to-be-impervious instinct
impetuosity, impetuosity instinct
impiety, impiety instinct
imploring, an-imploring-look instinct
imploring, imploring instinct
imposing, someone-or-something-is-imposing instinct
imprecation, imprecation instinct
impress, to-impress instinct
impress, you-impress-something-on-someone instinct
impressed, to-be-impressed-by-someone-or-something instinct
impression, to-get-an-impression instincts
impression, your-impression-of-a-person instinct
impression, your-impression-of-a-place instinct
impression, your-impression-of-a-situation instinct
impression, your-impression-of-a-thing instinct
imprinting, imprinting instincts (imprinting is learning; all instincts are learning instincts)
imprudence, imprudence (imprudent behavior or speech) instinct
impulsion, impulsion (a desire that you cannot control) instinct
impulsive, impulsive-behavior instinct (impulsiveness instinct)
impulsive, impulsive-violence instinct
impulsiveness, impulsiveness instinct
inadvertent, an-inadvertent-action instinct
inane, inane-remarks instinct
inattention, selective-inattention instincts
inbreeding, inbreeding-avoidance instincts
incest, incest-barrier instincts
incest, the-incest-avoidance instinct
incongruity, the-detection-of-incongruity instinct

incredulity, incredulity instinct
inculcate, you-inculcate-something-in-someone's-mind instinct
indebtedness, indebtedness instinct
indecision, indecision instinct
independent, to-like-being-independent instinct
indignant, indignant-dispute instinct
indignant, you-are-indignant instinct
indignation, indignation instinct
indignation, moral-indignation instinct
indignity, to-feel-indignity instinct
indoctrinability, indoctrinability instinct
indoctrination, indoctrination instinct
indolence, indolence (laziness) instinct
indolent, an-indolent-smile instinct
indomitable, an-indomitable-spirit instinct
induction, induction instinct
indulgence, indulgence instincts
infantile, infantile-play instinct
infatuation, infatuation instinct
inference, inference instincts
inferiority, inferiority-feeling instinct (= feelings-of-inferiority instinct)
infidelity, infidelity instinct
infidelity, our-anger-in-reaction-to-infidelity instinct
information, information-talking instinct
in-group, in-group-solidarity instinct
inhibition, inhibition instincts (e.g. signals that inhibit attacks within the social group)
inhibitions, our-inhibitions-about-killing-fellow-humans instinct
injustice, a-sense-of-injustice instinct
innovativeness, innovativeness instincts
inquisitive, to-be-inquisitive instinct (= inquisitiveness instinct)

insecurity, the-feelings-of-insecurity instinct

insecurity,   we-cry-if-we-are-faced-with-a-high-degree-of-insecurity instinct

insensitivity, insensitivity-and-lack-of-tact instinct

insight, sudden-insight instincts (= a-burst-of-insight instincts)

insincerity, insincerity instinct

insinuation, insinuation instinct

insist, to-insist-on-something instinct

inspect, to-inspect-one's-environment-with-one's-eyes instinct

inspiration, inspiration instinct

inspirited, feeling-inspirited instinct

institutionalizing, institutionalizing-the-moral-values-of-the-community instinct

insularity, insularity instinct

insulting, insulting-gestures instincts

insulting, insulting-remark instinct

insulting, to-become-angry-at-an-insulting-person instinct

insult-signals, insult-signals instincts (disinterest signals, boredom signals, impatience signals, the tight smile, the cheek crease, mock-discomfort signals, dominant nose-in- air display, mockery signals, spitting aimed directly at the insulted person, pushing, flicking, flapping, swiping, holding the nose as if protecting oneself from a bad smell, obscene comments, a sneering, contorted face thrust close to our own, etc)

intellection, intellection (conception, comparison, abstraction, generalization, reasoning) instincts

intellectual, intellectual-fight instinct

intelligence, "everyday intelligence" instincts

intelligence, intelligence instincts (linguistic intelligence, mathematical intelligence, musical intelligence, visual-spatial intelligence, bodily intelligence, intrapersonal intelligence, interpersonal intelligence, emotional intelligence, etc)

intent, intent instincts

intention, intention instincts

intentionality, intentionality instincts

interest, interest-in-the-normal,-standard-activities-of-living instinct

interpreting, interpreting instincts

intimacy, the-feelings-of-intimacy instinct (the-need-for-intimacy instinct)

intimate, intimate-extended-cuddlings,-fondlings,-kissings,-strokings instinct

intimidate, to-intimidate-one-another instinct (= intimidating-behavior instinct)

intimidated, to-feel-intimidated instinct

intimidation, postures-of-intimidation instincts

intonation, intonation instincts

intrepidity, intrepidity instinct

intrigued, to-be-intrigued-by-something instinct

introspection, the-capacity-for-introspection instincts

introversion, introversion instinct

intuition, intuition instincts

intuition, intuition-based-on-emotion instincts

invariant, invariant-right instinct (The rule of the «invariant right» is a tendency to veer that way after entering a store. Even Brits who drive on the other side of the road obey the rule of the «invariant right»)

inventiveness, inventiveness instinct

investigation, investigation instincts

invigorated, to-feel-invigorated instinct

invocation, invocation instinct

iophobia, iophobia (fear of being poisoned/rusty objects) instincts

irascible, irascible-outbursts instincts

irony, irony instinct

irritability, irritability instinct

irritable, irritable-mood instinct

irritated, the-irritated-head-toss instinct

irritation, irritation instinct

irritations, sudden-scratchings-or-nibblings,-directed-at-specific-irritations instinct

isolation, a-sense-of-isolation instinct

itchy feeling, itchy-feeling instinct

J

j, the-j-speech-sounds instinct (The j speech sounds are the minimal units of instinctual speech sounds that correspond roughly to the letter j of the alphabet)

jabber, to-jabber instinct

jaded, to-get-jaded instinct

jaundiced, a-jaundiced-attitude instinct

jaw, jaw-dislocating instinct

jealous, jealous-rage instinct

jealousy, jealousy instinct

jealousy, sexual-jealousy instinct

jeer, to-jeer-at-someone instinct

jerk out, to-jerk-out-a-remark-or-comment instinct

jest, jest instinct

jest, you-say-something-in-jest instinct

jibe, jibe instinct

jibe, the-sarcastic-jibe-of-hatred-and-insult instinct

jingoism, jingoism instinct

jitters, getting-the-jitters instinct

jocularity, jocularity instinct

joke, laugh-at-a-visual-or-verbal-joke instinct

joke, to-joke-or-to-say-or-do-something-jokingly instinct

jokes, to-share-acerbic-jokes instinct

jollity, jollity instinct

joviality, joviality instinct

joy, joy instinct
joy, joy-of-life instinct
jubilation, jubilation instinct
judge, judge-people-fairly-accurately-on-first-appearances instinct
judgment, judgment-and-emotion-are-deeply-intertwined instinct
justice, justice instinct
justice, the-desire-for-social-justice instinct

K

k, the-k-speech-sounds instinct (The k speech sounds are the minimal units of instinctual speech sounds that correspond roughly to the letter k of the alphabet)

kainophobia, kainophobia (fear of new things/new experiences/new situations) instincts

keenness, keenness instinct

keeping your distance, keeping-your-distance (defending your personal space) instinct

kenophobia, kenophobia (fear of empty spaces) instinct

keraunophobia, keraunophobia (fear of lightning/thunder) instincts

kick, to-get-a-kick-from-something instinct

kick, to-kick-against-a-situation instinct

kid, to-kid-someone instinct

kid, to-kid-yourself instinct

kill, to-say-that-you-will-kill-someone instinct

kill prey, the-urge-to-kill-prey instinct (it keeps reappearing with startling regularity in the playful activities of young boys, but in the adult world it is subjected to powerful cultural suppression)

kindliness, kindliness instinct

kindness, kindness instinct

kindness, to-value-kindness instinct

kinesthetics, kinesthetics (feeling of motion) instincts

kinship, the-extent-and-formalization-of-kinship-ties instinct

kiss feeding, kiss-feeding (non-milk feeding) instincts (the mother's kiss-feeding instinct and the baby's kiss-feeding instinct). Mothers wean their children by chewing up their food and then passing it into the infantile mouth by lip-to-lip contact. Our species probably practiced it for a million years or more.

kissing, kissing instinct

kleptomania, kleptomania instinct

knocking, your-heart-is-knocking-with-fright instinct

knot, your-stomach-knots-because-you-are-afraid-or-excited instinct

knowing, a-knowing-look-instinct

knowing, feeling-of-knowing instinct

knowing, to-enjoy-knowing-how-things-work instinct

knowledge, love-of-knowledge instinct

knowledge, the-quest-for-knowledge instincts

kopophobia, kopophobia (fear of becoming fatigued or exhausted) instincts

L

l, the-l-speech-sounds instinct (The l speech sounds are the minimal units of instinctual speech sounds that correspond roughly to the letter l of the alphabet)

labor, cooperatve-division-of-labor-between-adult-males-and-females instincts

lackey, lackey instinct

lalophobia, lalophobia (fear of speaking/stammering or committing errors while speaking) instincts

lament, you-lament-something instincts

lamentation, lamentation instinct

lamenting, lamenting-the-misfortune instinct

language, language instincts

language, language-perception instincts (Language perception is reflexive: fast, automatic, and innate, like reflexes)

languid, to-be-languid instinct

languishing, languishing instinct

languor, languor instinct

lash, to-lash-out-at-or-against-someone instinct

lash, to-lash-out-with-your-hands-or-with-a-weapon instinct

lassitude, lassitude instinct

laterality, laterality instincts

laugh, he-laughs-through-clenched-teeth-at-jokes-about-him instinct

laugh, the-baby's-laugh instinct

laugh, to-laugh-at-yourself instinct

laugh, to-laugh-out-loud instinct

laugh, to-laugh-to-scorn instinct

laugh, to-laugh-very-heartily instinct

laughing, laughing-at-someone instinct

laughter, an-uncontrollable-bout-of-laughter instinct

laughter, laughter-of-scorn instinct

laughter, the-contagiousness-of-laughter instinct

laughter, to-burst-into-laughter instinct

laxness, laxness instinct

lay the blame, to-lay-the-blame-on-someone-or-something instinct

laziness, laziness instinct

lead, to-take-the-lead-in-a-particular-situation-or-group instinct

leader, to-be-a-leader instinct

leaders, intense-attention-toward-leaders instinct

leading males, attention-structure-is-centripetal-on-leading-males instinct

league, league instinct

learning, learning instincts (Associative learning, ideational learning, learning without awareness, motor learning, observational learning, pattern learning (relational learning), perceptional learning, response learning (place learning), rote learning, stimulus-response learning, stimulus-stimulus learning, to learn from experience, trial-and-error learning, learning by imitation, "X always immediately preceded Y" learning, learning from the consequences of your behavior, "we can benefit from the experiences of others" learning, insight learning, etc, are merely learning situations. Remember that only instincts can learn. We don't have to learn to learn because we have learning instincts.

> leave, thoughts-leave-your-mind instinct
> lechery, lechery instinct
> leering, leering instinct
> leering, leering-looks instinct
> leisure, the-need-for-leisure instinct
> lesbianism, lesbianism instinct
> letdown, letdown instinct
> lethargy, lethargy instinct
> levity, levity instinct
> levophobia, levophobia (fear of things being on the left side of one's body) instinct
> lewdness, lewdness instinct
> liberality, liberality instinct
> lick, lick-one's-wounds instinct
> lick, lick-our-lips instinct
> licking, the-general-licking instinct
> light, light-heartedness instinct
> lighting, to-regard-objects-as-having-colors-independent-of-lighting instinct
> liking, liking instinct
> liking, liking-a-person instinct
> limb, limb-movements instincts
> limb, limb-position instincts

limp, if-you-step-on-a-thorn-you-know-that-you-need-to-limp instinct

lingering, the-lingering-feelings-for-a-lost-love instinct

lip, lip-eroticism instinct

lips, men-desire-women-with-full-lips-and-small-chins instinct

lips, to-bite-one's-lips instinct

listening, listening instinct

liveliness, liveliness instinct (= to-be-lively instinct)

loathing, loathing instinct

locality, locality-survey instinct

locating, locating-a-sound-source-in-the-environment instinct

locating, locating-a-stimulus-in-the-visual-field instinct

locating, locating-the-point-of-stimulation-on-the-skin instinct

location, to-expect-an-object-to-have-a-location,-even-when-it-is-not-presently-perceivable instinct

locomotion, a-striding,-bipedal-locomotion instinct

locomotion, locomotion instincts (the slither, the crawl, the totter, the walk, the stroll, the shuffle, the hurry, the run, the jog, the sprint, the tiptoe, the march, the goose-step, the jump, the hop, the skip, the climb, the swing, acrobatics, the baby's swimming)

logical, logical-reasoning instincts (= logical-thinking instincts)

loneliness, a-feeling-of-loneliness instinct

lonely, to-feel-lonely instinct

longing, longing (a rather sad feeling of wanting something very much) instinct

longing, longing-for-something instinct

look, look-hard-at-somebody instinct

look, to-be-too-ashamed-or-embarrassed-to-look-at-someone-directly instinct

look, we-prefer-to-look-at-patterned-stimuli-with-sharp-contours instinct

looking, looking-towards-the-sound instinct

looks, angry-looks instinct
looks, leering-looks instinct
looks, loving-looks instinct
looks, suspicious-looks instinct
looks, tender-looks instinct
looks, understanding-looks instinct
loquacity, loquacity instinct
losing, to-hate-losing instinct
lost, to-be-lost-in-thought,-a-thing,-etc instinct (e.g. to become «lost» in a beautiful sunset)
loud, loud-and-intrusive-noises-irritate-and-annoy-you instinct
loudly, to-speak-loudly-and-angrily instinct
lounge, to-lounge-about(-or-lounge-around) instinct
lousy, to-feel-lousy instinct
love, a-kid-needs-love instinct
love, love-at-first-sight instinct
love, love-bites instinct
love, love-nibble instinct
love, parental-love instinct
love, to-be-in-love instinct
love, to-be-in-love-with-being-in-love instinct
love, to-fall-out-of-love instinct
lovers, lovers'-baby-talk instinct
loving, the-love-of-loving instinct
lowering, the-lowering-of-the-body-in-relation-to-the-dominant-individual instinct (e.g. groveling, prostrating, kneeling, bowing, curtsying)
loyalty, loyalty-in-fighting instinct
loyalty, loyalty-on-the-hunt (or work) instinct
loyalty, loyalty-to-duty instinct
lubrication, vaginal-lubrication instinct
lubricity, lubricity instinct
ludicrous, you-describe-someone-or-something-as-ludicrous instinct

lying, lying instinct

lynch, lynch-mobs instinct (remember: all instincts are situational!)

lyricism, lyricism instinct

M

m, the-m-speech-sounds instinct (The m speech sounds are the minimal units of instinctual speech sounds that correspond roughly to the letter m of the alphabet)

machismo, machismo instinct

macrophobia, macrophobia (fear of large objects) instinct

magnanimity, magnanimity instinct

magnetic, magnetic-compass instinct

main meals, main-meals instinct

maintain, ability-to-maintain-concentrated-attention instinct

make up, to-make-up-your-mind-about-something instinct

malaise, malaise (slight bodily discomfort) instinct

male chauvinism, male-chauvinism instinct

male-grouping, the-male-grouping-hunting-tendency-of-our-species instinct

male status, male-status instinct

male violence, male-violence instinct

maleness, maleness instincts

malevolence, malevolence instinct

malice, malice instinct

malignancy, malignancy instinct

malleability, malleability instinct

mammalingus, mammalingus instinct

mania, mania instincts. Manias are abnormal instincts. There are an enormous number of manias

manipulate, to-manipulate,-handle-and-explore-objects instinct manipulate, to-manipulate-others-through-violence-and-reconciliation instinct

manipulation, psychological-manipulation instinct

manipulation, resisting-psychological-manipulation-instinct

map, a-mental-map-of-reality instincts

masculinity, masculinity instinct

masochism, masochism instinct

mass-contagion, mass-contagion (fads, fashions, dress styles, political movements, etc.) instinct

mass suggestion, mass-suggestion instinct

massacre, massacre instinct (remember: instincts are situational)

mastering, the-pleasure-of-mastering-something-new instinct

masticating, masticating instinct

masturbation, masturbation instinct

masturbation, masturbation-fantasies instinct

mate, mate-for-life instinct (Nine out of ten mammals that mate for life are unfaithful. Man is not genetically monogamous. Only two primates are genetically monogamous: the marmoset and the tamarin. Research suggests left-handed people (like Bill Clinton) are more prone to compulsive sex addiction.)

mate, mate-selection instincts

mate, the-qualities-man-prefers-in-a-mate:-Men-pay-more-attention-to-youth-and-beauty,-women-to-wealth-and-status instincts

matechoice, matechoice instincts (mate choice reveals a distinct gender gap)

matechoice copying, matechoice-copying instinct (women are more likely to express an interest in going out with a man if they are told that other women also find him attractive)

maternal, maternal instincts

maternal, maternal-care instincts

maternal mood, the-baby-is-acutely-responsive-to-maternal-mood instinct mathematical, mathematical-intuition instincts (an-intuitive-grasp-of-mathematics,-even-of-mathematical-theorems instincts)

mathematical, mathematical-reasoning instincts

maudlin, to-become-maudlin instinct

mawkish, a-mawkish-pride instinct

mawkishness, mawkishness instinct

mayhem, mayhem instincts

meals, main-meals instinct

mealtimes, mealtimes instinct

meaning, finding-meaning instinct

meaningfulness, a-feeling-of-meaningfulness instinct

meaninglessness, a-feeling-of-meaninglessness

meat, the-urge-to-eat-meat instinct (our old primate omnivory)

mechanical, mechanical-ability instincts

meddle, to-meddle-in-something instinct

medical, medical-care instinct (Woolly monkeys can diagnose their own illnesses and choose to eat plants that provide the perfect cures. When you send them away to another country with its own set of plant life, the woolly monkeys adapt. Instincts are situational!

meditation, meditation instinct

meekness, meekness instinct

melancholy, melancholy instinct

melodramatic, melodramatic-behavior instinct

melody, melody instinct

memories, retrieval-of-long-term-memories instinct

memories, retrieval-of-short-term-memories instinct

memories, the-formation-of-new-memories instincts

memorization, rote-memorization-of-details instinct

memory, auditory-sensory-memory instinct

memory, declarative-memory instinct (= semantic and episodic memory)

memory, eidetic-images-memory instinct

memory, emotional-memory instinct

memory, episodic-memory instinct (= memory for information about specific experiences)

memory, flashbulb-memories instinct

memory, location-memory instinct

memory, long-term-memory instinct

memory, memory-consolidation-during-REM-sleep instinct

memory, memory-for-words instinct

memory, motor-memory instincts

memory, musical-memory instinct

memory, object-memory instinct

memory, olfactory-memory instinct

memory, procedural-memory instinct (= memory for motor movements, skills, and other procedures)

memory, semantic-memory instinct (= memory for meaning)

memory, visual-memory instinct

mental set, mental-set instincts (= a habitual way of approaching or perceiving a problem)

mercy, mercy instinct

merriment, merriment instinct

merry, to-make-merry-with-friends instinct

meticulousness, meticulousness instinct

microphobia, microphobia (fear of small objects) instinct

microsynchrony, microsynchrony-of-small-movements-when-a-pair-of-friends-are-in-a-condition-of-strong-rapport instinct

militancy, militancy instinct

mime, mime instinct

mimicry, mimicry instinct

mince, you-do-not-mince-your-words instinct

mince, you-mince-your-way-somewhere instinct

mind, the-ability-to-form-a-theory-of-mind-about-another-person instinct

miracle, to-treat-as-a-miracle instinct
mirth, mirth instinct
miser, miser instinct
miserable, to-be-made-miserable-by-your-mistakes instinct
miserable, to-feel-miserable instinct
misgivings, you-have-misgivings-about-something instinct
miss, you-miss-someone instinct
missing, the-feeling-of-missing-the-loved-one instinct
missionary, missionary-enthusiasm instinct
moaning, moaning instinct
mob, bloodthirsty-lynch-mob instinct
mob, to-mob-someone instinct (There are cases daily in schools round about of pupils being mobbed by fellow pupils. Also adults and animals mob.)
mock, mock-aggression instinct
mock, mock-fight instinct
mock, to-mock-a-person-or-something-that-they-do instinct
mocking, mocking instinct
model, to-model-yourself-on-someone instinct
moderate polygyny, moderate-polygyny instinct (We are moderately polygynous. About three-fourths of all human societies permit the taking of multiple wives, and most of them encourage the practice by law and custom. The monogamous societies fit that category in a legal sense only.)
moderation, moderation instinct (moderate-behavior instinct)
modesty, modesty instinct
modesty, to-value-modesty instinct
monophobia, monophobia (fear of being left alone) instinct
monopolize, males-monopolize-their-mates,-and-vice-versa instinct
mood, bad-mood instincts
mood, good-mood instincts
mood, lousy-mood instincts
mood, mood instincts

mood, mood-talking instincts (e.g. the words 'I am hurt' are whined or screamed, the words 'I am furious' are roared or bellowed)

mood, to-feel-the-mood-of-others instinct (to-sense-people's-moods instinct)

mood, you-are-in-no-mood-for-something instincts

mood, you-are-in-the-mood-for-something instincts

moodiness, moodiness instinct

moral, a-moral-sense instinct

moral, to-construct-a-moral-order instincts

moral, tribal-moral-codes instincts

morally, to-feel-morally-responsible instinct

morbid, to-be-morbid instinct

mordant, mordant-humor instinct

morose, a-morose-facial-expression instinct

morphemes, morphemes instincts (morphemes are the smallest units of meaning in a language)

mortification, mortification instinct

mortified, to-be-mortified instinct

motherese, motherese (the speech of adults to young children) instinct

mothers, mothers-feel-attachment-to-their-newborn-babies instinct (mothers who feel no attachment to their newborn babies may lack a neural pathway that is normally triggered by the act of giving birth, a new study of mice suggests)

motion, motion instincts (see locomotion instincts)

motion, to-perceive-motion-as-continuous instinct (Although our visual perceptions of objects are discrete because of our saccadic movements, we perceive objects as moving continuously. Perceiving motion as continuous may have evolved very early among vertebrates.)

motionless, motionless-postures instincts

motivated, motivated-forgetting instinct

motor, involuntary-motor-movements instincts

motor, motor-control instincts
motor, motor-coordination instincts
motor, voluntary-motor-movements instincts
mourning, mourning instinct
mouth, orienting-the-mouth instinct
moved, being-moved instinct
moved, to-be-moved-by-music instinct
movements, the-involuntary-movements-of-the-limbs-and-body instincts
movements, the-voluntary-movements-of-the-limbs-and-body instincts
mugging, mugging instinct
mumbling, mumbling instinct
murder, our-inhibitions-against-murder instinct
murmuring, murmuring instinct
muscle, maintaining-muscle-tone-and-muscular-coordination instincts
muscle, muscle-eroticism (pleasure in bodily activity) instinct
muscle, muscle sensation,
muse, to-muse-about-something instinct
musement, musement instinct
musement, the-play-of-musement instinct
music, music instinct
music, our-love-of-music instinct
musical, musical-ear instinct
musical, musical-harmony instinct
musical, musical-melody instinct
musical, musical-scale instinct
muster, to-muster-all-your-self-control instinct
muster, to-muster-up-your-courage instinct
mute, you-mute-your-feelings,-emotions,-or activities instincts
muttering, muttering instinct
muttering, muttering-to-himself/herself instinct

mysophobia, mysophobia (fear of dirt/contamination) instincts

mystique, an-atmosphere-of-mystique instinct

N

n, the-n-speech-sounds instinct (The n speech sounds are the minimal units of instinctual speech sounds that correspond roughly to the letter n of the alphabet)

nagging, a-doubt-is-nagging-at-you instinct

nagging, a-worry-is-nagging-at-you instinct

naked, photographs-of-naked-or-almost-naked-women-in-a-way-which-is-intended-to-please-men,-is-offensive-to-many-women instinct

name, name-calling instinct

name, to-give-someone/something-a-name,-and-call-someone/ something-by-this-name-afterwards instinct (= naming instinct)

names, infants-respond-positively-to-the-sound-of-their-names instinct

nap, nap instinct

narcissism, narcissism instinct

nastiness, nastiness instinct

nationalism, nationalism instinct

natter, to-natter instinct

natural kinds, we-are-predisposed-to-name-kinds-of-entities-and-to-expect-that-the-objects-of-a-kind-that-is-recognized-by-superficial-properties-will-have-additional-properties-in-common instinct

nature, our-love-for-nature instinct (= biophilia instinct)

nature, to-enjoy-beautiful-nature instinct

nature, to-feel-at-one-with-nature instinct

naughtiness, to-enjoy-stories-about-naughtiness instinct

nausea, nausea instinct

navigation, men-generally-navigate-paths-by-pure-guesses-of-relative-distances-and-angles instinct

navigation, the-general-navigation instinct

navigation, women-generally-navigate-paths-by-recognizing-particular-landmarks instinct

nearing, nearing-a-baby instinct

neat, a-feeling-that-something-is-neat instinct

neat, to-be-neat-and-tidy instinct

necking, necking (kissing each other passionately) instinct

necrophilia, necrophilia instinct (an abnormal instinct indeed)

necrophobia, necrophobia (fear of death/dead things/dead human corpses) instincts

negative, negative-self-feeling instinct (remember: instincts are situational)

negotiation, negotiation instinct

neophilia, neophilia (a desire for the new and novel and/or a tendency to try new foods) instincts

neophobia, neophobia (fear of the new/the novel/new foods) instincts (If we lost our neophilia, we would stagnate. If we lost our neophobia, we would rush headlong into disaster)

nepotism, nepotism instinct

nervous, nervous-anticipation instinct

nervous, nervous-excitement instinct

nervous, nervous-panic instinct

nervous, nervous-tension instinct

nervousness, nervousness instinct

neutral, neutral-voice instinct

new, the-fear-of-the-new instinct

new, the-pleasure-of-mastering-something-new instinct

new, the-urge-to-investigate-the-new-and-the-novel instinct

new, to-like-learning-new-things instinct

new, to-like-looking-at-new-things instinct

news, to-ask-for-news-of-mutual-acquaintances instinct

nibblings, minor-nibblings-between-our-main-meals instinct

nice, people-tend-to-be-nice-to-those-who-are-nice-to-them instinct nice-looking, a-feeling-that-someone-is-nice-looking instinct

nicknaming, nicknaming instinct (= naming instinct)

niggle, niggle (a small worry or doubt that you keep thinking about) instinct

nightmares, to-get-nightmares instinct

nihilism, nihilism instinct

nits, picking-nits instinct

no, a-wagging-forefinger-for-'no' instinct

no, the-head-shake-for-'no' instinct

nobleness, nobleness instinct

nocturnal, nocturnal-orgasm instinct

nodding, nodding-and-smiling-in-the-private-conversation instinct

noise, newborns-are-easily-perturbed-by-noise-and-movement instinct

noise, noise-rejection instinct (Certain appearances are «noise», e.g. shadows. We are predisposed to regard shadows as «noise» and to ignore the edges of shadows.)

noises, noises-irritate-and-annoy-you instinct

nonchalance, nonchalance instinct

non-conformity, non-conformity instinct

non-verbal, non-verbal-communication (prosody, vocal paralanguage, non-vocal paralanguage, etc) instincts

non-violence, non-violence instinct

non-vocal, non-vocal-paralanguage (body postures, motion, touch, facial expressions, chemical communication, etc) instincts

normal mood, normal-mood (tranquility, a pleasant relaxed state) instinct

nose, orienting-the-nose instinct

nosiness, nosiness instinct

nosism, nosism instinct

nosophobia, nosophobia (fear of illness/acquiring some specific illness) instincts

nostalgia, nostalgia instinct

note, note (a particular quality in someone's voice that shows how they are feeling) instincts (e.g. a note of uncertainty)

notion, notion instinct

novelty, novelty-seeking instinct

novelty, the-need-for-novelty-and-excitement instinct

nude, males-are-sexually-aroused-by-watching-(photographs-that-display-)the-nude-body-of-a-member-of-the-opposite-sex instinct

nude, women-are-less-excited-by-(the-image-of-)anonymous-nude-males instinct

nudge, to-nudge-someone-into-doing-something instinct

number, the-number-sense instinct (People have lost their number sense as a result of brain damage. Many nonhuman animals have been shown experimentally to have a number sense.)

numbing, psychological-numbing (a reaction of surviving victims) instinct

numinous, numinous-perception instinct

nurse, nurse-your-grief,-anger-and-discontent-deep-inside-you instinct

nursing, nursing instinct

nursing, nursing-your-pride instinct

nurturance, nurturance instinct

nurturant, women-are-more-nurturant-than-men instinct

nurture, nurture instinct

nurturing, to-be-nurturing instinct

nuzzle, to-nuzzle-someone-or-something instinct

nyctophobia, nyctophobia (fear of night/the dark/darkness) instincts

nymphomania, nymphomania instinct

O

o, the-o-speech-sounds instinct (The o speech sounds are the minimal units of instinctual speech sounds that correspond roughly to the letter o of the alphabet)

obduracy, obduracy instinct

obedience, obedience-to-authority instinct

obeisance, the-obeisance-of-subordinates instinct

obey, the-tendency-to-obey-social-rules-and-laws instinct

obeying, obeying-orders instinct

obfuscation, obfuscation instinct

object, object-directedness instincts

object, object-permanence instinct

objection, objection instinct

objects, the-ability-to-distinguish-objects instinct

objects, the-infant-takes-great-pleasure-in-pushing,-pulling,-and-mouthing-objects instincts

objects, to-assume-that-objects-are-solid-and-therefore-two-objects-cannot-occupy-the-same-space-at-the-same-time instinct

objects, to-examine-and-manipulate-objects instincts

objects, to-identify-objects instinct (to-identify-a-part-of-the-current-stimulus-pattern-as-coming-from-an-object instinct)

obligated, to-feel-obligated-to-do-something instinct

obscene, being-obscene instinct (= obscenity instinct)

obscene, obscene-signals instincts

obsequiousness, obsequiousness instinct

observation, observation instinct

obsession, obsession instincts. Obsessions are abnormal instincts

obsession, obsession-compulsion-control instincts

obsessiveness, obsessiveness instincts

obstinacy, obstinacy instinct

ochlophobia, ochlophobia (fear of crowds/crowded places) instincts

odium, odium instinct

odontophobia, odontophobia (fear of teeth/having one's teeth worked on by a dentist) instincts

odor, falling-in-love-involves-a-kind-of-fixation-on-the-specific-individual-odor-of-the-partner's-body instinct

odor, odor instincts (seven primary odors are assumed: camphorous, musky, floral, minty, ethereal, pungent, putrid)

odor preferences, before-puberty-there-are-preferences-for-sweet-and-fruity-odors instinct

odor preferences, from-puberty-there-are-preferences-for-flowery,-oily-and-musky-odors instinct

odor stimuli, certain-odor-stimuli-play-a-sexual-role instincts

odors, seven-primary-odors instincts (resinous, floral, minty, ethereal, musky, acrid, putrid)

off-key, music-is-off-key instinct

offences, to-attack-offences instinct

offend, to-offend-someone instinct

offended, to-be-offended instinct

oh, 'oh' instinct (a response or a comment on something that has just been said)

olfaction, olfaction (the sense of smell) instincts

olfactory, olfactory-eroticism (sexually exciting sensations associated with the sense of smell) instinct

ombrophobia, ombrophobia (fear of rainstorms) instinct

one-upmanship, one-upmanship instinct

onomatophobia, onomatophobia (fear of a particular word or name) instinct

onomatopoeia, onomatopoeia instinct

ooh, 'ooh' instinct (people say ooh when they are surprised, etc)

oops, 'oops' instinct (people say oops to indicate a mistake, etc) open spaces, dread-in,-and-of,-open-spaces instinct

open, to-open-one's-mouth-in-order-to-express-surprise-or-shock instinct

openness, openness instinct

openness, openness-to-experience instinct

openness, openness-to-feelings instinct

operant conditioning, Note: (general) operant conditioning doesn't exist because learning is always specialized and content-dependent. All instincts are learning instincts, and only instincts can learn.

ophidiophobia, ophidiophobia (fear of snakes) instinct

opinion, to-have-a-high/low-opinion-of-someone instinct

opinions, get-cross-at-opinions-expressed-by-others instinct

opinions, opinions-are-difficult-to-shake instinct

opportunism, opportunism instinct

opposites, "opposites attract" instinct

opposition, opposition instinct

oppression, oppression instinct

optimism instinct

oral, oral-drive instinct

oral, oral-eroticism instinct

oral, oral-sadism (the desire to inflict pain through oral means) instinct

order, order instinct

order, to-order-someone-to-do-something (e.g. 'Sit down!') instinct

order, you-order-someone-to-do-something instinct (normal behavior needs to be explained)

orderliness, orderliness instinct

orders, obeying-orders instinct

organ, organ-eroticism instinct

organizing, organizing instinct (= organization instinct)

orgasm, nocturnal-orgasm instinct

orgasm, orgasm instinct

orientation, orientation instinct
orienting, orienting-response instinct
orienting, orienting-the-nose instinct
orthodoxy, orthodoxy instinct
orthography, orthography instincts (making-words instincts)
ostentation, ostentation instinct
ostracizing, ostracizing-someone instinct
other, a-sensitivity-to-the-feelings-of-other-people instinct
ouch, 'Ouch!' instinct (expressing sudden pain)
ouch, the-"ouch"-part-of-the-experience-of-pain instinct
out, to-feel-out-of-it instinct
outcry, outcry instinct
outlet, subsidiary-outlet-for-emotional-feelings instinct
outpourings, outpourings instinct
outrage, outrage instinct
outspokenness, outspokenness instinct
ovation, ovation instinct
overawed, to-be-overawed-by-someone-or-something instinct
overcompensation, overcompensation instinct
overconfidence, overconfidence instinct (a version of an instinct)
overreaction, overreaction instinct
ow, 'Ow!' instinct (people say 'Ow!' when they suddenly feel a pain)
ownership, ownership instinct (even Karl Marx had this particular
instinct)
ownership, the-rituals-of-property-ownership instincts
ownership, to-gain-and-hold-ownership-over-things instinct

P

p, the-p-speech-sounds instinct (The p speech sounds are the minimal
units of instinctual speech sounds that correspond roughly to the letter p
of the alphabet)

pain, avoiding-pain instinct

pain, distressing-pain instinct

pain, psychological-pain instinct (Here: psychological = instinctual !!) pain, the-emotional-and-behavioral-aspects-of-pain-sensations instincts

pain, to-feel-pain instinct (= the-feeling-of-pain instinct)

pain, to-show-strength-in-the-face-of-pain instinct

pained, a-puckered,-pained-expression instinct

pair bonding, pair-bonding instincts

palavering, palavering instinct

palm, to-palm-someone-off-with-an-excuse-or-a-lie instinct

palmar response, palmar-response instinct

palpitation, palpitation instinct

panache, panache instinct

panic, a-feeling-of-panic instinct

panic, a-surge-of-panic-instinct

panic, nervous-panic instinct

panic, panic-attack instinct

panic, the-panic-face instinct

pan(t)ophobia, pan(t)ophobia (fear of everything) instinct (a most unpleasant abnormal instinct)

parental, parental-affection instinct

parental, parental-care instinct

parental, parental-control-and-restraint instinct

parental, parental-devotion instinct

parental, parental-games instincts (peek-a-boo, hand-clapping, rhythmical knee-dropping, lifting high, tickling, play-hiding, play-fleeing, play-catching, etc.)

parental, parental-love instinct

parents, parents-smile-softly-at-the-baby instinct

parochialism, parochialism instinct

parsimony, devotion-to-parsimony instinct (= parsimony instinct) part, to-take-someone's-part instinct

partiality, partiality instinct

parting, smiling-at-the-parting instinct

partition, partition-other-people-into-friends-and-aliens instinct

partners, how-we-attract-partners instincts

partners, women-choose-partners-from-a-wish-to-have-healthy-children instinct

parts, to-recognize-parts-of-an-object-and-their-relations-to-the-others instinct

parturiphobia, parturiphobia (fear of childbirth) instinct

party, party (social event) instinct

pass down, to-pass-down-stories,-traditions,-etc-to-a-younger-generation instinct

passion, a-feeling-of-very-strong-sexual-attraction-for-someone instinct

passion, a-passion-for-something/someone instinct

passion, passion (violent emotional outbreak) instinct

passionate, to-be-passionate-about-something instincts

passive, passive-resistance instinct

passive, passive-submission instinct

passiveness, passiveness instinct

pat, to-give-someone-a-pat-on-the-back (you tell them that you approve of what they have done or are trying to do) instinct

paternal, paternal instincts

pathos, pathos instinct

patience, patience instinct

patient, patient-tolerance instinct

patriotism, patriotism instinct

patrolling, patrolling-the-natural-environment instinct

pattern, pattern-detection instincts

pattern, pattern-discrimination instincts

pattern, pattern-recognition instincts

patterns, to-wish-to-discover-beautiful-patterns instinct

pay,   to-pay-someone-back-for-doing-something-unpleasant-to-you instinct

peace, a-feeling-of-peace instinct

peace, peace-with-yourself instinct

peacemaking, peacemaking instinct

peccatophobia, peccatophobia (fear of committing a sin) instinct

peck, to-peck-someone-on-the-cheek (you give them a quick, light kiss) instinct

pecking order, pecking-order instincts

peckish, feeling-peckish instinct

peculiar, feeling-peculiar instincts

peculiar, seeing-blood-make-you-feel-a-bit-peculiar-inside-you instinct

pedantry, pedantry instinct

peddle, to-peddle-an-idea-or-information instinct

pedestal, to-knock-someone-off-their-pedestal instinct

pedestal, to-put-someone-on-a-pedestal instinct

pedophilia, pedophilia instinct (is an abnormal instinct)

peep, to-peep-at-something instinct

peer, peer-rejection instinct

peering, peering instinct

pelt, to-pelt-someone-with-something instinct

penal, penal-sanctions instinct

penance, penance instinct

penitence, penitence instinct

pep talk, pep-talk instinct

perception, perception instincts (visual perception, perception of time, etc)

perception, person-perception instinct

perception, self-perception instinct

perceptions,   our-perceptions-are-influenced-by-our-emotions instincts perceptual, perceptual-constancy instincts (brightness constancy, color constancy, size constancy, shape constancy)

perceptual, perceptual-integration instincts

perceptual, perceptual-process instincts. Perceptual processes are similar to reflexes. They are also fast, automatic, and innately specified, like reflexes. Remember that reflexes and instincts can learn

perfect pitch, to-have-perfect-pitch instinct

perfectionism, perfectionism instinct

permanence, object-permanence instinct

permissiveness, permissiveness instinct

perplexed, to-be-perplexed instinct

persecution, persecution instincts

perseverance, belief-perseverance instinct

perseverance, perseverance instinct

persistence, persistence instinct

persistent objects, to-expect-that-persistent-objects-exist instinct (having this prejudice is fundamental to the survival of humans and other land vertebrates)

person, person-perception instinct

personal attack, personal-attack instinct

personal identity, personal-identity (feeling of being the same person) instinct

personal mark, the-need-to-leave-personal-mark-in-your-home-territory instinct

personal sincerity, personal-sincerity instinct (= that a man deal honestly with himself)

personal space, defending-your-personal-space instinct

personal space, personal-space instinct

personal territory, personal-territory instinct

personal vanity, personal-vanity-and-pride instinct

personhood, feeling-of-personhood instinct

perspective, a-sense-of-perspective instinct

persuade, to-persuade instinct (normal behavior needs to be explained!)

persuaded, to-be-persuaded instinct (normal behavior needs to be explained!)

persuasion, persuasion instinct (= to-persuade instinct)

persuasion, wheedling-persuasion instinct

perversity, perversity instincts. Perversities are abnormal instincts. There are an enormous number of perversities

pessimism, pessimism instinct

pestering, pestering instinct

pet, pet-idea instinct

pet, pet-name instinct

pettiness, pettiness instinct

petting, petting instinct

petulance, petulance instinct

phasmophobia, phasmophobia (fear of ghosts) instinct

pheromones, excreting-pheromones instincts

pheromones, reaction-to-pheromones instincts

phi, phi-phenomenon instinct

philanderer, philanderer instinct

philanthropy, philanthropy instinct

philia, philia instincts. Philias are abnormal instincts. There are an enormous number of philias

phlegmaticism, phlegmaticism (emotional coldness) instinct

phobophobia, phobophobia (fear of fear/acquiring a phobia) instincts

phoneme, phoneme-formation instincts (The English language has 44 phonemes)

phonemes, basic-phonemes instincts

phonophobia, phonophobia (fear of sound/the sound of one's own voice) instincts

physical attack, physical-attack intinct

physical attractiveness, the-sense-of-physical-attractiveness instinct

physical pain, the-emotional-and-bahavioral-aspects-of-the-feeling-of-physical-pain instinct

physical pain, we-cry-if-we-are-in-physical-pain instinct

physical strength, admiration-for-physical-strength-and-prowess instinct

pick a fight, to-pick-a-fight-or-quarrel-with-someone instinct

picking, picking-nits instinct

picking, picking-on-someone instinct

picture, to-picture-something-in-your-mind instinct

pictures, the-deriving-of-erotic-stimulation-from-viewing-sexually-oriented-pictures-or-films instinct

piety, piety instinct

pigheaded, to-be-pigheaded-and-determined instinct .

piloerection, piloerection instinct

pilomotor, pilomotor-response ('goose-bumps') instinct

pine, to-be-pining-for-something instinct

pine, to-pine-for-someone-who-has-died-or-gone-away instinct

pique, pique instinct

pit, to-pit-your-wits-against-someone instinct

pitch, to-have-perfect-pitch instinct

pitifully, to-act-pitifully instinct

pitiless, pitiless instinct

pity, to-feel-pity-for-someone instinct

placate, to-placate-someone instinct

placidity, placidity instinct

plainspeaking, plainspeaking instinct

plaintive, a-plaintive-voice instinct

planning, planning instinct (= the-capacity-for-planned-action instinct)

platonic, platonic-friendship instinct

play, boys-play-more-with-"masculine"-toys instincts (genetic exceptions exist, e.g. most homosexuals)

play, girls-play-more-with-"feminine"-toys instincts (exceptions: e.g. tomboys (genetic!) and homosexuals (genetic, directly or indirectly))

play, play instincts (thrill play, muscle play, love-play (in the broadest sense), mechanical play, fantasy play, day-dreaming, clever play, creative play, locomotory play, vertigo play, neophilic play, play-fighting, play-chasing, play-fleeing, etc)

play, play-fighting instinct

play, play-talking instinct

play, rough-and-tumble-play instinct

play, the-mother/father-plays-with-her/his-baby instinct (making funny faces at the baby, tickling the baby, swinging the baby playfully up into the air, playing peekaboo, play-fleeing, play-hiding, play-discovering, pretending to drop the baby, etc)

play, the-play-face instinct

play, to-play-a-joke-or-a-trick-on-someone instinct

play, to-play-aggressively instinct

play, to-play-around-with-the-idea-of-doing-something instinct

playfulness, playfulness instinct (= a-sense-of-playfulness instinct)

plea, plea instinct

pleading, pleading instinct

pleasant, pleasant-imagery instinct

pleasantness, pleasantness instinct

pleasantry, pleasantry instinct

please others, to-please-others instinct

pleasure, pleasure instinct

pleasure, pleasure-hunting instinct

pleasure, providing-pleasure instinct

pleasure, vengeful-pleasure instinct

pleasure, we-experience-pleasure-in-our-daily-lives instincts

pleasures, general-interest-in-the-pleasures-of-life instinct

plod, to-plod-along instinct
pluck, to-pluck-up-the-courage-to-do-something instinct
plug away, to-plug-away-at-something instinct
plume on, to-plume-oneself-on-something instinct
plunge, to-plunge-into-an-activity instinct
poignancy, poignancy instinct
pointing, pointing instincts (the forefinger point, the hand point, the head point, the body point, the secretive eyes point, etc.)
poise, poise instinct
poison, to-poison-one's-mind-against-another-person instinct
poker face, poker-face instinct
polarizing, a-polarizing-opinion instincts
polemics, polemics instinct
politeness, politeness instinct
political, political-attack instinct
political, to-play-political-games instincts
polygynous, mildly-polygynous instinct
pomposity, pomposity instinct
ponder, to-ponder instinct
pong, pong (an unpleasant smell) instinct
ponophobia, ponophobia (fear of pain/work/being overworked) instincts
pooh, 'Pooh!' instinct (expressing disapproval or scorn)
position, to-keep-track-of-the-position-of-the-head-relative-to-the-stimulus-after-the-light-goes-out instinct
positive, positive-self-feeling instinct
possession, possession instinct
possessiveness, possessiveness-about-things instinct
possessiveness, possessiveness-towards-persons instinct
postural, postural-movements-associated-with-the-senses instincts
posture, posture instincts
posture, to-maintain-an-upright-posture instinct

pounds, your-heart-pounds-with-joy instinct
pouting, pouting-mouth instinct
power, power-assertion instinct
power, power-play instincts
power, power-struggle-for-dominance-within-the-group instinct
power, thirst-for-power instinct (= the-desire-for-power instinct)
power, will-to-power instinct
powerlessness, a-feeling-of-powerlessness instinct
practical, practical-joke instinct
practical, practical-reasoning instinct
practical, practical-understandings-of-things instincts
pragmatism, pragmatism instinct
praise, to-praise-someone-or-something instinct
prance, prance instinct
praying, praying-to-God instinct (also atheists and agnostics pray
to God when reality steps in; instincts are situational)
preattentive, preattentive-processing instinct
precaution, precaution instincts
precious, precious-memories instinct
precious, precious-possessions instinct
precognition, precognition instinct
precoital, precoital-behaviors instincts
preconceived, preconceived-feelings instincts
preconception, preconception instincts
predators, escaping-from-predators instinct
prediction, prediction instincts
predictions,   to-make-predictions-about-what-other-people-are-
thinking instinct
preening, preening instinct
pregnancy, pregnancy-sickness instinct
prejudice, group-prejudice instincts
prejudice, prejudice instincts

preludes, dance-and-music-and-poetry-are-common-preludes-to-sex instincts

premeditation, premeditation instinct

premonition, premonition instinct

preoccupation, preoccupation instinct

preparedness, preparedness instincts

preparing, preparing-the-body-for-violent-activity instincts

presence, to-feel-another-person's-presence-in-the-room instinct

present, the-sense-of-the-present instinct

presentiment, presentiment instinct (foreboding instinct)

preservation, self-preservation instinct(s) (see: Introduction)

pressure sensation, the-emotional-and-behavioral-aspects-of-the-pressure-sensation instinct

pressure, the-pressure-of-too-great-expectation instinct

pressure, the-skin-is-sensitive-to-pressure instinct

prestige, prestige instinct

prestige, social-prestige instinct

presumption, presumption instinct

pretence, pretence instinct

pretension, pretension instinct

pride, ethnic-and-national-pride instinct

pride, nursing-your-pride instinct

pride, pride (a sense of dignity and self-respect) instinct

pride, to-have-pride-in-something-that-you-have instinct

pride, to-take-pride-in-something-that-you-do instinct

primacy, the-primacy-effect instinct (= early-presented information has an undue influence on final judgment)

principle of mediocrity, principle-of-mediocrity instinct (we can learn about our own capabilities from observing others, and we can learn about others by putting ourselves in their places)

privacy, the-sense-of-privacy instincts

privacy, the-sense-of-privacy-that-surround-sexual-feelings instinct private, human-sex-is-a-private thing instinct

problem, problem-solving-activity instinct

problem, problem-solving-strategies instincts (trial-and-error reasoning, algorithmic reasoning, heuristic reasoning, logical reasoning)

problems, to-enjoy-solving-problems instinct

procedural, procedural-memory instinct (= memory for motor movements, skills, and other procedures)

prodding, prodding instinct

profanity, profanity instinct

promiscuity, promiscuity instinct (30 per cent of all white males have a gene for promiscuity. Human males in general have a tendency towards promiscuity, and females a tendency towards monogamy, as we would predict on evolutionary grounds.)

promise, to-promise-that-you-will-do-something instinct

proneness, proneness instinct

pronunciation, pronunciation instincts

propensity, propensity instinct

property, personal-property-and-space instincts

property, property instinct

property, property-rights instincts

property, we-tend-to-fight-tenaciously-for-property-which-we-have-put-great-effort-into-acquiring instinct

propitiation, propitiation instinct

proportion, rules-of-proportion-and-composition instincts

proprietarily, to-behave-proprietarily-toward-your-mate instinct

proselytize, to-proselytize instinct

prosody, prosody instincts (prosody = tone, tempo, rhythm, loudness, pacing, and other qualities of voice that modify the meaning of verbal utterances)

prostrate, you-prostrate-yourself instinct

prostrating, prostrating instinct

prostration, prostration instinct

protect, to-protect-your-territory instinct

protective, protective-feelings instincts

protective, to-feel-protective-of-a-baby-or-child instinct

protest, protest instinct

proud, to-feel-proud instinct

proudest, someone's-proudest-possession instinct

provocability, provocability instinct

provocability, the-victim's-provocability instinct

provocation, provocation instinct

prowess, admiration-for-physical-strength-and-prowess instinct

prowl, to-prowl instinct

proximity, the-principle-of-proximity instinct (the viewer perceives things that are close together as belonging together)

prudence, prudence instinct

prudery, prudery instinct

prudery, sexual-prudery instinct

prudishness, prudishness instinct

prurience, prurience instinct

pseudopresentiment, pseudopresentiment instinct

psychic pain, psychic-pain instinct

puckering, puckering instinct (= a-part-of-your-face-puckers instinct)

pugnacity, pugnacity instinct

pull, pull-oneself-together instinct

punctiliousness, punctiliousness instinct

punishment, punishment instinct

pupil, pupil-dilation/constriction-signals instincts (e.g. if a female/male feels emotionally attracted towards a male/female companion, her/his pupils dilate)

puppy, puppy-love instinct

purge, you-purge-your-thoughts-of-something-undesirable-such-as-hatred-or-envy instinct purpose, a-sense-of-purpose instinct

purposive, purposive-activity instinct

purr, to-purr (speak in a soft, gentle voice) instinct

pusillanimity, pusillanimity (timidity and the fear of taking risks) instincts

put down, to-put-someone-down instinct

puzzle over, to-puzzle-over-something instinct

puzzled, creasing-the-forehead-when-you-are-puzzled instinct

puzzled, to-be-puzzled instinct

pyrophobia, pyrophobia (fear of fire) instinct

Q

q the-q-speech-sounds instinct (The q speech sounds are the minimal units of instinctual speech sounds that correspond roughly to the letter q of the alphabet)

quake, quake instinct

qualm, qualm instinct

quarrel, a-quarrel-consisting-of-an-interchange-of-insults-and-rebukes instinct

quaver, someone's-voice-quavers (sounds unsteady, uncertain and nervous) instinct

queasy, feeling-queasy instinct

queer, a-queer-feeling instinct

queer, a-queer-sensation instinct

queerness, queerness instinct

quest, quest instinct

question, question instinct

questioning, to-have-a-questioning-expression-on-one's-face instinct

questions, children's-questions instinct

quibble, to-quibble-about-something instinct

quiescence, quiescence (a feeling of restfulness) instinct
quietness, quietness instinct
quietness, quietness-of-authority instinct
quizzical, a-quizzical-expression instinct
quizzical, a-quizzical-glance instinct
quizzical, a-quizzical-look instinct
quizzical, quizzical-amusement instinct
quizzical, to-stare-quizzically instinct

R

r, the-r-speech-sounds instinct (The r speech sounds are the minimal units of instinctual speech sounds that correspond roughly to the letter r of the alphabet)
    rabble, rabble-rousing instinct
    racial, racial-consciousness instinct
    racial, racial-prejudice instinct
    racism, racism instinct (Remember: instincts can learn)
    raconteur, raconteur instinct
    radicalism, radicalism instinct
    rage, feeling-of-rage instinct
    rage, rage instinct
    rage, rage-at-ego-injury instinct
    rage, uncontrollable-rage instinct
    rage, violent-rage instinct
    raillery, raillery instinct
    raise, to-raise-one's-voice instinct
    raising, raising-eyebrows-in-surprise instinct
    rancor, rancor instinct
    rank, networks-of-rank-and-status instinct
    rank, the-struggle-for-rank instinct
    rapid, rapid-eye-movement (REM) instinct

rational, ordinary-rational-control instincts
rational, rational-willing instinct
rationalization, rationalization instinct
reality, reality-feeling instinct
reality, to-construct-physical-reality instincts
rearing, child-rearing instinct
reason, reason-is-the-slave-of-the-passions instincts
reasoning, reasoning instinct
reassurance, a-sense-of-reassurance instinct
reassured, to-be-reassured-by-someone instinct
rebel, to-rebel-against-parental-authority instinct
rebellious, rebellious-behavior instinct
rebellious, the-rebellious-teenage-years instinct
rebelliousness, rebelliousness instinct
rebuke, you-rebuke-someone instinct
recall, recall instincts (e.g. to-recall-facts instinct)
recall, we-are-sometimes-unable-to-recall-some-very-unpleasant-or-threatening-memories instinct
recklessness, recklessness instinct
reclaiming, reclaiming instinct (Natural, spontaneous behavior is instinctual behavior!)
recognition, pattern-recognition instincts
recognition, recognition instinct
recognition, the-use-of-the-face-for-personal-recognition instinct
reconciliation, reconciliation instinct
recrimination, recrimination instinct
recriminatory, recriminatory-arguments instinct
rectitude, rectitude instinct
redirected, redirected-activities instinct (actions diverted on to a bystander)
redirected, redirected-aggression instinct (sometimes the redirection process is greatly delayed in its expressions)

reflection, reflection instinct (considering instinct)

reflectively, to-scratch-one's-chin-reflectively instinct

reflex, reflex instincts. Reflexes are instincts ("little instincts"), but instincts are not necessarily reflexes. Reflexes can learn. There are an enormous number of reflexes. More than 70 infant reflexes have been identified.

reflexive, reflexive-behavior instincts (e.g. «Reflexively, he stepped backwards»)

regression, regression instinct (e.g. a 12-year-old child may show regression by thumb sucking)

regret, to-regret instinct (= regret instinct)

rejection, rejection instinct (normal behavior needs to be explained!)

rejoicing, rejoicing-behavior instinct

relationship, a-love-hate-relationship instincts

relationships, the-need-to-have-relationships-with-others instinct

relaxation, a-sense-of-relaxation instinct

relaxation, a-state-of-calm-relaxation instinct

relaxation, deep-relaxation instinct

relaxation, relaxation-feeling instinct

relaxation, the-postures-of-relaxation instincts (nightly sleep, the full sleeping pattern, dozing, the forty winks, the catnap, the snooze, the vertical lean, the arms support, the head support, the sitting down, the body slump, the lying-down, the full limbs sprawl, the one-leg stand, the knee-kneel, the double knee-kneel, the all-fours rest, the squat-kneel, the flat-footed squat, the tiptoe squat, the squat-sit, the full legs-fold posture, the lotus position, the simple leg side-curl, breaks, 'a change is as good as a rest', etc)

relaxation, the-relaxation-response instinct

release, feeling-of-release instinct

relief, comic-relief instinct

relief, feelings-of-relief instinct

relief, relief instinct

relief, to-sigh-with-relief instinct

religion, religion-affiliation instinct

religious, a-moment-of-sudden-religious-insight-or-awakening instinct

religious, religious-belief instinct

religious, religious-emotion instincts

religious, religious-trance instinct

reluctance, to-do-something-with-a-feeling-of-reluctance instinct (= a-feeling-of-reluctance instinct)

REM, non-REM-dreams instincts (non-REM-dreams are ordinary instincts at work during non-REM sleep)

REM, REM-dreams instincts (REM-dreams are ordinary instincts at work during REM sleep)

REM, REM-erections instinct (= erections during REM sleep = erection instinct; see above)

remember, to-remember instinct

remembrance, remembrance instinct

reminder, reminder instinct

remonstrate, to-remonstrate instinct

remorse, feelings-of-remorse instinct

remorse, remorse instinct

repartee, repartee instinct

repentance, repentance instinct

reply, reply instinct

repression, repression instincts (Remember: instincts can learn)

reprisal, reprisal instinct

reproach, reproach instinct

reproduction, reproduction instinct(s) (see: Introduction)

reproductive, reproductive instincts

reproof, reproof instinct

repudiation, repudiation instinct

repugnance, repugnance instinct

reputation, reputation instinct (Think! Reputation is an instinct!)

reputation, to-be-concerned-to-protect-one's-personal-reputation instinct

resentment, resentment instinct
resentment, to-feel-a-twinge-of-resentment instinct
reserved, to-be-reserved instinct
resignation, resignation instinct
resist, to-resist-the-urge instinct(s)
resistance, passive-resistance instinct
resistance, resistance instinct
resistance, resistance-to-temptation instincts
resolution, resolution instinct
respect, respect-for-"rank and wealth" instinct
respect, respect-of-others instinct
respecting, respecting-a-person instinct
respond sexually, to-respond-sexually-to-hemispherical-buttocks-and-red-labia-and-hemispherical-breasts-and-red-lips instincts
responsibility, a-sense-of-moral-responsibility instinct
responsibility, diffusion-of-responsibility instincts
responsibility, our-willingness-to-ascribe-responsibility instinct
responsible, holding-responsible instinct
responsible, to-be-responsible instinct (= a-sense-of-responsibility instinct)
rest activity cycle, rest-activity-cycle instincts
restlessness, restlessness instinct
restrain, to-struggle-to-restrain-one's-natural-impulses instinct (is natural!)
retaliation, retaliation instinct
retention, retention-of-information instinct
reticence, reticence instinct
retribution, the-fear-of-retribution instinct
retroactive, retroactive-association instinct
returning, returning-a-kindness instinct
revelling, revelling instinct
revenge, revenge instinct

revenge, to-nurture-thoughts-of-revenge instinct
revenge, to-plan-revenge instinct
revenge, you-feel-a-desire-for-revenge instinct
reverence, reverence instinct
reverie, reverie instinct
revile, you-revile-someone-or-something instinct
revulsion, revulsion instinct
reward, reward-dependence instinct
reward, to-reward-someone instinct
rhetorical, rhetorical-speech instinct
rhypophobia, rhypophobia (fear of defecation—the process/defe-
cation—the product) instincts
rhyming, rhyming instinct
rhythm, rhythm instincts
rhythms, biological-rhythms instincts
ridicule, ridicule instinct
right and wrong, , the-sense-of-right-and-wrong instinct
righteousness, righteousness instinct
rigidity, rigidity instincts
riot, riot instinct
ripe language, ripe-language instinct
riposte, riposte instinct
risk taking, risk-taking instinct
ritual, ritual instinct(s) (see: Introduction)
rivalry, rivalry instinct
rivalry, sibling-rivalry instinct
rivet, people-or-things-rivet-you instinct
roar, a-roar-of-anger instinct
roasting, to-give-someone-a-roasting instinct
rock, the-infant-is-held-and-either-rocked,-patted-or-stroked instinct

rock,   we-rock-back-and-forth-on-our-feet-when-we-are-in-a-state-of-conflict instinct

rock, to-rock-with-anguish instinct

rock, to-rock-with-laughter instinct

romance, romance instinct

romantic, a-romantic-fling instinct

romantic, romantic-intimacies instincts

romantic, romantic-love instinct

romantic, romantic-relationship(s) instinct

romantic, to-be-romantic instinct (romanticism instinct)

romping, romping instinct

rooting, the-rooting-reflex instinct (the rooting reflex enables the baby to take its mother's nipple in its mouth and nurse)

rote learning, rote-learning instinct

rotten, to-dread-the-odor-of-rotten-eggs,-vegetables,-etc instinct

rough, rough-and-tumble-play instinct

row, a-family-row instincts

rub, to-rub-one's-chin-thoughtfully instinct

rude, a-readiness-to-be-rude instinct

rude, rude-gesture instincts (e.g. to put one's tongue out)

rude, to-be-rude-to-people instinct (rudeness instinct)

rule, rule-worship instinct

ruling, a-ruling-idea-or-feeling instinct

rumination, quiet-sessions-of-rumination instinct

rumination, rumination instinct

rumor, rumor instinct

rumors, to-peddle-rumors instinct

run away with, a-feeling-runs-away-with-you instinct

running, running instinct

rush, a-rush-in-someone's-physical-feelings-or-emotions instincts

ruthlessness, ruthlessness instinct

S

s, the-s-speech-sounds instinct (The s speech sounds are the minimal units of instinctual speech sounds that correspond roughly to the letter s of the alphabet)

saccadic movement, saccadic-movement instinct

sacredness, sacredness instinct

sacrifices, to-make-sacrifices-for-something instinct

sadism, sadism instinct

sadness, sadness instinct

sadness, the-sadness-that-accompanies-a-setback instinct

safety, to-strive-for-safety-and-security instinct

saliva, the-ceasing-of-secretion-of-saliva-on-intense-excitement instinct

salivation, salivation instincts (e.g. the mere thought of food makes you start to salivate)

saltiness, to-sense-saltiness instinct

salutation, salutation instinct (we are, in general, incapable of beginning or ending any kind of encounter without performing some type of salutation)

sanctification, sanctification instinct

sanctions, penal-sanctions instinct

sanctity, the-sanctity-of-something instinct

sanguine, you-are-sanguine-about-something instinct

sarcasm, sarcasm instinct

sarcastic, sarcastic-remark instinct

sardonic, sardonic-behavior instinct

sardonic, sardonic-humor instinct (= grim-humor instinct)

satiety, the-feeling-of-satiety-after-a-meal instinct

satire, satire instinct

satisfaction, job-satisfaction instinct

satisfaction, satisfaction instinct

satisfaction, the-restful-satisfaction-from-an-altruistic-act-well-and-truly-placed instinct

satisfying, satisfying-emotional-experience instinct

savagery, savagery instinct

savor, to-savor-food-or-drink instinct

scaling, scaling-of-responses-in-aggressive-interactions instincts

scapegoating, scapegoating instinct

scolding, scolding instinct

scolding, the-scolding-charges-of-racism-and-sexism instinct (Natural, spontaneous behavior is instinctual behavior)

scar, an-unpleasant-experience-scars-one's-mind instinct

scared, the-scared-face instinct

scared, to-be-scared instinct

scene, to-make-a-scene instinct

scent, scent (a pleasant smell) instinct

scent, you-scent-something (you begin to feel that it is going to happen)

scoffing, scoffing instinct

scolding, scolding instinct

scopophilia, scopophilia (the deriving of sexual pleasure from visual sources) instinct

scopophobia, scopophobia (fear of being seen by others) instinct

scorn, laughter-of-scorn instinct

scorn, scorn instinct

scorn, to-laugh-to-scorn instinct

scotophobia, scotophobia (fear of the dark/darkness) instincts (not used for the common condition in children and adults)

scourge, you-scourge-someone instinct

scout, to-scout-the-surrounding-area instinct

scrap, to-love-a-scrap instinct

scratch, to-scratch-a-part-of-one's-body instinct

scream, to-scream instinct

scream, to-scream-in-terror instinct
screaming, screaming-child instinct
scrutinizing, scrutinizing instinct
scuffle, scuffle instinct
scuttle, to-scuttle-somewhere instinct
search, to-search-one's-mind-for-something instinct
searing, to-feel-a-searing-pain instinct
seasickness, seasickness instinct
secure, to-feel-secure instinct (= the-feeling-of-security instinct)
seditious, seditious-behavior instinct
seduce, to-charm-and-seduce-the-sex-object instinct
seduction, seduction instinct
seeing, seeing instincts
seize, to-seize-something instinct
selective, selective-attention instinct
selective, selective-inattention instinct
self, a-sense-of-self-and-other instinct
self, feeling-of-self instinct
self, negative-self-feeling instinct
self, positive-self-feeling instinct
self-abandonment, self-abandonment instinct
self-abasement, self-abasement instinct (feeling-of-inferiority instinct)
self-abnegation, self-abnegation instinct
self-absorption, self-absorption instinct
self-accusation, self-accusation instinct
self-activity, self-activity instinct
self-actualization, self-actualization instinct
self-advertisement instinct
self-assertiveness, self-assertiveness instinct
self-assurance, self-assurance instinct
self-attention, self-attention instinct
self-attribution, self-attribution instinct

self-awareness, self-awareness instinct
self-blame, self-blame instinct
self-complacency, self-complacency instinct
self-conceit, self-conceit instinct
self-conception, self-conception instinct
self-condemnation, self-condemnation instinct
self-confidence, self-confidence instinct
self-consciousness, self-consciousness instinct
self-control, self-control instinct
self-correction, self-correction instinct
self-criticism, self-criticism instinct
self-deceit, self-deceit instinct
self-deception instinct
self-defense, self-defense instincts
self-degradation, self-degradation instinct
self-denial, self-denial instinct
self-directedness, self-directedness instinct
self-discipline, self-discipline instinct
self-discovery, self-discovery instinct
self-display, self-display instinct (positive-self-impulse instinct)
self-distrust instinct
self-doubt, self-doubt instinct
self-effacing, self-effacing instinct
self-efficacy, a-sense-of-self-efficacy instinct
self-entertainment instinct
self-esteem, self-esteem instinct
    self-evaluation, self-evaluation instinct
self-expression, self-expression instinct
self-grooming, self-grooming instincts
self-identity, self-identity instinct
self-image, self-image instinct
self-importance, a-sense-of-self-importance instinct

self-improvement, the-concern-with-self-improvement instinct

self-indulgence, self-indulgence instinct

self-intimacies, self-intimacies instincts (the hair clasp, the mouth touch, the temple support, the cheek support, the chin support, the jaw support, interlocking the fingers, clasping one palm with another, clasping one hand tightly in the other, the folded arms, the self- hug, leg-hugging, thigh-clasping, the touching finger tips, the head-lowered-on-to-shoulder posture, rock ourselves back and fourth, etc)

self-love, self-love instinct

self-perception, self-perception instinct

self-pity, self-pity instinct (= the-mood-of-self-pity instinct)

self-possessed, to-be-self-possessed instinct

self-preservation, self-preservation instinct(s) (see: Introduction)

self-realization, self-realization instinct

self-recognition, self-recognition instinct

self-recrimination instinct

self-renunciation instinct

self-repression instinct

self-reproach instinct

self-respect, self-respect instinct

self-restraint, self-restraint-with-respect-to-bodily-discharges instinct

self-restraint, self-restraint-with-respect-to-sexual-impulses instinct

self-righteousness, self-righteousness instinct

self-sacrifice, self-sacrifice instinct

self-satisfaction, self-satisfaction instinct

self-sentiment, self-sentiment instinct

selfish, to-be-selfish instinct

selfish, to-be-unselfish instinct

selflessness, we-universally-admire-and-praise-selflessness,-but-we-simply-do-not-practice-what-we-preach instinct

semantic, semantic-memory instinct (memory for meaning)

semantic, to-infer-semantic-meaning instinct

semismile, a-semismile-expression instinct

semiwakeful, a-semiwakeful-state instinct

sensation, sensation-seeking instinct

sensationalism, sensationalism instinct

sensitized, sensitized-hand instinct (the-sensitive-nature-of-our-hands instinct)

sensory, sensory-seeking instincts

sensual, sensual-pleasure instincts

sentences, memory-for-tacit-implications-of-sentences instinct

sentences, to-speak-in-sentences instinct

sentience, sentience need (need for sensual pleasures) instinct

sentimentality, sentimentality instinct

sentimentalizing, sentimentalizing instinct

separation, infant's-separation-anxiety instinct

separation, separation-anxiety instinct

serenity, serenity instinct

serial, serial-monogamy instinct

sermonizing, sermonizing instinct

servility, servility instinct

seven-plus-or-minus-two, seven-plus-or-minus-two instinct (the term denotes the number of discrete pieces of information that can be held in short-term memory at one time)

sex appeal, the-feel-of-sex-appeal instinct

sex experimentation, sex-experimentation-among-children instinct

sex feeling, sex-feeling instinct

sex play in children, sex-play-in-children instinct (overt sex-play romping)

sexiness, sexiness instinct

sexual activity, sexual-activity-continuous-through-menstrual-cycle instinct

sexual advertisement, sexual-advertisement instinct

sexual arousal, sexual-arousal instinct

sexual desire, sexual-desires instinct
sexual ecstasy, sexual-ecstasy instinct
sexual excitement, sexual-excitement instinct
sexual fantasies, sexual-fantasies instinct
sexual flush, sexual-flush instinct
sexual gratification, sexual-gratification instinct
sexual identity, sexual-identity instinct
sexual intimacy, sexual-intimacy instincts
sexual jealousy, sexual-jealousy instinct
sexual masochism, sexual-masochism instinct
sexual orientation, sexual-orientation instincts
sexual passion, sexual-passion instinct
sexual pleasure, sexual-pleasure instincts
sexual response, the-sexual-response-cycle instinct
sexual restrictions, sexual-restrictions instinct
sexual sadism, sexual-sadism instinct
sexual violence, sexual-violence instinct (Remember: instincts can learn)
shade, to-shade-one's-eyes instinct
shaking, shaking-a-fist-at-someone instinct
shaking, the-baby-is-shaking-its-head-from-side-to-side (= no, no, no) instinct
shame, shame instinct
shamefaced, to-be-shamefaced instinct
shape, by-feeling-the-physical-thing-you-determine-its-shape instinct
share, disrespect-for-those-who-would-not-share instinct
share, to-feel-a-need-to-share-your-excitements instinct
share, to-share-an-enthusiasm-or-an-interest instinct
share, to-share-food instinct
sharp, sharp-remarks instinct
shelter, finding-shelter instinct
shiver, a-shiver-of-excitement instinct

shivering, to-be-shivering-because-you-are-cold instinct

shivering, to-be-shivering-because-you-are-frightened instinct

shock, the-need-to-shock-others instinct

shoo, to-shout-'Shoo!'-at-an-animal-in-order-to-make-it-go-away instinct

short temper, short-temper instinct

short term memory, short-term-memory instinct

shorter, men-seek-shorter-wives instinct

shoulder, to-put-an-arm-around-a-friend's-shoulder instinct

shout, to-shout instinct

shout, to-shout-encouragement-to-people instinct

shout, to-shout-something-out instinct

show, show-someone/something-off instinct

show, to-show-someone-round instinct

shriek, to-shriek-in-alarm instinct

shriek, to-shriek-with-laughter instinct

shriek, to-shriek-with-pain instinct

shriek, to-shriek-with-terror instinct

shrillness, shrillness instinct

shrug, to-shrug-one's-shoulders instinct

shudder, to-shudder instinct

shush, to-say-'shush'-when-you-are-telling-someone-to-be-quiet instinct

shy, a-shy-smile instinct

shy, to-be-too-shy-to-speak instinct

shyness, shyness instinct (Note: infants show shyness)

sickness, feelings-of-"sickness" instinct

sides, to-take-sides (with someone) instinct

sigh, to-sigh instinct

sight, the-sight-of-food-triggers-a-desire-to-eat instinct

sign language, sign-language instincts

silent, silent-emotion instinct

similarity, the-principle-of-similarity instinct (the viewer perceives similar things as being related)

simplification, simplification instinct

simulate, to-simulate-a-feeling-or-an-action instinct

sincerity, sincerity instinct

singing, singing instinct

sisterhood, sisterhood instinct

situation, to-identify-the-current-situation-as-being-of-a-certain-kind instinct

skepticism, skepticism instinct

skin, like-the-feel-of-something-on-your-skin instinct (= skin-pleasure instinct)

skin, skin-contact instinct (= body-contact instinct)

skin, skin-eroticism instinct

skin, the-naked-skin-of-the-woman-is-used-as-a-sexual-releaser instinct

skin, the-skin-sense instinct

skip, to-skip instinct

slap, you-slap-someone-on-the-back instinct

sleep, non-REM-sleep instinct

sleep, REM-sleep instinct

sleep, sleep-wake-schedule instinct

sleep, the-postures-of-sleep instincts

sleepiness, the-feeling-of-sleepiness instinct

sleepwalking, sleepwalking instinct

slight, to-slight-someone instinct

slobbering mouth, the-slobbering-mouth-of-the-intensely-inhib-ited-assault instinct

sloppiness, sloppiness instinct

sloth, sloth instinct

slurp, to-slurp-a-liquid instinct

sly, to-give-a-sly-gesture instinct

sly, to-give-a-sly-look instinct

sly, to-give-a-sly-remark instinct
slyness, slyness instinct
smack, to-smack-one's-lips instinct
small, small-talk instinct
smell, beautiful-women-smell-nice instinct
smell,   the-emotional-and-behavioral-aspects-of-smell-sensation instincts
smell, the-sense-of-smell-contributes-to-the-sense-of-taste instinct
smell, the-smell-of-food-triggers-the-desire-to-eat instinct
smells, certain-smells-remind-you-of-certain-places instinct
smells, something-smells-pleasant/unpleasant instincts
smile, a-beaming-smile instinct
smile, a-big,-happy-smile instinct
smile, infants-smile-at-the-faces-of-their-caregivers instinct
smile, the-smile-on-the-face-of-a-fighting-boy instinct
smiles, smiles-of-admiration instinct
smiling, smiling instincts
smiling, smiling-child instinct
smiling, the-smiling-face instinct
smirk, to-smirk instinct
smugness, smugness instinct
snake, the-snake-reaction instinct
snakes, our-fascination-with-snakes instinct
snap, to-snap-at-someone instinct
snarl,   the-open-mouthed-snarl instinct (the-intention-move-ments-of-biting instinct)
snarl, to-snarl-something instinct
sneer, sneer (the facial expression) instinct
sneer, to-sneer-at-someone-or-something instinct
snicker, to-snicker instinct
snide, a-snide-comment-or-remark instinct
snigger, to-snigger instinct

snobbery, snobbery instinct
snobbishness, snobbishness instinct
snore, snore instinct
so what, a 'so what?'-feeling instinct
sob, to-sob instinct (= sobbing instinct)
social, social instincts
social, social-bonding instinct
social, social-facilitation instinct
social, social-hierarchy instinct(s) (see: Introduction)
social, social-imitation instinct
social, social-intimacies instinct
social, social-loafing instinct
social, social-phobia instincts (= fear of social situations)
social, social-status instinct
social, social-stigma instinct
social, social-tension instincts
social, to-avoid-social-stigma instinct
social, to-calculate-social-obligations instinct
social, to-interpret-social-situations instincts
socialization, socialization instincts (perhaps most instincts are socialization instincts)
soft, to-be-soft-hearted instinct
soft, to-get-a-sensual-pleasure-from-touching-soft-things instinct
softly, to-cry-softly instinct
solace, solace instinct
solemnity, his/her-mask-of-solemnity instinct
solemnity, the-sense-of-solemnity instinct
soliciting, soliciting-behavior instinct
solicitude, your-solicitude-for-someone instinct
solidarity, in-group-solidarity instinct
solidarity, solidarity instinct
solitude, the-terror-of-absolute-solitude instinct

solving, problem-solving-activity instincts

solving, to-enjoy-solving-problems instinct

soothing, soothing instincts (e.g. we employ stroking and patting movements to soothe an agitated individual)

soothing, soothing-a-baby-ain't-no-cure-for-the-baby-blues instinct

sore, a-sore-point instinct

sore, if-part-of-your-body-is-sore,-it-causes-you-pain-and-discomfort instinct

sore, you-are-sore-about-something instinct

soreness, a-feeling-of-body-soreness instinct

sorrow, a-feeling-of-sorrow instinct

sorry, to-be-sorry-about-a-situation instinct

sound, localization-of-sound instinct

sound, the-reflexive-turning-of-the-head-and-eyes-in-the-direction-of-a-sudden-or-alarming-sound instinct

sounds, sounds-conjure-up-memories-for-you instinct

sounds, sounds (represented by the letters of the alphabet)-in-a-language instincts

sounds, the-elementary-sounds-of-human-nonlinguistic-communication instincts

sourness, to-sense-sourness instinct

space, space-perception instincts (position,-direction,-form,-and-magnitude instincts)

space, space-time-matter instincts

spaces, dread-in,-and-of,-open-spaces instinct

spaces, dread-of-confined-spaces instinct

spank, to-spank-a-child instinct

spatial, spatial-orientation instinct

spatial, spatial-reasoning instinct

spatial, spatial-skills instincts

speciesism, speciesism instinct

speculation, speculation instinct

speculative, speculative-interpretation instinct

speech, speech-rhythm instinct

speech, to-produce-speech-sounds instincts

spider, the-spider-reaction instinct

spit, the-disgust-that-makes-you-spit-out-bad-tasting-food instinct

spit, to-spit instinct

spite, spite instinct

spontaneous friendship, spontaneous-friendship-formation instinct

spree, spree instinct

sprint, to-sprint instinct (see locomotion instincts)

squabble, family-squabble instinct

squabbling, squabbling instinct

squealing, squealing instinct

squeamishness, squeamishness instinct

squeeze, when-a-man-and-a-woman-have-to-squeeze-past-each-other,-the-man-twists-towards-the-woman,-while-she-twists-away-from-him instinct

stage fright, stage-fright instinct

stamina, stamina instinct

stamp, people-stamp-their-feet-when-they-are-angry instinct

stand, stand-with-more-weight-on-one-leg-and-stick-out-one-hip-more-than-the-other instinct

stand up fight, stand-up-fight instinct

standing, standing-your-ground instinct

stare, a-hostile-stare instinct

stare, stare-fixedly-into-space instinct

stare, to-feel-that-somebody-stare-at-you instinct

stare, to-give-somebody-a-hard-stare instinct

stare, to-stare-angrily-at-somebody instinct

staring, staring-at-interesting-visual-stimuli instinct

startle, startle-response instinct

startle, the-startle-posture instinct

stasibasiphobia, stasibasiphobia (fear of standing erect and walking) instinct

stasiphobia, stasiphobia (fear of standing) instinct

static sense, the-emotional-and-behavioral-aspects-of-the-static-
sense instincts

statistics, reasoning-about-statistics instinct

status, men-demonstrate-their-prowess-in-order-to-generate-sta-
tus instinct

status, status-differentiation instinct

status, status-seeking instinct

status, the-display-of-status instinct

status, to-be-conscious-of-his/her-status-among-colleagues instinct

stay, to-stay-in-love instincts (having fallen in love, he/she would
have to stay in love)

stench, stench (a strong and very unpleasant smell) instinct

stereotyping, stereotyping-people instinct

stern, a-stern-look-or-expression instinct

sternness, sternness instinct

stew, to-be-in-a-stew instinct

stiff, to-keep-a-stiff-upper-lip instinct

stiffness, a-feeling-of-body-stiffness instinct

stimulus generalization, stimulus-generalization instinct

stinginess, stinginess instinct

stinginess, to-be-intolerant-of-stinginess instinct

stirred, to-be-stirred instinct

stories, we-love-to-hear-stories instinct

story, telling-a-particular-story instinct

straight, to-keep-a-straight-face instinct

strain, mental-strains instinct

strange, to-feel-a-bit-strange instinct

strangeness, to-feel-the-strangeness instinct

stranger, stranger-anxiety-reaction-of-the-baby instinct

strangers, fear-of-strangers instinct

strangers, suspicion-of-strangers instinct

stray, your-thoughts-stray instinct

strength, a-sense-of-strength instinct

stress, reactions-to-stress instincts (the-stress-response instincts)

stress, the-stress-management instincts

stress, to-be-vulnerable-to-stress instincts

stress, to-feel-stress instinct

strictness, strictness instinct

strife, strife instinct

strike, an-idea-or-thought-strikes-you instinct

strike back, to-strike-back instinct

strike on, to-strike-on-a-solution,-answer,-plan,-etc (to unexpectedly think of it) instinct

stroke, to-stroke-someone-or-something (e.g. he stroked her hair affectionately) instinct

stroll, the-stroll-is(-also)-the-gait-of-the-man-pacing-up-and-down,-deep-in-thought instinct

strong language, strong-language instinct

struggling, struggling-for-success instinct

strut, to-strut (to walk in a proud way) instinct

stubbornness, stubbornness instinct

study, to-study instinct (in the widest sense of the word "study")

subdued, subdued-feelings instinct

sublimation, the-sublimation-of-a-strong-desire-or-feeling instinct

submission, passive-submission instincts (is much the same as in other mammals: cringing, crouching, groveling, whimpering, verbal pleading and begging for mercy, attempts to protect the most vulnerable parts of the body, etc)

subordination, subordination instincts (e.g. a subordinate (male or female) adopts a attitude of "femininity" towards a dominant individual)

subservience, subservience instinct

substitutes, our-tendency-towards-accepting-symbolic-substitutes-for-the-real-thing instinct

succeed, to-want-to-succeed instinct

success, enjoying-success instinct

success, fear-of-success instinct

success, striving-for-success instinct

sucking, sucking instinct

suckle, a-mother-suckles-a-baby instinct

sudden, sudden-body-movement instinct

suffer, to-suffer-pain-in-one's-body instinct

suffer, to-suffer-pain-in-one's-mind instinct

suffering, dread-of-suffering-or-disease instinct

sugary, to-prefer-sugary-foods instinct

suggestibility, suggestibility instinct

sullenness, sullenness instinct

sum people up, sum-people-up-after-a-first-meeting instinct

summon, to-summon-all-the-"will power" instinct

sunbathe, a-strong-tendency-to-sunbathe instinct

superior, feeling-superior instinct (= feelings-of-superiority instinct)

supernatural, beliefs-about-the-supernatural instinct

superstition, superstition instinct (superstition is a form of protective response unique to man)

supplication, supplication instinct

support, social-support instinct

support, the-need-of-a-sympathizing-support,-or-of-objects-of-admiration-and-reverence instinct

supportiveness, supportiveness instinct

suppressing, suppressing-thoughts instinct

suppression, a-deliberate-suppression-of-personal-feelings,-or-personal-likes-and-dislikes instincts

suppression, suppression instinct

sure, to-be-sure-about-one's-feelings,-wishes,-or-intentions instincts

sure, to-feel-sure instinct

surmise, you-surmise-that-something-is-true instinct

surprise, raising-eyebrows-in-surprise instinct

surprise, surprise instinct

surreptitious, surreptitious-behavior (e.g. he looked surreptitiously at his watch) instinct

survey, locality-survey instinct

survival, survival instincts («all» instincts are survival instincts)

survivor guilt, survivor-guilt instinct

suspicion, suspicion instinct

suspiciousness, suspiciousness instinct

suss, to-suss-someone-out (to discover what their true character is) instinct

swagger, to-swagger instinct

swanking, someone-is-swanking instinct

swear, to-swear instinct

sweet, a-strong-positive-response-to-sweet-tasting-objects instinct

sweet, a-sweet-smell-is-pleasant instinct

sweet, a-sweet-sound-is-pleasant instinct

sweet, to-eat-sweet-things-purely-for-pleasure instinct

sweetness, the-sweetness-of-freedom instinct

sweetness, to-sense-sweetness instinct

swim, babies-can-swim-when-only-a-few-weeks-old instinct

symbol, an-object-can-be-understood-both-as-a-thing-itself-and-as-a-symbol-of-something-else instinct

symbolophobia, symbolophobia (fear of symbols/symbolic representations) instincts

sympathy, sympathy instinct

synchrony, synchrony-of-movement-between-two-or-more-persons instinct

syncretism, syncretism instinct

synesthesia, synesthesia instincts (synesthesia is an involuntary joining in which the real information from one sense is joined or accompanies a perception in another)

syntax, syntax (the grammatical arrangement of words) instinct

T

t, the-t-speech-sounds instinct (The t speech sounds are the minimal units of instinctual speech sounds that correspond roughly to the letter t of the alphabet)

tact, tact-and-sensibility instinct

tactical, tactical-deception instinct

tactile, the-emotional-and-behavioral-aspects-of-the-tactile-sensa-tions instincts

tactile, the-tactile-sensation-experienced-in-the-skin-when-a-hair-is-touched-or-moved instinct

take risks, take-risks instincts

taking, taking-sides instinct

talkativeness, talkativeness instinct

talking, exploratory-talking instinct

talking, play-talking instinct

talking. "talking back" instinct

tampering, tampering instinct

tantrum, tantrum instinct

tantrum, temper-tantrum instinct

tap, we-tap-our-feet-or-fingers-in-time-to-music instinct

taphephobia, taphephobia (fear of graves/being buried alive) instincts (also called taphophobia)

taphophobia, taphophobia (fear of graves/being buried alive) instincts (also called taphephobia) taste, taste-sensations (sweet, sour, salty, bitter, umani) instincts (the proportions of the five basic tastes contained in the food give the food its basic flavor)

tastes, sexual-tastes instinct (Note: instincts are situational, and instincts can learn)

tasting, to-enjoy-tasting-food instinct

taunt, you-taunt-someone instinct

teaching, teaching instinct (teaching is a method of learning)

team, team-play instinct

team, team-spirit instinct

tears, the-bursting-into-tears-for-bodily-pain instinct

tears, the-bursting-into-tears-for-joy instinct

tears, the-bursting-into-tears-for-sorrow instinct

tears, to-burst-into-tears instinct

teasing, teasing instinct

teeth, to-grit-one's-teeth-with-anger instinct

telepathy, telepathy instinct

tell off, to-tell-someone-off instinct

temper, temper instinct (inborn versions: a quick temper, a violent temper, a mild temper, etc)

temper, temper-tantrum instinct

temper, to-lose-your-temper instinct

temperature, the-emotional-and-behavioral-aspects-of-the-temperature-sensations instinct

temperature, the-feeling-of-temperature-across-the-entire-skin-surface instinct

tempo, personal-tempo instinct

temptation, giving-in-to-temptation instincts (or rather the effect of instincts?)

temptation, temptation instincts (or rather the effect of instincts?)

temptation, to-resist-temptation instincts (or rather the effect of instincts?)

tenacity, tenacity instinct
tender, tender-feelings instinct
tender, you-are-tender-hearted instinct
tenderness, feeling-of-tenderness instinct
tense expectancy, tense-expectancy instinct
tenseness, tenseness instinct
tenseness, to-feel-a-tenseness instinct
tension, nervous-tension instinct
tension, tension instincts
territorial, territorial instinct(s) (see: Introduction)
territorial, territorial-behavior instinct
territorial, territorial-spacing instinct
territorial, the-territorial-imperative instinct
territoriality, territoriality instinct(s) (= territorial instinct(s))
territory, to-protect-your-territory instinct (= territorial-defense instinct)
terror, a-feeling-of-terror instinct
terror, terror (extreme degree of fear) instinct
thalassophobia, thalassophobia (fear of the sea) instinct
thanatophobia, thanatophobia (fear of death/dead things, especially human corpses) instincts
thank, to-thank instinct
thankfulness, thankfulness instinct
theatrical, theatrical-behavior instinct
theophobia, theophobia (fear of God/retribution from God for one's sins) instincts
theorizing, theorizing instinct
things, enjoying-things instincts
things, possessiveness-about-things instinct
things, the-desire-to-attain-things instinct
thinking, abstract-thinking-style instincts
thinking, concrete-operational-thinking instincts

thinking, concrete-thinking-style instincts

thinking, formal-operational-thinking instincts

thinking, thinking instincts

thirst, thirst instinct

thoughtfulness, thoughtfulness instinct

threat displays, the-facial-expressions-of-threat-displays instincts

threat gesture, threat-gesture instincts (the raised-fist threat, the stiff forefinger threat, an attack is performed in mid-air, a man can puff up his chest and draw himself up to his full height, obscene signals used as threatening devices, etc)

threat, postures-of-threat instincts

threat, the-threat-face instinct

threat, the-threat-of-punishment instinct

threat, the-threat-stare instinct

threat, threat-of-death instinct (Note: instincts are situational, and instincts can learn)

threat, vocal-threat instincts

threaten, to-threaten-away-rivals instinct

threatening, threatening-someone/something instinct

three-dimensional objects, the-innate-knowledge-about-three-dimensional-objects instincts (e.g. a baby doesn't have to learn that a picture of a dog in a book is the same kind of object as a real dog)

three dimensional vision, the-emotional-and-behavioral-aspects-of-three-dimensional-vision instincts

thrift, thrift instinct

thrill, the-thrill-of-the-chase instinct

thrilled, to-be-thrilled instinct

thrills, seeking-thrills instinct

throwing, throwing instinct

thumb, thumb-sucking instinct

thunder and lightning, the-normal-dread-of-thunder-and-lightning instinct tickling, tickling instinct

tidiness, your-concern-with-tidiness-and-punctuality instinct

tie sign, tie-sign-reading instincts

tie-signs, body-contact-tie-signs instincts (the kiss, the hand-in-hand, the arm link, the pat, the hand shake, the shoulder embrace, the full embrace, the waist embrace, the body support, the body-guide, the caress, the hand-to-head, the head-to-head, the mock-attack, body proximity, etc)

tight lipped, the-tight-lipped-threat-glare instinct

timbre, timbre instinct (noises have their timbre, from which we may infer what is going on)

time, time-sense instincts (= innately-given-knowledge-of-time instincts) The brain has many timing skills: mechanism for measuring short time intervals in the seconds to minutes range, perception of the passing of hours, days, weeks and years, etc

timidity, timidity instinct

tingling, to-feel-tingling-in-one's-limbs instinct

tirade, tirade instinct

tiredness, feelings-of-tiredness-and-drowsiness instinct

titter, to-titter instinct

tittle tattle, tittle-tattle instinct

toddle, a-child-toddles instinct

togetherness, the-feeling-of-female-togetherness instinct

togetherness, the-feeling-of-male-togetherness instinct

tolerance, patient-tolerance instinct

tolerance, tolerance-of-pain instinct

tolerant, to-be-tolerant/intolerant instincts (= tolerance/intolerance instincts)

tomfoolery, tomfoolery instinct

tongue, the-tip-of-the-tongue-phenomenon instinct

tool, to-perceive-a-suitable-design-of-tool-for-a-certain-job instincts

tool, tool-making instincts

tool, tool-using instincts

torment, to-torment-someone instinct (Note: instincts are situational, and instincts can learn)

torment, torment instinct

touch, the-emotional-and-behavioral-aspects-of-the-touch-sensations instincts

touch, the-sense-of-touch (pressure) instinct

touch, to-be-pleasant/unpleasant-to-the-touch instincts

touch, to-reach-out-gently-to-touch-someone-in-reassurance instinct

touched, to-be-emotionally-touched-by-something instinct

touching, touching instinct

toughness, toughness instinct ("it is important to be tough")

toxophobia, toxophobia (fear of poisons/being poisoned) instincts

traditions, to-pass-on-traditions instinct

train, a-train-of-thoughts instinct

training, training (learning the skills that you need for a particular activity) instincts

trance, trance instinct

transvestism, transvestism instinct (an "abnormal" gender-identity instinct)

travel sickness, travel-sickness instinct

tremophobia, tremophobia (fear of trembling) instinct

trepidation, trepidation instinct

trial and error, to-do-something-by-trial-and-error instinct

tribal territory, tribal-territory instinct

tribalism, tribalism instinct

trichopathophobia, trichopathophobia (in women, fear of facial hair) instinct

trichophobia, trichophobia (fear of hair) instinct

trifle, you-trifle-with-someone-or-something instinct

trill, a-trilling-laugh instinct

triskaidekaphobia, triskaidekaphobia (fear of the number that results from the operation of subtracting 1 from 14) instinct

triumph, a-feeling-of-triumph instinct
triumph, a-note-of-triumph-in-his-voice instinct
triumph, punching-the-air-or-throwing-up-their-hands-in-triumph instinct
trophy, trophy instinct
troubled, a-troubled-facial-expression instinct
troubled, to-be-troubled instinct
trust, basic-feeling-of-trust/distrust instincts
trusting, trusting/distrusting-people instincts
truth, disregard-for-truth instinct
truth, love-of-truth instinct
try, to-try instinct (= trying instinct)
tumble, rough-and-tumble-play instinct
turn, to-turn-his/her-eyes-in-our-direction-and-check-us-out instinct
type, "She's/he's my type" instinct

U

u, the-u-speech-sounds instinct (The u speech sounds are the minimal units of instinctual speech sounds that correspond roughly to the letter u of the alphabet)
um, um (a sound that people make when they are hesitating) instinct
umbrage, to-take-umbrage instinct
unappetizing, unappetizing-food instinct
uncertainty, a-feeling-of-uncertainty instinct
uncomfortable, to-feel-uncomfortable instinct
unconscious sight, unconscious-sight-is-more-accurate-than-conscious-sight instinct
unconsidered, unconsidered-thoughts-and-actions instinct
uncooperativeness, uncooperativeness instinct (instincts are situational!)
unctuous, to-be-unctuous instinct

undertone, to-say-something-in-an-undertone instinct

undying love, undying-love instinct

unease, a-feeling-of-unease instinct

unfair, to-be-upset-by-unfair-behavior instinct

unfocused, someone's-eyes-are-unfocused (they are open, but not looking at anything) instinct

unfriendly, the-unfriendly-face (curling down the mouth corners) instinct

unfriendly, to-be-unfriendly instinct

unhappiness, unhappiness instinct

unified, we(most of us)-wish-to-have-unified-attitudes-as-well-as-unified-beliefs instinct

uninhibited, to-be-uninhibited (used showing approval) instinct

unity, to-feel-a-sense-of-unity-with-the-world(universe) instinct

universal grammar, universal-grammar instinct

unkind, to-be-unkind instinct

unmusical sounds, unmusical-sounds-are-unpleasant-to-listen-to instinct

unpalatable, unpalatable-food instinct

unpleasant, unpleasant-feeling instinct

unreality, feeling-of-unreality instinct

unrest, to-feel-a-sense-of-unrest instinct

unroll, a-series-of-events-unroll-in-one's-memory instinct

unselfishness, unselfishness instinct

unsympathetic, to-be-unsympathetic instinct

unwillingness, unwillingness instinct

upset, to-be-upset-by-unfair-behavior instinct

upset, to-get/be-upset instinct

upset, to-intend-to-upset-people instinct

us, the-feelings-of-"us"-versus-"them" instinct

used, to-get-used-to-something-or-someone instinct

V

v, the-v-speech-sounds instinct (The v speech sounds are the minimal units of instinctual speech sounds that correspond roughly to the letter v of the alphabet)

    vacant, a-vacant-look-or-expression instinct

    vaginal, vaginal-lubrication instinct

    vain, to-be-vain instinct

    vainglorious, vainglorious-behavior instinct

    valor, valor (great bravery in battle) instinct

    vanity, vanity instinct

    vehemence, vehemence instinct

    veiled, a-veiled-expression-on-one's-face instinct

    venerate, you-venerate-someone instinct (= veneration instinct)

    veneration, a-sentiment-of-veneration instinct

    vengeance, vengeance instinct

    vengeful, vengeful-pleasure instinct

    vengefulness, vengefulness instinct (= you-are-vengeful instinct)

    venturesome, a-venturesome-spirit instinct

    veracity, veracity instinct

    verbal, verbal-communication(language) instincts (= the utterance of words and sentences)

    verbal, verbal-violence instinct

    versions, our-ability-to-imagine-different-versions-of-events instinct

    vertigo, vertigo instinct

    vexed, a-vexed-frown instinct

    vexed, to-be-vexed instinct

    vibrancy, vibrancy instinct

    vibrant, a-vibrant-voice instinct

    vibration sensations, the-emotional-and-behavioral-aspects-of-vibration-sensations instincts vice, hating-vice instinct

vicious, vicious-language instinct

victimize, to-victimize-someone-because-you-do-not-like-their-beliefs instinct

victory, victory-celebration instinct

views, to-get-angry-if-people-do-not-agree-with-your-political-or-religious-views instinct

vigilance, vigilance instinct

vigilante, a-vigilante-group instinct

vigorated, to-feel-vigorated instinct

vileness, vileness instinct

vindictiveness, vindictiveness instinct

violence, physical-violence instinct

violent, men-are-more-violent-than-women instinct

violent, preparing-the-body-for-violent-activity instincts

violent, violent-behavior instinct

violent, violent-rage instinct

virtue, loving-virtue instincts

virulence, virulence instinct

visceral, visceral-sensation instinct

vision, vision (a mental picture) instinct

visiting, visiting instinct (normal behavior needs to be explained!)

visual, visual-awareness instinct

visual, visual-grasp-reflex instinct

visual, visual-illusions instincts

visual, visual-imagery instinct

visual, visual-sensation-and-perception instincts

visualization, visualization instinct

vitriol, vitriol instinct

vocal, vocal-paralanguage instincts (grunts, giggles, laughs, sobs, cries, etc)

vocal, vocal-stress-in-a-spoken-sentence instinct

vocational, vocational-interests instincts (= vocation instincts)

voice, neutral-voice instinct

voice, people-rely-on-facial-expression-and-tone-of-voice-to-judge-a-person's-emotional-state instincts

voice, to-raise-one's-voice instinct

voice, tone-of-voice instincts

voice, voice instincts (see examples above)

void, an-aching-void-in-one's-heart instinct

volition, volition instinct

vomiting, the-emotional-and-behavioral-aspects-of-vomiting instinct

vow, you-vow-to-do-something instinct (normal behavior needs to be explained!)

voyeurism, voyeurism instinct

vulgar, to-scream-vulgar-insults instinct

vulgar, vulgar-gestures instinct

vulgar, vulgar-insults instinct

vulgar, vulgar-remarks instinct

vulnerability, vulnerability instincts (many instincts are vulnerable)

vulnerable, vulnerable-to-stress-and-pressure instincts (many instincts are vulnerable)

W

w, the-w-speech-sounds instinct (The w speech sounds are the minimal units of instinctual speech sounds that correspond roughly to the letter w of the alphabet)

wail, to-wail instinct

waist, men-everywhere-find-women-with-a-waist-to-hip-ratio-of-0.7-sexually-alluring instinct

waiting, waiting instinct (instincts are situational, and instincts can learn!)

wake, the-sleep-wake-schedule instinct

waking, waking-up instinct

wander, one's-thoughts-wander instinct

wander, to-let-the-mind-wander,-or-go-blank,-while-continuing-to-nod-and-smile-automatically instinct

wandering, wandering,-unguided-conversations instinct

wandering, your-mind-is-wandering instincts

wanderlust, wanderlust instinct

want, want-to-succeed instinct

wanting, wanting instincts

wanton, senseless-and-wanton-cruelty instinct

wanton, wanton-aggression instinct

wanton, wanton-violence instinct

warfare, intertribal-warfare instinct (Remember: war is not inevitable, but as long as people dream about violent revolutions—leftist or rightist, then …and…and…and…)

warlike, warlike-behavior instinct

warm, to-be-warm-hearted instinct

warm, to-feel-warm instinct

warm, warm-thoughts instinct

warmth, the-emotionally-and-behavioral-aspects-of-warmth-sensations instincts

warning, warning instinct

wary, you-are-wary-about-something instinct

washing, washing-with-water instinct

watch, to-watch-for-signs-of-possible-danger-and-compare-current-information-with-information-stored-in-memory instinct

watching, to-enjoy-watching-someone/something instinct

water, to-like-cold-drinking-water-better-than-warm-drinking-water instinct

wave, to-wave-one's-hand (e.g. to wave for silence) instincts

weakness, to-feel-weakness-in-one's-limbs instinct

weariness, weariness instinct

weep, weep-(copiously-)when-emotionally-disturbed instinct

welcome, to-welcome-someone instinct

welfare, to-care-about-the-welfare-of-others instinct

well-being, the-feeling-of-well-being instinct (= the-sense-of-well-being instinct)

wetness, the-emotional-and-behavioral-aspects-of-wetness-sensations instincts

wetness, to-sense-wetness instinct

whacked, to-be-whacked instinct

wheedling, helpless-little-girl-actions-as-part-of-a-wheedling-process instinct

wheedling, wheedling-persuasion instinct

whim, "his/her tendency to change his/her mind at whim" instincts

whimper, to-whimper instinct

whims, momentary-whims instincts

whining, the-child's-whining instinct

whining, whining instinct (= someone-whines-about-something instinct)

whisper, to-whisper instinct

white lie, white-lie instinct

whole, to-want-to-understand-a-thousand-"little things"-to-make-a-great-whole instinct

whoop, to-whoop-with-delight instinct

whoops, people-say-'Whoops!'-when-they-have-a-slight-accident-or-see-someone-else-having-one instinct

wild, to-be-wild-with-excitement instinct

wild, to-have-wild-eyes (a wild look) instinct

will, feeling-free-will-exist instinct (the-intuitive-belief-in-free-will instinct)

will, feeling-of-will instinct

win, like-to-win instinct

wince, to-wince instinct (= wincing instinct)

wind, to-wind-someone-up instinct

wink, to-wink-at-someone instinct

wishful thinking, wishful-thinking instinct

wishing, wishing instincts

wistfulness, wistfulness instinct

wit, wit-in-speech instinct

witty, a-witty-remark-or-joke instinct

witty, to-be-witty instinct

woe, woe instinct

wonder, a-feeling-of-wonder instinct

wonder, the-extreme-sense-of-wonder-which-we-all-feel-when-confronted-with-highly-complicated-machinery instinct

work, a-desire-to-understand-how-things-work instinct

working, working-memory instinct

worry, worry instincts

worry, worry-about-looking-foolish instinct

worry, worry-about-the-safety-of-relatives-and-close-friends instinct

worry, worry-about-what-other-people-think-about-you instinct

worship, hero-worship instinct

worship, to-worship-our-gods instinct

worship, worship instincts

worship, worship-of-authority instinct

wow, you-say-'Wow!'-when-you-are-very-impressed-by-something-or-very-pleased-about-something instinct

wrath, wrath instinct

wrestling, good-natured-wrestling-among-the-boys instinct

wretchedness, a-feeling-of-wretchedness instinct

wry, a-wry-smile instinct

X

x, the-x-speech-sounds instinct (The x speech sounds are the minimal units of instinctual speech sounds that correspond roughly to the letter x of the alphabet)

    xenophobia, xenophobia (fear of strangers) instinct (both humans and animals show xenophobic behavior)

    xenophobic, our-propensity-for-xenophobic-killing-of-other-human-groups instinct

Y

y, the-y-speech-sounds instinct (The y speech sounds are the minimal units of instinctual speech sounds that correspond roughly to the letter y of the alphabet)

    yammer, to-yammer instinct

    yarn, someone-spins-you-a-yarn (they tell you a story which is not true, (often) as an excuse for something) instinct

    yawning, yawning instinct

    yawning, yawning-(really-)is-infectious instinct

    yearn, to-yearn-for-something instinct

    yell, babies-yell-when-they-are-being-fed-too-little instinct

    yelp, a-flinching,-lurching,-terrified-yelp instinct

    yelp, a-yelp-of-pain instinct

    yes, the-head-nod-for-'yes' instinct

    youthful, youthful-rebellion instinct

Z

z, the-z-speech-sounds instinct (The z speech sounds are the minimal units of instinctual speech sounds that correspond roughly to the letter z of the alphabet)

    zealous, to-be-zealous instinct
    zest, the-zest-of-flavors instinct
    zest, zest instinct
    zonked, to-feel-zonked instinct